ILLUSTRATING COMPUTER DOCUMENTATION

The Art of Presenting Information Graphically on Paper and Online

William Horton

John Wiley & Sons, Inc.
New York ▪ Chichester ▪ Brisbane ▪ Toronto ▪ Singapore

1991 $32.95

Copyright © 1991 by William Horton

Published by John Wiley & Sons, Inc.

Library of Congress Cataloging in Publication Data:

Horton, William K. (William Kendall)
    Illustrating computer documentation: the art of presenting information graphically on paper and online/William Horton

        p.   cm.

    Includes bibliographical references and index.
    ISBN 0-471-53846-9. — ISBN 0-471-53845-0 (pbk.)
    1.   Computer graphics.   2.   Visual communication.
I.   Title.
T385.H695   1991
006.6—dc20   91-15425

Printed in the United States of America

10 9 8 7 6 5 4 3 2 1

Trademarks

Stone and Lucida are trademarks of Adobe Systems Incorporated. Aldus and Aldus Freehand are registered trademarks of Aldus Corporation. Palatino is a registered trademark of Allied Corporation. Apple and Macintosh are registered trademarks of Apple Computer, Inc. HyperCard is a trademark of Apple Computer, Inc. Canvas is a registered trademark of Deneba Systems, Inc. Intergraph and I/EMS are trademarks of Intergraph Corporation. Linotronic is a trademark of Linotype. Microsoft, Microsoft Excel for the Macintosh, and Microsoft Word for the Macintosh are registered trademarks of Microsoft Corporation. Windows is a trademark of Microsoft Corporation. EndNote Plus is a registered trademark of Niles & Associates, Inc. Pictionary is a registered trademark of Pictionary, Inc. Digital Darkroom is a trademark of Silicon Beach Software, Inc. Tektronix is a registered trademark of Tektronix, Inc.

PREFACE

WHAT IS THIS BOOK ABOUT?

This book is about authoring images, about communicating, about making things understandable. It is about ideas: how to reach out and grab ideas, how to make them tangible, how to shape and sculpt them so you can share them with others. It is emphatically not a guide to making pretty pictures.

WHO SHOULD READ IT?

Illustrating Computer Documentation is for those who design, create, and edit illustrations for computer documentation:

- All writers and editors eager for new techniques to ensure that documents are noticed, read, and understood.

- "Word people" who feel the need to express ideas visually and those who strive to wrap words around an essentially visual concept.

- Artists, illustrators, graphic designers, and others responsible for the display of graphic and textual information on the page and screen.

- Computer programmers and others who design computer-generated information displays.

WHY DID I WRITE IT?

For years I have prowled bookstores looking for a book like this one. I came across many good books on how to produce particular kinds of graphics—especially statistical graphics—but none of these books explained where specific techniques could most appropriately be used. I also encountered many books that explained how to use particular drawing instruments or computer programs to create graphics. Though valuable, these books are quickly dated by the next round of computer drawing programs. Many books told how to make stunningly beautiful images. But that was not the most important thing I wanted to do. I wanted to learn to use graphics to communicate difficult technical information clearly. Toward this end I found some useful information in journals of perceptual and cognitive psychology and proceedings of conferences on ergonomics and human factors. These works required considerable deciphering, as they were quite esoteric and written (properly so) to suit the needs of researchers, not practitioners.

WHY IS IT NEEDED?

In preparing this book, I examined hundreds of manuals and thousands of illustrations for computer hardware and software. I considered illustrations for peripheral devices, semiconductor chips, circuit boards, integrated systems, operating systems, utilities, and application programs. These documents spanned mainframe computers, minicomputers, microcomputers, engineering workstations, and laptop and notebook computers. Some were superbly illustrated, but most suffered from four common problems:

1. **Few illustrations**. Many manuals intimidate or bore their users with gray walls of unbroken text. Words may be necessary, but they are seldom the best way to explain interactive, visual, and spatial concepts.

2. **Wrong kinds of illustrations**. Many illustrations communicate the wrong kind of information. In far too many manuals, over 90 percent of the illustrations were unannotated screen snapshots. Though valuable to help users confirm their location in a program, they are no substitute for a conceptual overview explaining how the program works.

3. **Clumsy and crude illustrations.** Poorly executed illustrations add more noise than information to the page. Oversized illustrations, as well as those with heavy lines, can overpower related text.

4. **Merely decorative illustrations**. When the sole purpose of the graphic is to look good, communication takes a back seat. Aesthetic features should not interfere with the

viewer's functional task of recognizing objects and patterns. Alas, it often does.

HOW IS IT DIFFERENT?

This book draws on my 15 years of experience designing and producing technical communications, including reams of computer manuals and megabytes of online documentation. This material has been refined over the past few years in numerous presentations and seminars for technical writers, graphic designers, and computer programmers.

Illustrating Computer Documentation is not scholarly. It does rely on research in cognitive and perceptual psychology, but it does not belabor the theoretical basis of communication. It does include references to other works for those interested in the research basis for what I say here.

Nor is *Illustrating Computer Documentation* primarily a how-to book. Bookstores are filled with how-to books on communications. This book concentrates on showing you what to do instead of telling you how to do it, and provides a conceptual understanding from which you can deduce rules and on which you can base design decisions. Effective graphics result from true visual literacy, not from memorizing rules or slavishly imitating examples. This book contains examples of applications of the techniques and references to sources of instruction on how to apply them.

Illustrating Computer Documentation is not about tools. True, tools, especially electronic publishing tools, do affect the quality and economy of the graphics we produce. It has always been so. The very word style derives from *stilus*, the writing implement of the Romans. Yet, we must not let tools dictate our style. Good style can be achieved with any tools. Ken Muse, the well-known cartoonist, uses No. 2 pencils he buys at the supermarket. For those more interested in the electronic tools, I recommend a subscription to one of the many magazines that showcase the latest drawing and word processing programs. Better make that a *weekly* subscription.

HOW TO READ THIS BOOK

Don't read this book cover to cover. It is intended more as a handbook than a quick read. Scan it. Skim it. Leaf through it, reading what catches your eye and fancy. Apply it. This is a book for doing, not just for reading.

How is it organized?

This book covers all the main issues of designing effective graphics.

Symbols used throughout the book

Throughout this book, you will encounter symbols in the margin. These mark special information that supplements the main discussion or theme.

The concepts in this book generally apply to all documents regardless of reader or medium. However, what holds true for black-and-white graphics appearing in paper documents for English-speaking people does not always apply when we go beyond these restrictions. Exceptions are flagged with symbols. They are also discussed in detail in Chapters 10, 12, and 13.

Additional symbols flag bits of advice, sources of additional information, and activities for you to pursue on your own.

 Activities. This symbol flags exercises and demonstrations that let you experience a topic directly.

 Color. This symbol flags information about the use of chromatic color beyond black, white, and shades of gray.

 International audiences. This symbol flags information that is especially important for documents to be translated and for those read by persons with another first language or with different cultural values.

 Online display. Displaying illustrations on the computer or television screen creates special requirements not faced on paper. This symbol flags these differences.

 Readings. Sources of additional information are listed for those who want to delve into particular techniques or explore background theory.

 Tips. This symbol flags suggestions, hints, and practical techniques.

Bibliographic references

References to other publications are included to let you continue your learning. They are included to show why you should believe something is so, how to apply a technique, where to find an example, and where to look for more details. I have tried to make them as unobtrusive as possible while letting you look outward to other sources of information.

HOW IT WAS PRODUCED

Producing this book required a range of talents and tools.

Who is responsible

Like all books, this one is a collaboration of many minds, hearts, and hands. Chief among them are:

Ideas and words	William Horton
Illustrations and graphic design	William Horton Katherine Horton
Editing and proofreading	Carol Kamback Editorial staff at Wiley

| Linotronic output | Carole O'Neal, O'Neal Business Forms |
| Insightful advice and special inspiration | John Brockmann, Gerald Cohen, Elizabeth Keyes, Philip Rubens, Marty Shelton, Edmond Weiss |

How it was produced

Production also required a rich collaboration of electronic tools. Text was entered on various Macintosh and PC-compatible computers and formatted in Microsoft Word 4.0 for the Macintosh. Body text was set in Palatino and headings in Lucida Sans. Graphics were drawn in Freehand 3.0 and Canvas 2.1 and then merged with text in Microsoft Word. Photographs were scanned on a Microtek scanner and edited with Digital Darkroom 2.0. The bibliography was created with End Note Plus. The resulting Microsoft Word files were printed on a Linotronic 300.

A SECRET

As a reward for reading this preface, I will share a secret with you. Though this book focuses on illustrations for computer documentation, the principles discussed here can be applied to just about any kind of graphic, regardless of the subject of the graphic or the type of document in which it appears.

CONTENTS

THE NEED TO SHOW

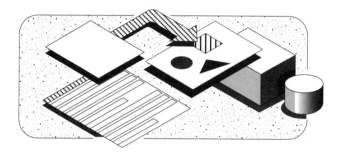

1

Daily the task of communicating information grows harder. Currently we communicate to the color TV generation who expect to be entertained with multihued, exciting images. Soon we must communicate with the videogame generation who expect to interact with beeping, buzzing, animated images. Merely flinging pages or screens of words at the users of your products will not suffice.

Almost every nonfiction published work, whether it is a highly technical paper for a scientific journal or the stockholder's report of a business, uses illustrations. Indeed, since the middle of the 20th century, graphics—including film and television—have assumed an increasingly large role in our everyday lives, with a correspondingly smaller role for the written word. You need to consider your graphics carefully, for they are likely to be at least an equal partner with words in your published work. (138, p. 23)

In documentation, graphics are no longer an option—they are required (46; 330). They are required by the subject matter and demanded by users. In surveys, computer users consistently demand more illustrations and less text (44; 203). The readers of computer documentation are more attuned to visuals than to text. Raised on a diet of television, movies, and videogames, today's user more willingly and skillfully interprets graphics (209).

"It can spell the difference between chaos and clarity, the difference between darkness and daylight, between confusion and communication. Yet it is conspicuous by its absence from technical manuals. It is graphics. Good graphics." (65, p. E-32)

"Videos, television, movies, and computers have changed the way people absorb information. Today printed documentation has to compete for the user's attention with information presented visually in graphically oriented documentation and training videos. Increasingly users prefer visually oriented manuals over classic text-intensive manuals." (140, p. VC-7)

WHY GRAPHICS MAKE DOCUMENTATION WORK BETTER

Graphics are often hard to design, difficult to create, and expensive to produce. So why bother? After all, we've gotten by with bare words and numbers for thousands of years. Do we really need graphics? The answer is a resounding yes, for the simple reason that graphics communicate.

Graphics aid job performance

"From cave-paintings to the Pioneer 10 Plaque, humans have always naturally turned to graphic communication when the task was vital or complex." (237, p. 334)

"The higher one looks in administrative levels of business, the more one finds decisions are based on data analyzed and presented in tabular or graphic formats." (89)

When displays are studied leisurely, graphics and color appear to offer little advantage. However, when viewers or readers are impatient or must make decisions quickly, color pictorial displays are more effective (258; 345). For tasks involving large numbers of concepts, graphics enable viewers to process information with almost mathematical precision and speed (24). Some examples from the research include:

- In a test, technicians made three times as many errors when using narrative instructions as when using a flowchart (124). Supplementing program listings with flowcharts of control flow simplified and speeded debugging (47).

- A better organized display reduced response time by 31 percent and errors by 28 percent. These improvements applied to both expert and novice users (53).

- A study of computer displays comparing narrative, tabular, monochrome graphic, and color graphic formats found that users achieved accurate performance sooner and demonstrated quicker response times with both of the graphic formats (316).

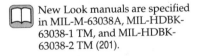 New Look manuals are specified in MIL-M-63038A, MIL-HDBK-63038-1 TM, and MIL-HDBK-63038-2 TM (201).

- The U.S. military, confronted with the task of training recruits with poor reading skills to operate and maintain sophisticated electronic and computer systems, slashed words and relied primarily on graphics. These New Look manuals (201; 209) and Functionally Oriented Maintenance Manuals (FOMMs) (183) are reportedly doing the job well.

Graphics help documents go global

Over the globe about 5000 languages and dialects are spoken, of which about 100 are used in business and technical pursuits (79). A product today may be designed in one country, manufactured in another, shipped through several others, and used in dozens of countries. The potential cost of translation is outweighed only by the potential cost of confusion. Graphics can reduce these costs.

Even if your document never crosses national boundaries, it may still have to communicate with immigrants from a vastly different culture who read English as a second language or not at all.

"… through its neutrality and its independence of separate languages, visual education is superior to word education. Words divide, pictures unite." (225, p. 217-220)

"If a picture can save you a thousand words, then that same picture can save you another ten thousand words if it is in a document that will be translated into ten other languages." (321, p. 330)

"Society will no longer accept the elitist attitude 'If the user can't read plain English, let them do without!'" (43, p. 19)

Graphics reach nonreaders

Increasingly the world seems divided between those who won't read and those who can't. The can't-reads, the illiterates, are growing in number at a frightening rate.

- In the last 10 years the percentage of Americans 18 to 29 years old who read newspapers regularly has dropped from 60 percent to 33 percent (265).

- Functional illiteracy in the United States is variously estimated at between 11 and 20 percent (281).

- In 1988 UNESCO estimated that 1 billion adults cannot read—one-third of the population of the world (186).

- Eighty percent of job applicants at New York Telephone Company failed a seventh-grade English comprehension test (128).

- In 1988, seventy-eight percent of 21- to 25-year-olds failed a simple reading test given as part of the National Educational Assessment Test (128).

"The bad news is that most of you who communicate with the printed word should be learning a new profession, because the need for your skills is declining rapidly. You're on the same path the dinosaurs took. Not extinct yet—but well on the way to becoming an endangered species." (281, p. 168)

Graphics seduce reluctant readers

When was the last time you saw a magazine or paperback book without an attractive graphic on the cover? Even staid technical journals, such as the *Journal of the American Medical Association*, are using graphics to seduce readers.

"Reading demands concentration and work; looking at images is fun." (335, p. 124)

"The best way to present an idea vividly and to communicate a point is through a picture. A picture displays an idea quicker, clearer, and more vividly than any other means of communication and in marketing, graphics can mean the difference between winning and losing a contract." (102, p. G&P-24)

"Readers look at the pictures before they read the words, and the words they read first are the ones in and about the graphic." (335)

 In Western cultures the word is sacred. Laws are recorded in words and religious truth is revealed through sacred texts. However, the whole world does not share this reverence for the written word. In Eastern cultures, for instance, it is the sound (the sacred syllable OM) or the visual image (the mandala) that is sacred.

"Eyesight is insight." (11, p. 46)

Graphics aid thinking

A survey of 100 undergraduate business students found that the format of the text determined their initial reactions to it. As compared with a traditional, formal, text-heavy format, they strongly preferred (86 percent) a format with more graphics, cartoons, white space, and color. They saw the more graphical format as less difficult (84 percent), as better preparation for the final exam (82 percent), and as more useful on the job (65 percent) (254).

When the state of Maine switched to a graphical format for a massive statistical report on the performance of local schools, the "report's graphics format communicated information so much more effectively than the table of statistics in earlier reports that it not only assisted local school boards in making budget decisions but also … influenced Maine voters" (184, p. 135).

Graphics add credibility

Seeing is believing. Most people believe that pictures don't lie (180). Robert Boyle of the British Royal Society called this "virtual witnessing" (285). So strong is our faith in vision that when what we feel with our hands disagrees with what we see with our eyes, the touch perceptions are unconsciously altered to make them consistent with vision (261). Showing something says that it is real, here and now. What otherwise might be vapor or "just words" becomes something real to the viewer.

Graphics aid thinking

In engineering, science, and business, clear thinking is often synonymous with visual thinking. Albert Einstein, in a letter to Jacques Hadamard, described his own thought process:

> The words or the language, as they are written or spoken, do not seem to play any role in my mechanism of thought. The psychical entities which seem to serve as elements in thought are certain signs and more or less clear images which can be "voluntarily" reproduced and combined. … The above mentioned elements are, in my case, of visual and some of muscular type. Conventional words or other signs have to be sought for laboriously only in a secondary stage, when the mentioned associative play is sufficiently established and can be reproduced at will. (87, p. 43)

Other thinkers also relied on visual images. Nikola Tesla's procedure for designing complex electrical devices was to "project before his eyes a picture, complete in every detail" and "more vivid than any blueprint" (229, p. 8). Benoit Mandelbrot, the discoverer of much of fractal geometry who was unable to remember the alphabet, debugged computer programs by forming mental pictures of them and looking for defects in the images (41). James Watson's discovery of DNA (328) and Richard Feynman's contribution to particle physics (231) relied heavily on visual imagery.

Graphics aid problem solving (247). Problem solving largely depends on finding a way of representing the problem that makes its solution transparent (289). Graphics provide memorable, easily manipulated symbols with which to represent ideas. Graphics also simplify problem-solving by visually recording facts the person would otherwise have to deduce or remember in short-term memory (339). By prechunking information, graphics and color enable people to handle more information, process it more efficiently, and apply simpler and more efficient decision-making strategies (258).

Graphics promote more efficient reading

Graphics can help a reader tackle even the daunting task of understanding an unstructured document. We've all read documents in which the author seems to be flinging facts helter skelter. In computer parlance, such a disgorging of raw information is called a *data dump* or *core dump*.

When we use words alone we often "fail to make explicit the diagrammatic structure underlying our explanations" (200, p. VC-34). Graphics can help readers see and comprehend complex patterns.

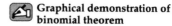

Graphical demonstration of binomial theorem

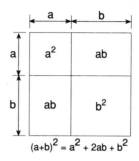

$$(a+b)^2 = a^2 + 2ab + b^2$$

"… in order to understand what we read we translate from the text into some kind of structure in our head which expresses the relationships among the various concepts that the text communicates." (238, p. VC-38)

Map of this book

Illustrating computer documentation

What does this say?

Smoking permitted in the three rows of tables between 2nd and 5th columns.

"... it is usually forgotten that without prints and blueprints, without maps and geometry, the world of modern sciences and technologies would hardly exist." (207, p. 145)

"Seeing comes before words.... No other kind of relic or text ... can offer such a direct testimony about the world.... In this respect images are more precise and richer than literature." (21, p. 7-10)

"The infant takes hold of the world with his eyes long before he does with his hands—an extremely significant fact." (105, p. 20)

Graphics can also guide efficient readers who do not need to read a document from cover to cover. Such readers often skim, skip, zoom in, and zoom out. Graphics can provide these readers with a global map of the document as well as flags to critical information. The map lets the reader grasp the organization of the document and plan a strategy for finding information. The local flags identify blocks of text so readers can find them quickly. They also remind readers of the larger context of discourse (327).

Graphics can explain visual and spatial concepts

Some concepts defy words. Other concepts can be expressed in words but are more efficient in pictures. Still others must be translated to visual images before they can be understood.

Images work better than words for expressing subtle spatial, color, or textural relations. They also work well for storing much information about appearances (166).

An architect once described the problem of describing visual systems with words: "It's like trying to design a building sitting on your hands" (290, p. VC-12).

WHY GRAPHICS WORK

Why does the mind prefer the more complex, dynamic, life-like image to the seemingly simpler verbal one? And how do graphics contribute to communications?

Vision is our dominant sense

Our species relies on vision over all other senses. We learn about 11 percent audibly and 83 percent visually (103). Drawing originated over 60,000 years ago—long before written language (97).

Six months before we are born into the light, our eyes begin tentative movements. By birth, our eyes move together in tandem. Within eight weeks we can accurately judge size, shape, orientation, and distance (36).

Consider the importance of vision and seeing throughout our language. We speak of someone as being *far-sighted* or *visionary* or a *seer*. When we agree, we *see eye-to-eye*. We are on the *lookout* for bargains and we relish the *sight for sore eyes*. Something that gets our attention is *eye catching* or *eye opening*. We trust *eyewitnesses* and hire *private eyes*. After *looking into* something, we develop our own *viewpoint*.

Graphics are compact

Graphics can say more in less space than words. When graphics serve as a storage medium for recording facts, they can be quite dense while still legible (24; 315). According to Lin Yu-tang, visual symbols have "the virtue of containing within a few conventional lines the thought of the ages and the dreams of the race" (68, p. 7).

 Try describing in words all the information in one square inch of a road map or a circuit diagram.

Graphics escape the limitations of linear text

Given the high expectations of readers, writers must seek ways to overcome the limitation of traditional pages and computer screens. Languages, human and computer, are all limited by a linear, word-after-word syntax (79; 110).

The structure of language implies certain assumptions about reality. Sentences, which are built from individual words, are one-directional. This structure of language can cause us to view the world as fragmented rather than continuous, as linear rather than complex. Such a restrictive concept also tends to screen out other ways of thinking.

"... contemporary scientific communications media are predominantly language-oriented and are no longer adequate for today's scientific research." (277, p. VC-18)

Graphics relate separate ideas

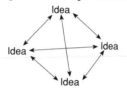

Graphics are readily understood

Properly designed graphics make their main point in a glance. Because they do not have to be read, analyzed, and interpreted, graphics improve the speed and accuracy with which information is learned and processed (11; 20). With graphics, comparisons become automatic and relationships obvious (32).

"A simple, quickly comprehended form or color, or combination of both, is translated to the brain faster and more directly than a written word. In an emergency or panic, the milliseconds saved in reaction time could save a man's fingers, his arm, his leg, or even his life." (79, p. 20)

"The visual dimension of pictures presents an entirely different way of showing the relationship of general and particular; memory is no longer necessary to make the connections because they can be displayed directly for the mind to grasp in a form closer to that in which they will be assimilated." (238, p. VC-38)

"Discourse will be ineffectual if it provides, on the one hand, only a set of unrelated particulars rattling around like a shoe box full of small parts, or on the other hand, a sequence of generalizations with no details to make them present in the reader's mind." (239, p. G&P-44)

 Compare narrative and graphical forms. Consider these two ways of representing the mutual likes and dislikes of a group of people:

Diane likes Charles and Suki but dislikes Jan. Andrea likes Paul but dislikes Charles and Jan. Jan likes Paul but dislikes Andrea. Suki likes Charles and Diane but dislikes Jan. Paul likes Andrea and Charles but dislikes Suki. Charles likes Diane, Suki, and Paul but dislikes Andrea.

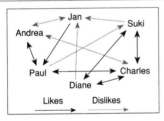

Which form makes answering the following questions quicker?

1. Who is the most popular?
2. Who is the least popular?
3. Is there a clique of people who all like each other?
4. Which people have their likes and dislikes reciprocated?

Graphics are understood more quickly than words (119) and are more easily related to the real world (201). Furthermore, graphics that reinforce the meaning of text increase comprehension (181).

Graphics improve comprehension both for children and adults. Adding graphics to children's materials increased comprehension 40 percent and boosted test scores (336). Teaching history in comic book form rather than from traditional textbooks improved test scores for high school students (44). Using annotated screen examples proved effective in training users of the Bell System's Telephone Office Planning and Engineering System, a complex, interactive computer-aided design system (15). Replacing a word-only handbook with a graphical learning aid reduced errors and increased proficiency for both low and high aptitude users in one test (37).

Graphics are remembered

Do you, like most other people, remember faces better than names? Tests have shown that we have almost unlimited recognition memory for graphic images and that concepts remembered visually are recalled better than those encoded verbally.

Graphics are recalled better

We remember what we form a mental image of. We can recall more objects presented as pictures than presented merely as words (166). In addition, we remember 20 percent of what we hear but 50 percent of what we both hear and see (103). A study by the University of Minnesota in 1989 showed that adding visuals to presentations increased recall by 43 percent (216). In another test, creating strong associative images increased recall 2.5 times over mere verbal repetition (80 percent versus 33 percent). When the images were distinct and vivid, recall soared to 95 percent (36).

Graphics are recognized almost perfectly

Our capacity for recognizing graphics appears unlimited (296). In an experiment, subjects looked at 2,560 slides over three days. Each slide was shown once, for ten seconds only. One hour after viewing the last slide, the subjects were tested by viewing 280 pairs of slides, each pair containing one slide from the original series and one new slide. Subjects were asked to identify which slide they had already seen. Even when the original slides were presented in mirror image in the second viewing and when the presentation rate was speeded up to one per second, the subjects still recognized 85 to 95 percent of the slides correctly (120). When the subjects were asked to select the one slide they had viewed earlier from 32 alternatives, they were still correct 92 percent of the time (296). When the pictures in the slide-recognition test were "vivid," recognition reached 99.6 percent (226).

"Visual intelligence conveys information with amazing speed, and if the data is clearly organized and stated, it is not only easier to absorb, it is easier to retain and utilize referentially." (76, p. 137)

"… these experiments with pictorial stimuli suggest that recognition of pictures is essentially perfect. The results would probably have been the same if we had used 25,000 pictures instead of 2,500." (120, p. 212)

Graphics are stored in multiple forms

Human beings process several "channels" of information simultaneously. Each channel has a different input stimulus, and is stored in a different part of the brain (123). The channels are:

- Written words or numbers
- Auditory inputs and vocal chord movements when reading aloud
- Graphics
- Manual writing or drawing movements when taking notes or making sketches
- Attitudes from the input or from memory
- Environmental information, such as noise
- Muscular processing, if interacting with the information

The more channels used to process the information, the more areas of the brain are activated and the more locations the information is stored in (123). By the mechanism of *conjoint retention*, properties of an image are stored in one memory channel and verbal information in another. Visual information is recorded in both (339).

"Pictures are more memorable because they are encoded both imaginally and verbally while words are only encoded verbally." (340, p. 304)

 Which of these lists is easiest to memorize?

zak	cure	marble
guv	peace	Cadillac
poj	vapor	whiskey
vig	color	Lassie
tra	animal	scarlet

"There is a tremendously large storage capacity for pictorial information and, therefore, visual contexts through which to associate other items for recall. While most memory loses detail, the meaning or sense of the representation is retained, with enough of the pattern to reconstruct most of the main elements portrayed in the picture." (123, p. 99)

Visual memories are highly linked

Not only are visual images stored in several forms, but the visual memories are tightly linked to one another and to other forms.

Purely verbal memories are stored in the *taxon* memory system where memories lack linkages to related memories. This system is unconnected to long-term memory sites, and information here fades rapidly unless used often. This is why cramming for an exam seldom produces true learning (123).

Visual memories are stored in the *locale* memory system, which includes linkages among memories. These linkages form a context of related events that provide more cues to trigger the visual memory and allow visual memories to trigger other memories of associated events and objects (45).

Graphics are self-correcting

The eye and mind are forgiving. Less than perfect graphics still manage to communicate well and with extra effort we can make sense of all but the worst graphics. The context of a graphic makes errors stand out and correct conclusions easy to infer (223). Furthermore, we can examine visual images suggested by explicit graphics more reliably than we can images formed by reading words. With words, the image must be constructed by the reader and it is never as vivid as the explicit image provided by a graphic (97).

WHY ARE MANY GRAPHICS BAD?

Despite the clear potential for graphics to aid in communicating difficult concepts, many documents use graphics poorly. The reasons stem from outdated attitudes and ignorance.

Give graphics their say

"The conservatives among us see the visual piece, in all its alluring forms, as nothing but the dependent auxiliary of the verbal element, as the jaunty parlourmaid among the reliable house staff." (46, p. 37)

Graphics are treated as secondary to words

The prevailing attitude expressed in most textbooks on technical writing and practiced in most publications departments is that graphics are secondary to words. Where graphics are used, they are generated after the text is complete (329). Graphics included in documents are often chosen on the basis of cost, ease of production, and attractiveness (45).

Even the plainest, least expensive medieval books were profusely and beautifully illustrated. Yet since the seventeenth century, visual thinking and expression have been held in low regard in Western cultures. Today, many illustrations in technical documents are "little more than afterthoughts included perhaps for the benefit of the mathematically illiterate" (231, p. 16). Many scientists "view our pictures only as ancillary illustrations of what we defend by words" (114, p. 8).

The potential effectiveness of graphics is often repressed by the way they are used on the page. Consider these common practices:

- Placing graphics in a separate, secondary part of the book or far from related portions of text

- Using boxes and borders to unnecessarily separate text and related graphics

- Distorting graphics to fit the page's text margins

- Making graphics merely recite what is already said in the text

Departmental practices and procedures also make clear that graphics are considered less than necessary:

- Hiring professional writers but having graphics done by amateur illustrators

- Writing the text first and adding graphics only as a second thought and at the last minute

- Omitting figures and trying to explain everything in words when deadlines are tight

- Failing to edit graphics—tolerating shoddy, even misleading, graphics while sweating over a comma that only an editor will ever notice

- Seeking training in verbal communication but not in visual communication

And, finally, many publishing specifications work against good graphics by prescribing a rigid format and typography that severely restrain the use of graphics (65).

"Graphics are dropped into a manuscript almost as an afterthought. Sort of like adding a squirt of vanilla to an already-baked cake." (65, p. E-32)

 What is wrong with this figure?

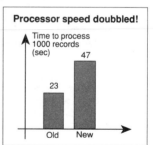

Did you find the typo but miss the fact that the title and the data disagree? Which is the more critical error?

"Unless facts are presented in a clear and interesting manner, they are about as effective as a television without a picture tube." (102, p. G&P-24)

"Showy but useless graphics are still encountered everywhere, even in scholarly journals and works devoted to graphic representation. Their main result is to hide the content of the information from the user, thus doing a real disservice to graphics. Experiments have shown that readers do not even look at them." (24, p. 260).

Graphics are used just to decorate

No one would suggest using an ugly graphic when an attractive one would work just as well. Many illustrators, however, do compromise or even defeat the effectiveness of graphics by considering only the aesthetics of the image. In technical graphics, form must follow function, and when it does, the results are usually pleasing to the eye. When function is ignored and graphics are used merely to decorate, viewers are frustrated, bored, or insulted.

"It is clear, therefore, that typographic and numerical skills, long thought sufficient for the professional communicator's tasks, are no longer enough." (231, p. 18)

Writers know words, not graphics

Most technical writers suffer from the twin diseases of logomania and graphophobia. They know and love words but not graphics. Students majoring in writing were less than half as likely (43 percent versus 87 percent) to use visuals when creating descriptions as were students with technical backgrounds. When creating consumer instructions, the same held true (100 percent versus 64 percent) (303).

"Editors who delve fearlessly into text may tread lightly over illustrations through lack of confidence." (8, p. W-147)

The writer or editor who would not tolerate a misplaced comma or misspelled word, often turns a blind eye to shoddy, confusing, or misleading graphics (276).

"The design community has failed to resolve the problem by incorporating the latest findings from the perceptual and cognitive sciences. Instead, they continue to employ 18th and 19th century design conventions to solve 20th century information problems. The result: a flood of poorly designed, inefficient, and ineffective information products." (116, p. 42)

Communicators lack training

Those charged with creating technical documents often lack training in creating functional graphics. Of the 100 or so textbooks on technical communication in print, many don't mention graphics at all and few devote more than a cursory chapter to the subject of graphics (46; 270). Degrees in technical communication are largely offered by the English department whose curriculum seldom includes more than an occasional course on page layout and typography.

"… the generation of graphics is shifting to individuals who are inexperienced in creating graphic output and lack formal training in graphic design, thereby increasing the possibility of a proliferation of hard-to-understand and misleading visuals." (149, p. 766)

Increasingly, technical writers with access to electronic publishing programs are expected to create their own graphics. Many publications groups have no full-time professional illustrators. Some have no access to illustration services at all.

Many companies have provided the writers of their documentation with computer drawing tools. The thinking is that these tools will enable writers to create effective graphics. But even though writers readily master the mechanics of operating such programs, they lack training in the effective use of graphics. They know *how to do* but not *what to do*. Instead of staring at a blank page of paper, they stare at a blank computer screen.

"At present, we seem to take visual literacy as a given despite the fact that our entire educational process aims at verbal literacy at the expense of the visual." (267, p. 7)

Writers and illustrators do not collaborate successfully

Even organizations that have illustrators produce ineffective graphics when writers and illustrators do not communicate clearly (42). Writers, lacking a clear visual sense, may fail to identify concepts that need graphics and may attempt to explain the concepts to be illustrated. Illustrators may misinterpret the writer's verbal description. Writers may resist the illustrator's suggestions for adding illustrations, and the illustrator may resent criticism of graphics by the writer.

There is no canon of excellence

There is no universally recognized canon of excellence for graphics. For verbal languages, the rules of grammar and spelling are firmly established, widely accepted, and thoroughly taught (295). Not so for graphics. Authorities disagree, sometimes bitterly. What one reveres, another reviles. Often the same image serves one authority with an example of how to do it right while another finds it an example of all that is wrong with graphics. For instance, compare page 32 of *The Designer's Guide to Creating Charts and Diagrams* (141) and page 34 of *Envisioning Information* (314).

"There have been insufficient guidelines for designing formats used in presenting information intended to communicate concepts, general information, or even simple procedures. ... Writers of technical manuals, designers of programmed instructions, and designers of equipment are continually faced with the problem of selecting among pictorial, schematic, and printed formats to communicate information, with little or no knowledge of the format's effect on understanding or comprehension of the information presented." (32)

Research is incomplete

The quest for research-based guidelines is thwarted by the lack of research on graphics and by the limitations of much of the research done so far. Several problems plague the existing research literature:

Not all research is flawed. Several technical journals routinely publish up-to-date, scientifically valid research on graphical formats:

- *Human Factors*, published by the Human Factors Society

- *Transactions on Professional Communication*, published by IEEE

- *Technical Communication*, published by the Society for Technical Communication

"At the same time, research into learning has made us recognize that people do not learn just by words but that a careful blend of visual and verbal messages is most likely to reach listeners." (119, p. 137)

Even blocks of text appear as graphics when surrounded by blank space or lines. Remember that lists and tables are graphical forms too.

- **Atypical test subjects**. Much of the research dating back to the 1920s was done in the British Civil Service and the U.S. Military, whose members may not represent current computer users (293).

- **Oversimplified tests**. Most graphics research has used short tests, typically less than two minutes (293), and dealt with only simple tasks with a short, linear path to a clear goal in a well-structured environment. Modern computer systems, especially those with graphical user interfaces, let users organize their own actions to navigate among countless paths to a goal they set (290).

- **Poor method**. Many early tests used questionable experimental methods and data-collection techniques (293).

WHEN TO USE GRAPHICS

Use graphics alone or with words as appropriate. Keep in mind that most research efforts comparing text and graphics have found that the proper combination of text and graphics outperforms either alone.

When do you need mostly words?	When do you need mostly graphics?	When do you need an even balance of both?
For abstract concepts, emotions, nuances (79)	To show what something looks like	For quicker, more accurate comprehension
To describe nonvisual sensory experience—touch, smell, and taste (173)	To clarify messages that may be misunderstood in text (119)	For complex subjects and critical tasks (258)
When cultural taboos limit use of visuals (97)	For objects that must be recognized reliably	When communicating to a diverse audience
	For objects with similar names but which must be remembered reliably (123)	When a word-picture is too vague (166)

VISUAL THINKING AND CREATIVITY

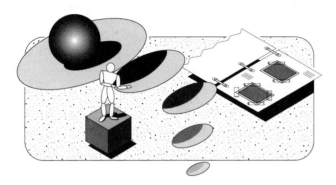

"I'm no artist," you say. "I can't draw a straight line, and even if I could draw, I couldn't think of anything to draw. I just don't think visually." Nonsense. We all think visually and with a little practice can conceive and carry out clear, effective graphics.

"Most aspects of imaging seem to be innate capacities that only require use to develop; and unlike language, even adults are usually able to develop these capacities fairly readily." (166, p. 186)

VISUAL LITERACY REQUIRES VISUAL THINKING

Visual literacy is the ability to understand, think, and create graphically (73). It is far more than the passive process of just taking in visual images. It involves highly active, pattern-seeking and pattern-making activities (206).

"Not only the transmission of ideas but the very ideas themselves are limited by the designer's sensitivity to visual relationships. Understanding is based upon a perception of pattern amidst the ebb and flow of visual stimuli." (19, p. 3)

Practice flexible thinking

More flexible thinking lifts you over the barriers to good communication.

Connect the dots

Without raising your pen or pencil from the paper, connect the following nine dots with just four straight lines. (Solutions are on page 26.)

Connect the dots again

Too easy, you say! Now connect the dots with just three straight lines.

Connect the dots yet again

Now that you've warmed up, try connecting the dots with just one straight line.

Advantages of visual thinking

Visual thinking gives not one but many languages in which to represent, manipulate, and express our ideas (206). Before we can write about a subject, we must understand it. And to understand it, we must visualize it. Francis Crick and James Watson could not explain the replication of DNA until they saw it as a double helix. Many feel that Einstein failed to make breakthroughs in his later life because he forsook concrete mental images for mathematical equations (329). Nikola Tesla, inventor of the AC generator and fluorescent lights, claimed he could "picture complete in every detail, every part of the machine. The pictures were more vivid than any blueprint" (166). Tesla claimed to use these images to conduct week-long simulations, after which he would examine the parts for wear.

We all think visually

We all think visually. In fact, we could not proceed from bed to breakfast without clear visual thinking (179). Sir Francis Galton, in 1883, reported that only about 12 percent of those he tested reported they could not form mental images. In a 1965 poll of Mensa members, only 3 percent reported they did not use visual images (166). A study of 500 people found that 97 percent reported experiencing visual images, while only 92 percent reported auditory images (205).

People vary in their ability to form and use images. They differ in these ways (166):

- Ability to find a part of a whole image
- Ability to hold an image in mind
- Ease of generating images
- Reliance on static versus dynamic images (children rely more on static images (242))
- Sharpness or graininess of the mental images and the size of the image

LEARN TO THINK VISUALLY

Learn to observe accurately

Often we have difficulty communicating visually because what we create is not what we or others really see. We create what we remember and we remember what we pay attention to, not what we see. Remember, to make objective, recognizable graphics, we must take care to draw the subject of the illustration, not our personal interpretation of that subject.

Learn to see. Consciously monitor the visions your eyes take in. Pay attention to and guide your daydreams (206). Watch TV and movies with the sound off. Look at pictures upside down. Trace famous works of art and effective print advertisements.

Get training

We all tend to feel uncomfortable doing a job for which we have inadequate training. Unfortunately, our Western educational system ensures that few of us receive training in creating graphics. Count the number of hours of training you have had in visual communication and compare it to the number in verbal communication. Include formal and informal classes and training sessions. Unless you are a professional artist with an educational background in the arts, you have probably had much more training in communicating verbally than visually.

The obvious solution is to get more training in graphical communication. Help is readily available. Examples include:

- Courses at community colleges, art associations, and museums

- How-to-draw books such as *Thinking With a Pencil* by Henning Nelms (223) and *Drawing on the Right Side of the Brain* by Betty Edwards (85)

- Computer drawing programs that make experimenting painless and even fun

 Draw what you see, not what you remember.

Without looking up from this page, sketch a human face on the oval.

Now compare your sketch to the faces of the people around you. Pay special attention to the position and spacing of the eyes. Most people sketch the eyes too high. Why? Because we pay little attention to the part of the face above the eyes. Now sketch the face again.

 Practice thinking visually

Imagine a cube. It is painted red and then cut into thirds vertically, horizontally, and longitudinally as shown.

1. How many of these 27 small cubes are red on three sides?
2. On only two sides?
3. On only one side?
4. How many are unpainted?

"This notion of building good visual habits suggests that sending writing majors to the art department for a graphic fundamentals class is not a sufficient response." (303, p. RET-129)

 Never publish a tracing of copy-righted images without permission of the copyright owner.

Standard geometric shapes

Common graphical objects

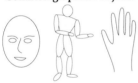

Draw on a grid

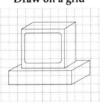

Draw blank space

Learn to draw

Professional illustrators have evolved a grab-bag of techniques to simplify and streamline drawing. These range from pragmatic to philosophical, but all can help boost your drawing abilities.

☐ Before starting, take a few slow, deep breaths. Establish a calm and observant state of mind (85; 206).

☐ Trace the original. This is not cheating. Often the tracing is adequate for many purposes. Tracing teaches us the nature of shapes and curves and helps us develop a sensitivity to curve and shape (223).

☐ Learn to draw basic geometric shapes, such as the cube, cylinder, cone, and sphere, and compose more complex shapes from these simpler building blocks (125). Throughout the centuries, teachers of drawing have instructed their pupils to compose realistic images by combining standard shapes and forms (schemata) and modifying them to achieve the meaning they would express (111).

☐ Learn to draw basic shapes and common objects, such as the human face, frame, and hands.

☐ Measure the proportions of the object, and transpose them to paper. A ruler and grid paper are usually all that is needed (125).

☐ View the original through a grid. Draw small squares of the original, one at a time. Also use the grid to compare relative lengths and sizes. Drawing through a grid prevents interpretive rearrangement (111).

☐ Turn the original upside down. Doing so blocks our tendency to draw what we interpret rather than what we see (85).

☐ Don't sketch the object directly. Instead sketch the spaces around and within the object (85).

☐ Use electronic aids:

- Computer drawing programs
- Scanners to pull paper art into the computer

- Automatic tracing programs that make editable versions of your scanned sketches

- Electronic (or paper) clip-art

☐ Draw sketchily, quickly, and broadly. Rough out the large forms. You can refine them and add detail later (125).

Keep a visual journal

Perhaps you keep a diary or journal of your activities, thoughts, or feelings. Why not add graphics to the words (206)?

☐ Sketch objects you might otherwise describe.

☐ Doodle to make your daydreams visible.

☐ Design a set of symbols to label your notes.

How many windows were in the kitchen of the house or apartment you lived in when you were nine years old?

Put visuals in the rest of your life

Visual thinking is not something restricted to the office. Make it a part of your home and leisure activities.

☐ Take up a visual hobby such as sketching, painting, or photography.

☐ Play visual games, such as *Pictionary.*

☐ Join visual design organizations and participate in their activities.

☐ Visit museums and art galleries.

☐ Associate with visually literate individuals, invite them to your parties, and attend theirs.

OBSERVE AND IMITATE

Keep a notebook of effective visuals

Graphics notebook

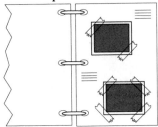

Collect illustrations, photographs, advertisements, cartoons, and other visual images you can use as models or inspiration (219; 125). Look for images you find effective, interesting, provocative, or especially bad (25). Cut or copy them from books, manuals, newspapers, and magazines. Label each example you have collected and record why you included it, and what it exemplifies. Also, identify the source of the example (77). Include multiple copies of an example that fits under several categories.

Study fine art

"Too many persons visit museums and collect picture books without gaining access to art. The inborn capacity to understand through the eyes has been put to sleep and must be reawakened. This is best accomplished by handling pencils, brushes, chisels, and perhaps cameras." (11, p. 1)

Studying art and composition is important for technical communicators because before reading a diagram, before seeing data in a chart, before looking up values in a table, the viewer confronts composition. Technical photographers, for instance, can learn much from the still lifes, close-ups, and portraits of great artistic photographers such as Edward Steichen (297).

How to learn from a museum

Go through the museum rapidly, giving each work no more than a glance, until … one work arrests your attention:

1. Stop and focus on this one work, forgetting the others you've seen.

2. Savor the feeling. Let your eyes go where they will. Be the passive observer, noting your reactions but not consciously controlling them.

3. Study the work. Only after experiencing it should you begin to figure out what grabbed your attention, what guided your eye, what drew attention to areas of fine detail.

4. Pick one technique from the work of art and apply it to something in your world of work.

Remember, it is better to know the few best works well than to know many mediocre ones moderately.

Seek models of graphical excellence

Carefully observe the techniques and strategies of documents that depend on effective visuals. Collect these. Subscribe to them. Study them. My collection includes the following:

- *Scientific American*

- *National Geographic*

- *Mad* Magazine

- *Classics Illustrated* comic books

- *The Way Things Work* by David Macaulay (189)

- *How to Keep Your Volkswagen Alive* by John Muir (217)

PUT PICTURES WITH WORDS

Write to encourage graphics

Often the way we create documents encourages words but not graphics. Take steps to make graphics as easy to create as words:

- Write your draft in two columns: one for words and the other for drawings (26).

- Swap lined paper for grid, ortho, or plain paper.

- Turn pages sideways to draw in landscape orientation.

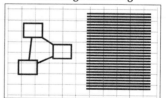

Encourage sketching

Convert words and numbers to graphics

More than any other factor, the type of information determines the most appropriate format for the purpose at hand.

Numerical values

Numbers rate, rank, quantify, and describe. The type of graphic best qualified to show numerical values depends on whether you want to show exact quantities or only general ratios. It also depends on how many numbers are involved.

For this type information:		Use this type graphic:
Exact values	Few	Chart annotated with values
	Many	Table
Relative values	Absolute	Bar or column chart
	Proportion	Pie chart
Correlation		Scatter chart with a correlation line
Trend		Line chart

Logical relationships

Several types of graphics are dedicated to showing the logical relationships among objects and concepts.

For this type information:		Use this type graphic:
Logical arguments, cause to effect		Words, supplemented with a diagram
Logical analysis, effect to cause		Words, supplemented with a diagram
Parts-whole relationships		Tree diagram, Chinese-box diagram, indented list
Interrelationships		Symbol-link diagram, box-border diagram
Relative importance		Numbered list
Decision rules	Single, simple decision	Bullet list, selection table
	Single, complex decision	Decision table, flowchart, decision tree

Procedures and processes

Another class of graphics tells us how to do something or how something is made or done.

For this type information:		Use this type graphic:
Action sequence	Performed in particular order	Numbered list
	Performed in any order, but all required	Checklist
	Performed by more than one person	Playscript
Decisions	Series of simple, independent decisions	Decision tree, selection tables, decision tables, indented list
	Network of simple, interrelated decisions	Flowchart

Visual and spatial characteristics

Many graphics simply show what something looks like or where it is located.

For this type information:		Use this type graphic:
Appearance	Simple subject	Photograph
	Complex subject	Line drawing
Shapes		Rendering
Spatial relationships	In two dimensions	Map
	In three dimensions	Line drawing
Internal components	For general information and a nontechnical audience	Cutaway
	For showing technician how to assemble an object	Exploded parts diagram
	For showing a professional how something is designed	Cross-section

Organizational relationships

Organizational relationships concern how parts make up a system. Graphics can help us see how various parts form a pattern of relationships. Four patterns are common: series, grids, hierarchies, and webs.

For this type information:		Use this type graphic:
Chain	Unordered	Bullet list
	Ordered or ranked	Numbered list
Grid		Table
Hierarchy		Indented list, tree diagram, organization chart, Chinese-box diagram
Web		Symbol-link diagram

Temporal relationships

Time is a powerful organizing principle, and many graphics are dedicated to showing how things change as time passes.

For this type information:		Use this type graphic:
Trend		Line chart
Simultaneous events		Timeline
Repeated patterns	Cyclic	Cycle diagram
	Alternating	Playscript
Narratives		Words, flowchart

Find graphical forms for what you have to say

For the kinds of documents you produce, you can identify common phrases, sentences, and paragraphs and select visual alternatives to them. For each of these verbal forms, you should try to identify a few different visual forms for use in different circumstances. You may want a formal graphic for a straight-laced technical journal and a casual one for a general-interest magazine. You may want a form that can be produced directly from your word processor and another that is highly visual. You may need one quick-and-easy form and another that is more polished.

The key to converting words and numbers to graphics is to first identify the kind of information the words and numbers express—or should express. Then you can usually find a matching graphical form. The following table gives some examples of words translated into graphics.

Words	Type information	Type graphic
Measured values for the alpha, beta, and gamma test sites were 13.667, 16.784, and 22.782, respectively.	Exact, absolute numbers	Table, graph annotated with exact values
The error rate for programs with online documentation was about one-half that of those without.	Relative numbers	Bar or column chart, table
Temperature rose continuously over the test period, but pressure plummeted at the flash point.	Trend, related changes	Line chart, series of visual symbols
… is composed of …. … is made up of …. … consists of … …comprises …	Parts-whole relationship	Organization chart, exploded parts diagram
First you…. Then you …. Next you …. Finally you ….	Step, by step instructions	Numbered list, checklist
… is proportional to … … varies inversely as … … and … show a high degree of correlation.	Correlation	Scatter chart, line chart
Make sure you have all of these tools before you begin: screwdriver, soldering iron, needle-nose pliers, voltmeter, and grounding strap.	Required items	Checklist with pictures of the required items
You can view your document in four ways: as an outline, in galleys, as individual pages, and as two-page spreads.	Alternatives, choices	Bullet list, visual symbols, pictures

Solutions to flexible-thinking exercises

Solution for four lines

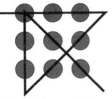

No one said the lines couldn't extend outside the area of the dots.

Solution for three lines

The instructions didn't specify that the lines had to pass through the center of the dots.

Solutions for one line

Paint the line with a wide brush.

Tear out the dots and paste them down in a straight line.

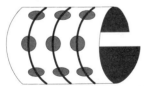

Bend the edges of the paper around and offset so that the ends of the three separate lines join to form one helical line.

Words	Type information	Type graphic
A does .... Then B does .... Next A does ..., and B does .... Finally A does ... and B does	Multiple person procedure	Playscript, procedure table
If ... and ..., then ...; otherwise	Rules for a complex decision	Decision table, selection table, decision tree
If ... then do .... Next, if ... do ...; otherwise do	Network of simple, interrelated decisions	Flowchart, series of decision tables
The test site is on Mount Madison, three miles north of Highway 41 just east of Miller's Ferry Road.	Geographic location, spatial relationships	Map, numbered instructions
The fuel-mixture sensor is located at the rear of the engine intake manifold, just below the injector plug.	Location, spatial relationships in three dimensions	Drawing, photograph
The wheel bearing surrounds the wheel shaft and is held in place by a thrust plate secured by three screws.	Spatial relationships	Exploded parts diagram
The budget was proportioned as follows: supplies 25 percent, salaries 36 percent, advertising 22 percent, shipping 14 percent, and reserve 3 percent.	Proportions	Pie chart, stacked bar chart
A requires B, which in turn requires C and D. E may be substituted for C and F may be substituted for A. However, E and F are not compatible.	Mutual relationships	Diagram, matrix

LANGUAGE OF GRAPHICS

3

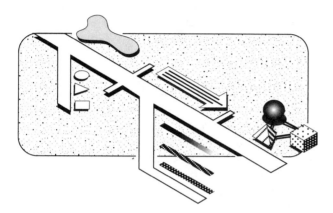

This chapter is both the simplest and most advanced in this book. It takes you "back to basics." It explores the fundamental elements and characteristics of graphics and shows how they combine to communicate specific kinds of messages. Understanding such fundamentals enables you to extend standard graphical forms and even create entirely new graphical forms.

THE COMPONENTS OF GRAPHICS

Every drop of ink, every pixel of a graphic either contributes to the meaning and effectiveness of the graphic or is noise.

> Graphic = message + redundancy + decoration + noise

The **message** is simply what you want to say. It is the meaning, the information, the signal you are trying to convey.

Redundancy means saying the same thing more than one way, such as signaling caution by a triangular shape and yellow color. Redundancy is not waste; it adds predictability. It resists misinterpretation and accommodates busy, varied, sometimes imperfect viewers (57). It is absolutely necessary in

"Like all good communication services, our senses rarely take chances with one signal alone. They make use of what engineers call 'redundancies,' the mutual confirmation of messages by repetition and cross reference." (111, p. 275)

Whether a component is message, redundancy, decoration, or noise depends also on the knowledge, goals, and interest of the viewer. A knowledgeable viewer may be annoyed or distracted by redundant elements. Likewise, decorative elements may actually hinder a highly motivated reader.

communication (330). In fact, English prose is about 75 percent redundant (210).

Graphical characteristics without meaning are either decoration or noise. **Decoration** draws the eye to the graphic. If decoration does not get in the way of meaning, it can be useful, motivating the reader to study the graphic in detail. Decorative aspects further the purposes of the graphic but do not represent information directly. **Noise** is anything that interferes with meaning.

These components are highly interrelated. Redundancy is necessary to overcome noise and to accommodate less than perfect viewers. The less noise there is, the less redundancy is required. Decorative elements that fail become noise. To gauge the decorative component of an illustration, identify features not strictly necessary to communicate factual information. For instance, if a component is drawn larger or in more detail than necessary, these features are either decorative or they are noise.

Consider a circuit diagram. In such a diagram, different types of components are identified by different shapes. Such shapes convey meaning. If the diagram also uses color to reinforce the distinctions among components, the use of color is redundant. . However, if colors were assigned, not to reinforce the shape codes, but merely to make the graphic more visually attractive, then the use of color would be decorative. If the diagram has a frilly border, that border is decoration. If the diagram is cluttered with many small notes of no interest to the viewer, then such notes are noise. If colors were assigned randomly, then they too would be noise.

GRAPHICAL LANGUAGES

Since the 1600s when Leibnitz proposed developing a universal language of visual symbols that could be combined and read with the precision and logic of mathematics, many graphical languages have been proposed. These have included Charles Bliss's Semantography (30), Christopher Alexander's Pattern Language (7), Otto Neurath's ISOTYPE (International System Of TYpographic Picture Education) (224), Yukio Ota's LoCos (234), Tom Zavalani's Jet Era Glyphs (281), and Picto by Jansen (213). Although these graphical languages have achieved limited success in specific disciplines, none have come to rival spoken or written languages. Nor do they encompass the many forms of graphics we use daily.

In this chapter I do not propose a new language but attempt to show how the many graphical forms achieve meaning and how we consciously and unconsciously use them. I treat graphics as a language, but as a language very different from English, French, or Chinese.

Though visual language has analogies with traditional literary rhetoric, an exact correspondence is unlikely (266). The human mind processes visual information in fundamentally different ways from how it handles heard or read words. Visual grammar is not like verbal grammar. The two do not share common parts of speech, syntax, and rules (257).

Imagine a language with only concrete nouns and adjectives—no verbs, no abstract nouns, no adverbs. Thus to convert a verbal expression to graphics, we must convert all verbs, abstract nouns, and adverbs to concrete nouns and adjectives. In graphics, we must represent tense, active and passive voice, and abstraction indirectly—by visual metaphor.

"Graphic representation constitutes one of the basic sign-systems conceived by the human mind for the purposes of storing, understanding, and communicating essential information." (24, p. 2)

"To produce high-quality graphics, we need to learn good graphic grammar. Just as there are grammatical rules for composing effective prose, there are rules for composing effective graphics." (118, p. VC-66)

On a scale of directness, we can show:
Objects (concrete nouns)
Characteristics of objects (adjectives)
Relationships between objects (adjectives)
Change (state of being or passive verbs)
Action on or by objects (action verbs)
Abstract concepts (abstract nouns)

Parts of a graphic

Every graphic consists of a context and backdrop in which graphical objects are set.

Context

Visual objects, such as words, depend on context for meaning. Their full meaning depends on the surrounding body of discourse of which they are a part (336). For a graphic, the context includes:

- Other images in the reader's field of view

- Active memories and expectations

- Biases, appetites, and interests of the viewer

In many ways what we see is influenced more by this context than by what is contained in the graphic itself.

Backdrop

The backdrop is the part of the graphic we don't notice consciously. It identifies the scope of the graphic and

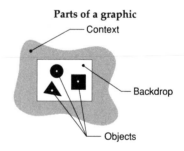

Parts of a graphic
Context
Backdrop
Objects

establishes a frame of reference against which the graphical objects are measured. It consists of:

- Frame or border around the graphic
- Background surface

Often the backdrop is simply blank space.

Objects

Graphical objects are the symbols we use to encode meaning in graphics. An object is something recognized by the viewer. It may be only a primitive point, line, or area, or it may be the likeness of a physical object. It may be an abstract symbol rife with emotional associations. It is whatever we process as a unit.

Objects are made up of:
- Other objects
- Graphical elements, which include
    - Points
    - Lines
    - Areas

Because an object is whatever we see as a meaningful unit, the definition of object changes as we view a graphic. An object may be a group of lower-level objects. Objects may overlap. A low-level object may belong to two or more higher-level groups.

Top-down processing

Top-down processing decomposes the graphic from the top of this hierarchy, first identifying the graphic in its context and separating backdrop from content. It then divides the whole graphic into groups and objects within groups. This decomposition may continue until the viewer finds the meaning desired.

Top-down processing

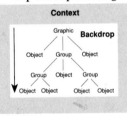

Imagine that you are standing at the corner waiting to cross the street and your eye is captured by a bright light in your peripheral vision. You turn your head and a large red shape momentarily fills your field of view. As you focus on it you quickly recognize it as an automobile. (The bright light was the glint off the windshield.) You notice that it is a four-door sedan, and because you are considering buying such a model, you continue to stare. As you study the car, you notice more details, such as the shape of the doors, the profile of the rear-view mirror, and the fact that the mirror is cracked. Someone merely interested in crossing the street without being run over might have stopped top-down processing after classifying the car as an obstacle or threat and would not have noticed or remembered any of the lower-level details.

THE BACKDROP SETS THE STAGE

The background and frame of the graphic help define its scope and provide a frame of reference for interpreting the graphical objects contained in the graphic.

Background

There is a tendency to think of the background as empty space; in other words, just what's left over after the graphical objects are drawn. Such thinking defeats the two clear purposes of the background: to provide a baseline reference for graphical objects and to separate and organize those elements.

The human perceptual system is poor at making absolute judgments of color, size, lightness, or other graphical characteristics. It does, however, make effective comparisons between nearby images. The background of the graphic thus sets the reference level against which graphical objects are evaluated. A white background will make gray objects appear darker while a black background will make them appear lighter. A background that too closely matches the characteristics of an object will swallow and hide that object.

It may seem odd to think of blank space as a graphical force. Blank space is not nothingness, not just what's left over, not insulation to keep ideas from touching. It isolates individual forms and shepherds the viewer's eyes about the design in a predictable path. Blank space can communicate. Using blank space actively, between and among objects, can signal (307):

- Relative importance of objects—put more blank space around more important objects.

- Groupings of objects—place related objects close together and unrelated ones farther apart.

- Interrelationships among objects.

Background is basis for comparison

"Genuine white space is an active participant in the design of the page (i.e., functional design—that works to get ideas off the page into the reader's mind)." (334, p. 47)

Blank space is "the most misused, misunderstood, abused material on the page." (334, p. 47)

Blank space shows relationships

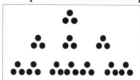

Frame directs view

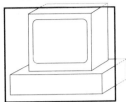

Frame

The frame of a graphic is the limit of the graphic within the viewer's field of view. The frame, visible or implied, is not a passive decorative feature. The frame isolates the enclosed area from its environment and places its contents "on show" (97). It affects the balance, force, relative importance, and weight of graphical objects within the frame (336) and imposes order upon them (304). It provides psychological security to viewers (19). The frame shows the limits of the visual symbology. If the subject extends to the frame, it is perceived as continuing beyond the borders of the illustration (24).

Should you put explicit borders around graphics? Many designs include a rectangular border to clearly show the extent of the figure. Others dispense with the border and let the margins and edges of surrounding text define the frame of the graphics. Still others integrate text and graphics in such a way that text flows tightly around the graphic, giving the graphic an irregular outline.

Reasons to box graphics	Reasons to avoid boxes around graphics
Some research suggests that users refer to boxed graphics more quickly and more often than unboxed ones (255).	A reluctance to cross borders may cause some readers to detour around boxed graphics.
The shape and style of the box can designate the type of information contained in the graphic.	Because the subject cannot extend all the way to the border, borders waste space (223).
Graphics that contain text, such as images of computer screens, can be placed closer to body text without confusion.	

You can make the border a meaningful part of the graphic by using it to reinforce and clarify the message of the graphic:

☐ Make the border of computer screens rounded like the screen itself (25).

☐ When showing reports, forms, screens, and windows, style the border of the graphic to resemble the border of the object shown.

Border sets context

Screen   Window   Report

☐ Show three-dimensional objects in a diamond or trapezoidal frame. The edges of the frame should converge toward imaginary vanishing points (24).

☐ To enhance the three-dimensionality of an object, let it protrude out and over the frame of the illustration.

Border adds depth

Violated border adds depth

GRAPHICAL ELEMENTS

Ultimately all graphics can be divided into simple graphical elements. Frame, background, and graphical objects are made up of points, lines, and areas.

Points

A point is the simplest graphical element. A point is a mark used to represent a position in space. The mark takes up space, but the position it represents does not. The mark may take on graphical characteristics to symbolize concepts that apply at the point's position (24). A geometric point would be invisible. A graphical point, however, is visible. A graphical point is any small mark perceived as a location in space. We seldom see dots as isolated points. Usually their meaning relates to another object (97).

The point is the basis of all graphical objects. A point is zero dimensional. A line is just a point in one dimension; an area, in two; a solid in three; and a moving solid, in four.

In practice, a point must be about 1.5 mm (0.06 in) to display color and 2 mm (0.08 in) to show shape. The most distinctive shapes for points are the circle, plus, and dash (24).

"In graphic terms the dot or point is a materialized area, recognizable by the human eye. It is the smallest graphic unit, as it were the 'atom' of every pictorial expression." (97, p. 23)

Distinctive point shapes

●   ✚   ▬

Lines

Lines outline and divide figures. Typically lines signify boundaries or directions of motion or force (24). Edge and curve lines represent discontinuities in texture, orientation, and value (11). The thin, uniform line is seen as a thread leading the eye, crossing out, framing, or bordering. It represents no physical presence. If the line's thickness changes, it loses its abstract character (97).

Lines can also include symbols along the entire length of the line, at ends, and at regular intervals along the line (180).

"The human eye, which is but an extension of the fingertips, enjoys travelling not only along a line but also between two that provide an open roadway." (19, p. 187)

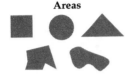

Areas

Areas

Areas are two-dimensional forms. They represent surfaces and two-dimensional extents. Areas can carry a full range of graphical characteristics, such as shape, color, texture, and pattern.

Areas are not entirely distinct from points and lines. At their smallest, areas are perceived as points. The edge of an area defines a line and any line that closes on itself or crosses itself encloses an area.

GRAPHICAL CHARACTERISTICS

Graphical characteristics refer to the visual attributes of graphical elements. Graphical characteristics serve two roles. They tell us something about individual objects that possess the characteristics and they show relationships among separate graphical objects (340).

Dynamics

This book is primarily concerned with static displays—ones in which graphical objects do not change over time. But for computer and television screens, dynamics dominate the display and without them the display would be dull and mute. Some of the dynamic graphical characteristics include:

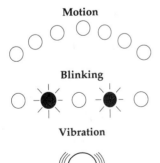

Motion

Blinking

Vibration

- **Motion**. The object may move about the display. It may move smoothly along a curve or zigzag erratically.

- **Blinking**. The object may alternate graphical characteristics; for instance, it may flash bright and dim or pulse first red and then green.

- **Vibration**. The object may shake in place, its size or shape alternating rapidly.

Dynamics are compelling. They are the only graphical characteristics completely effective in peripheral vision. A moving or blinking object demands attention. Dynamics should be used sparingly and only for the true subject of the graphic.

Position

We judge the position of a graphical object relative to ourselves, to the frame of the graphic, and to other objects in the graphic.

Vertical position strongly affects when the element is noticed, as most graphics are scanned top to bottom. It may also suggest the importance of the object or its place in sequence. A higher vertical position strongly suggests priority in importance and in sequence. In realistic scenes, higher objects are seen as farther away. In composing scenes, keep in mind that the optical center of a graphic is actually about five percent above the true center. This is why we typically leave a larger border at the bottom of a graphic.

Horizontal position may also affect when an object is noticed. In cultures that read left to right, more important items are placed to the left of lesser objects, as in an indented outline. However, horizontal position is less powerful than vertical position. Left and right are nearly equal. For primitive man, food or attack was equally likely from left as from right. Modern man has trouble distinguishing b from d (11).

As important is the object's position relative to other objects. Objects close together are seen as related. The eye naturally jumps from object to nearby object. The clustering of small objects around a large one portrays the large object as dominating and protecting the smaller ones (19).

In positioning objects in space, it is useful to think of them as governed by forces of gravity and magnetism. The eye is drawn to the center of an object or cluster of objects (the center of gravity). Objects close together seem linked to one another (magnetic attraction).

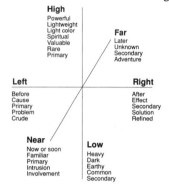

Position and its associated meanings

Meanings associated with positions. (11; 24; 68; 69; 111; 336; 339; 340)

Clustering objects

Value

Value refers to the contrast of an object with its background. For printed documents, value corresponds to the lightness of the ink. Value contrast is essential for us to clearly see an object. At low value contrast, we can see fewer sizes, colors, shapes, orientations, and textures (24).

Dark-adapted eyes can detect a 10 percent lightness difference. In a bright environment eyes require a 70 percent

Value variation

difference (309). When two objects of unequal lightness are shown, the lighter will appear white and the darker, gray or black. As the lightness ratio increases, the lighter area becomes luminous like a glowing full moon (326).

The general lightness of the graphic affects its overall tone. A light tone suggests a friendly, playful mood. A dark tone suggests a somber, serious, or ominous mood. White is aggressive, while black is passive and recessive (91).

Size

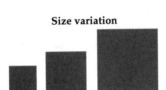

Size variation

Enlarging or reducing an image changes the way it is perceived. We attach significance to the size of an object. In general, we pay more attention to larger objects and attribute more power and importance to then. Consider these phrases indicating the importance conferred by size: *bigger is better, the big picture, large-minded, big deal, big business, Mr. Big, Big Daddy, Big Mama, big cheese, big wheel, big-league, big top, big shot, big man on campus, the Big Ten, small potatoes, small fry, small change, small-minded, smalltime,* and *small talk.*

Color

Color is one of the most powerful graphical characteristics. It is so important—and difficult to use well—that Chapter 13 is devoted to using color to communicate.   What we speak of as color is really three separate graphical characteristics: hue, lightness, and saturation.

- **Hue.** When most people speak of the color of an object, they are referring to its hue. Hues are red, yellow, green, blue, and so forth.

- **Lightness.** Lightness refers to the degree of illumination of the color. Zero lightness would be black. Lightness corresponds to the characteristic we called value.

- **Saturation.** Saturation is the purity of a color. For instance, red has higher saturation than pink. Saturated colors are vivid and strong; less saturated colors are paler and are considered weaker.

Texture

When we refer to the texture of a piece of fabric, we are concerned with how it feels to the touch. Is is smooth or coarse? Are threads fine and closely spaced or large and loosely woven? When we refer to the visual texture of an area, we are likewise concerned with the fineness or coarseness of the constituents of an object. Texture is usually described in terms of the number of lines or marks for a given area. It results from varying the scale of a pattern of marks, but not the pattern of marks itself. Varying texture does not change the overall balance of light and dark (the value) of an area. Technically it is defined as "variation in the fineness or coarseness of the constituents of an area having a given value" (24, p. 61).

At the limit of fineness, we can identify no individual marks in a texture. These limits of fine texture are determined by the display medium. Photography, microfilm, typesetting, laser printing, and computer displays all impose different limits. As scale changes, repeated objects become pattern, texture, and eventually value (179).

Medium values of texture produce a shimmering or vibratory effect of reversing figure and ground. This powerful effect is highly selective but is most annoying when misused or when it occurs by accident. The effect seems most prominent with a 1 mm texture of 50 percent value (24).

Gradual changes in texture indicate changes in the orientation of the surface relative to the viewer or the source of light. The pattern of changes tells whether a surface is flat or curved. Sudden changes of texture indicate edges, folds, or creases (222).

Pattern

Pattern refers to a repeated visual characteristic along a line or over an area. Patterns can be regular or irregular (179).

Variation in texture

Shimmering texture

Changes of texture

Variation of pattern

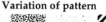

Regular and irregular patterns

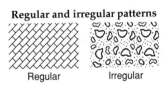

Regular   Irregular

Pattern provides valuable clues about the world. Patterns can represent tactile sensation (69). Patterned areas are usually solid, but unpatterned ones are sky or water. Graininess suggests coarseness, crudeness, vulgarity, and violence (91). All of these clues help us decide where to step, how to grasp, and when to duck (107). In technical graphics, they represent characteristics of surfaces, thereby making objects more recognizable.

Shape

Shape provides the outline of any object we perceive. Shapes can be classified along two scales:

Variations of shape

Straight-edged   Rounded

Regular

Irregular

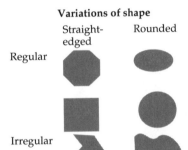

Straight-edged versus rounded

Shapes may be bounded by straight or curved edges. Straight edges are easier to draw and easier for the eye to follow.

Hard edges represent man-made creations; soft edges, living organisms.

A sharp edge maintains contrast; a soft edge weakens it (69).

Regular versus irregular

Areas also vary in the simplicity and predictability of their edges. Regular shapes are quickly perceived and easily remembered—as well as easily reproduced. However, they are less exciting and eye-catching than irregular shapes.

Simple, regular geometric shapes have more weight than more complex, irregular shapes (11).

For abstract concepts and categories, use simple regular shapes. More complex shapes will carry more associations (69).

Visual flow into convex and out of concave shape

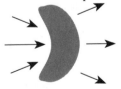

Shapes can also be classified as concave or convex. Concave shapes draw the eye inward, while convex shapes push outward (11).

Our perception of angles is not precise. Angles are seen as acute (less than 90 degrees), right (90 degrees), or obtuse (between 90 and 180 degrees). Angles of 180 degrees are seen as straight lines. Reflex angles (over 180 degrees) are seen as smaller internal angles (19).

Basic categories of angle

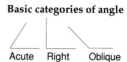

Acute   Right   Oblique

Consider the meaning conveyed by the shape of balloons in cartoons: Puffy thought balloons, smooth-edged speech balloons, and jagged-edged balloons for speech from a radio or telephone (219).

Orientation

The angle or orientation of a figure relative to the viewer and other objects gives it an identifiable character (19). Usually we are vertical when awake, horizontal when sleeping, and diagonal when falling. Therefore, a horizontal orientation of a figure suggests stability and repose; a vertical orientation offers energetic potential; and a diagonal orientation conveys instability and excitement.

Variations of orientation

Orientation also strongly affects how well objects are recognized. We cannot recognize upside-down faces quickly or accurately (94). Recognition for text, shapes, and faces deteriorates with increasing rotation (260).

Combinations

Applying graphical characteristics to graphical objects and elements is tricky. Some objects work better than others with certain characteristics. The following table offers advice.

	Element		
	Point	**Line**	**Area**
Dynamics	The eye can easily follow a moving point—provided the point is large enough and the motion is not too fast or too erratic. Blinking and vibration are quite effective in drawing attention to a small point.	The eye can follow the motion of only a small line segment. Keep moving lines short and simple and make their motions straight and direct.	Moving areas are difficult to follow, unless the area is small (almost a point) and the motion is simple.
Value	Use up to three levels of value.	Use up to four levels of value.	Use up to five levels of value.
Color	Because points are small, limit them to no more than four distinctive colors.	Because lines are thin, use only six contrasting colors.	Positive areas can use six to eight distinct colors.
Size	People can distinguish only about four sizes of points. Drawn too large, points are seen as shapes, not points.	Viewers can distinguish about four widths of lines. Thin lines, especially in a grid, connote scientific and technical precision (141). Broad, clear lines convey a sense of confidence and strength. Delicate, flimsy lines can appear weak and indefinite, as if the ideas they present were tentative (102). Use heavier lines for the shaded side of an object (118). Use different line weights to distinguish overlapping objects (118).	Areas can vary freely in both length and width. In general, viewers can distinguish five sizes.
Texture	Points are too small to display texture well. Limit texture to two or three values.	Lines display texture as a dashed or dotted line, produced by regular breaks in the line. Use up to four line textures.	Areas can use texture freely. Use four or five textures.
Pattern	Points can display only two or three distinctive patterns.	Use dashed or dotted lines for imaginary or hidden lines (118). Limit line patterns to solid and one or two dash patterns.	Use up to four patterns.

	Element		
	Point	**Line**	**Area**
Shape	Points can take on only a few simple shapes. Complex shapes are easily confused. For overall selection, use circles, dashes, and crosses as they are the most distinguishable shapes. Make the dash four times as long as wide. The cross may produce a shimmering effect (24). To be legible as a shape, a mark must be at least 2 mm in size (24).	Lines can be straight, jagged, or curved. The slight irregularities of a freehand line give it a natural, human quality in contrast with the mechanical precision of the smooth, uniform line of the draftsman (150). Use straight lines to suggest a simple, monotonic change. Use jagged lines to indicate that only part of an object is shown and to suggest abrupt, dynamic change. Use smooth lines to suggest continuity and to make following the line easier.	A triangle implies upward movement (when point is upward), downward movement or slowing (when point is downward), stability, the number 3, a trinity. Square shapes imply stability, solidity, firmness, balance, order, the number 4. Rectangular shapes imply security, rationality, grounding—especially if the base is broader than the height. Circles imply unity, oneness, permanence, continuity, eternity, marriage.
Position	Points can be positioned vertically, horizontally, and relative to other objects.	Lines can be positioned vertically, horizontally, and relative to other objects.	Areas can be positioned vertically, horizontally, and relative to other objects.
Orientation	To convey orientation, a point must have a 4:1 height:width ratio (24). For selective tasks, restrict orientation of points to four values: horizontal, vertical, 30 degrees, and 60 degrees (24).	Lines can be horizontal, vertical, or diagonal. Most lines we encounter in daily life are horizontal or vertical (11). For selective tasks, restrict orientation of lines to directions parallel and perpendicular to the line (24). The only oblique line we can gauge with any accuracy is 45 degrees (97).	Shapes may be rotated to any orientation. Rotation may make the shape less recognizable or even transform it into another shape.

PRINCIPLE OF DATA-MAPPING

For a thorough discussion of data-mapping, see *The Semiology of Graphics* by Jacques Bertin. Unfortunately this work is out of print, so check used-book stores and libraries for a copy.

All technical graphics are built on a principle so simple that you probably know it already but have never paused to examine it. When you do, you realize that it can explain the tremendous variety of technical graphics in use and can suggest creative new graphical forms. The principle of data-mapping is:

> Use graphical objects to represent concepts and graphical characteristics to represent corresponding dimensions or traits of these ideas.

For most graphics, we are not aware of the mapping because it is determined either by the conventions of a standard graphical form, such as a perspective drawing or line graph, or because it is supplied by the instincts of a creative designer.

How to encode visual meanings

Assigning symbols for concepts involves an iterative process.

1. **Pick a graphical symbol** for the concept. For example, to compare the speed of various processors, you might select a bar to represent each processor.

2. **Pick a graphical characteristic**. Decide which graphical characteristics will represent characteristics of the concept. Here the length of the bar will represent the speed.

3. **Choose a scaling function**. Define an algorithm, procedure, or heuristic to assign graphical values for data values. The scaling function can be linear, logarithmic, or geometric.

4. **Choose a scaling parameter**. Calibrate the assignment of graphical characteristics to the particular display.

Graphical symbol

298X

298CX

Graphical characteristic

|◄——— Speed ———►|

Scaling function
length = scale factor x speed

Scaling parameter
1 mm = 1 MHz

Pick a graphical symbol for the concept

Showing concepts as visually separate objects keeps them from getting jumbled or blurred in memory (123). In notational symbol systems, each symbolic object in the graphic directly represents one object of the subject. Maps, for instance, use clearly distinguishable symbols, while in nonnotational photographs smooth gradations of tone and texture make distinguishing one object from another difficult (340).

In mapping concepts, don't forget practical considerations, such as the size of the graphic, the size of the mark necessary for perceptually separable symbols, and the number of categories that the reader can readily recognize (24).

The strategy for selecting graphical objects will blend techniques of analogy, projection, aggregation, and filtering.

Mimicry

The most direct form of mapping is to ensure a physical similarity between real-world and graphical objects. With mimicry, the graphical object looks like its counterpart.

We must distinguish between illustrations that show *what is* and those that show *what something looks like*. This is the philosophical distinction between knowing and seeing. Pictures show the appearance from one viewpoint at one moment. Symbolic illustration, such as diagrams, show the essential facts that apply universally.

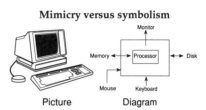

Use mimicry to teach and to focus attention. For initial teaching of concepts show critical features realistically. Also use realistic details to focus attention on individual objects rather than overall patterns (340).

Analogy

Analogy is the direct representation of the characteristics of the object but not of its visual appearance. It is appropriate when it is more important what something is or does than what it looks like. Analogy is thus useful in computer documentation where we must make the invisible inner workings of hardware and software comprehensible. Analogy is also useful when a procedure can be performed in several ways, but we are only interested in the results. Use analogy to create simplified visual symbols, diagrams, and drawings (340):

- To explain how something works

- After initial learning when only recognition is needed

- If the viewer must focus on the big picture and process the graphic holistically

When using visual analogy, make clear the limitations of the analogy before releasing the readers (340).

Projection

By the technique of projection, we create a deliberately ambiguous visual image onto which viewers can project their own interpretations, much like a Rorschach ink blot. Projection is a risky technique because some viewers may project an image quite different from the one you intended. Still, projection is useful provided:

- Graphics are not specific
- Viewers can supply missing details
- Missing details are not essential to the point you are making

For example, if your program runs on many different models of computer, you might present an ambiguous shape with only enough details to clearly suggest a computer but not enough details to represent a particular brand or model.

Aggregation

Aggregation simplifies a graphic by letting one object represent multiple concepts. Forms of aggregation include:

- **Generalization**. To generalize a graphic, omit identifying details. To show a particular object or event, include and emphasize identifying details (223).
- **Categorization**. Divide objects into categories and show all members of the same category with identical symbols.
- **Grading**. Let each graphical object represent a range of numerical values; for instance, bands of color on television weather maps represent ranges of temperature.

Generalization

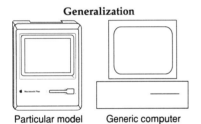

Particular model   Generic computer

Filtering

Filtering selects which objects and details are included and which are not. In general:

Seek out and include	Exclude
Essential concepts, facts	Nice-to-know information
Crucial details, such as edges and creases in drawings	Irrelevant and distracting details
Trends and overall patterns	Anomalies and exceptions (unless they are the subject)

Pick a graphical characteristic

The graphical characteristics you assign to each object depend on the meaning you want to convey. For example, here are how some common graphics use graphical characteristics:

Type of graphic	Dimension or characteristic in the data or subject of the graphic	Corresponding graphical characteristic
Column chart	Category of data	Horizontal position of the bar
	Data value	Height of the bar
List	Sequential order of an item	Vertical position in the list
	Nature of the item	Shape of bullet or other mark
Table	First indexing category	Horizontal position of column
	Second indexing category	Vertical position of row
	Subcategories	Indentation of row head
Diagram	Type of concept	Shape of symbol
	Type of relationship	Style of line connecting symbols
Line drawing	Outer edges of the subject	Heavy lines
	Inner edges of the subject	Moderate lines
	Creases in the subject	Light lines
	Position of the subject	Position in the drawing
Photograph	Position in field of view	Position in graphic
	Lightness of subject	Lightness in photograph
	Color of subject	Color or lightness in photograph
Map	North-south position	Vertical position
	East-west position	Horizontal position
	Type of feature	Shape, color, size

The characteristic chosen must be able to represent fully the corresponding real-world characteristic or dimension. For instance, a continuous variable, such as time or location, cannot be represented by a characteristic with spaces or gaps.

Likewise a ranked series needs a characteristic with as many discriminable steps as the series (24).

Some general recommendations follow:

	What you need to express			
Charac-teristic	**Similarities**	**Categories**	**Order**	**Quantity**
Position	■	■	■	■
Size	□	□	■	■
Value	□	□	■	
Texture	■	■	■	
Pattern	■	■		
Color	■	■		
Orientation	■	■		
Dynamics	■	■		
Shape	■			

Note: ■ = recommended, □ = possible but not recommended

Remember that you are not limited to one graphical characteristic per concept. Double-cue or redundant coding, can help users work with complex displays by giving users a second way to spot or recognize symbols. Redundant coding works well even on extremely complex displays (160).

Choose scaling functions

The next step is to define an algorithm, procedure, or heuristic to assign graphical values for data values. This scaling function is most easily identified in statistical graphics where, for instance, the length of a bar might be proportional to the numerical value it represents.

In many graphics the scaling function is provided by the production process. The optics of the camera ensure that what is vertical in the scene is vertical in the photograph. In mapping, conventions ensure that a northward direction is mapped to a vertical direction on the paper or screen. In drawing, rules of perspective rendering ensure correspondence between subject and image.

For the sake of the designer and the viewer of the graphic, the scaling function should be simple and direct. A logarithmic or geometric scaling of data values often confuses or misleads unsophisticated chart readers.

Choose scaling parameters

Calibrate the assignment of graphical characteristics to the particular display. The scaling factor is chosen to fit the range of information to the space available and to ensure that all symbols are legible. The scaling parameter may just be a scale factor, such as 1 cm on the map representing one kilometer on the earth, or as sophisticated as a compression or expansion of the range of gray tones in a photograph (1; 2; 3; 4; 5). In scaling characteristics (24):

- Make the lowest value sufficient to stand out from the background and visual noise.

- Limit the highest value to prevent overpowering other parts of the graphic or losing identity of individual objects.

- Express the necessary steps between highest and lowest value.

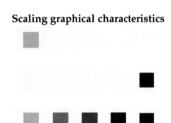

Scaling graphical characteristics

Strive for direct mappings

Graphical objects express meaning by association or mapping. Direct associations which work by visual analogy rely on human pattern matching and require little learning. Arbitrary associations rely on memory and require learning.

We can arrange all graphic associations on a scale from the most direct to the most arbitrary. Using this progression, here are some associations found in graphics:

- Lightness in photographs

- Positions of lines in line drawings

- Length of bars in bar charts

- Shapes and textures in cartoons

- Visual symbols based on simplified physical objects, such as road signs

- Visual symbols based on arbitrary shapes, as in schematic diagrams

- Text and mathematical symbols

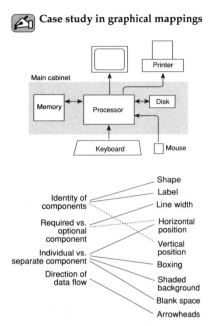

Case study in graphical mappings

Notice that identity is redundantly represented by shape and label. This meaning is reinforced by vertically positioning objects as they might appear in the user's field of view: The monitor is above the cabinet and the keyboard is below. Horizontal position is used both to separate components and to suggest that those to the right are optional. These mappings are not consistent, because the disk is separate but not optional. Confusion is avoided by ensuring that horizontal position is used only as a redundant, secondary mapping.

"The use of the literal, obvious, or clichéd solution should not be shunned. It often communicates the idea fastest." (141, p. 123)

Analyze graphical mappings

One of the best ways to study and improve graphical mappings is to study the mappings of existing graphics. To analyze the mapping of an existing graphic:

1. In one column list the meaning the graphic should express.
2. In another column, list the graphical characteristics used in the graphic.
3. Draw lines from each meaning to the graphical characteristics used to represent it.
4. Draw lines for each characteristic to the meanings it represents.

Now review the results. Meanings with no corresponding characteristics will not be conveyed. Meanings with multiple characteristics are redundantly encoded and are more likely to be understood. Characteristics representing multiple meanings are ambiguous and can lead to confusion. Characteristics with no corresponding meaning are either decoration or noise.

Follow standard mappings

Each graphical idiom has its own rules. In the Venn diagram, overlap represents relationship. In the organization chart, relationship is shown by position on the page and by lines of authority. In a flowchart, arrows symbolize relationships in time (206). If there is an established, expected form for what you have to say, use it. Don't be afraid to use visual clichés. If no standard form exists for what you have to say, create one using the principle of mapping.

MAKING VISUAL STATEMENTS: A BASIC PHRASEBOOK

Of the millions of combinations of graphical elements and characteristics, not all are equally effective for a given purpose. This section provides guidelines for creating effective graphical structures. It reviews strategies for helping viewers find and remember the information they seek.

This exists: Make an object stand out from the background

For us to even perceive an object, we must see it as distinct from the background. The graphic must have good figure-ground contrast. Background contrast is the most important factor in legibility and recognizability of images and their colors (309). Photographs with distracting clutter and trees growing out of people's heads result from the photographer's tendency to ignore the background and attend to the subject.

If text or pictures are superimposed on a background graphic, the original may become unrecognizable and just distract the reader from the real subject. For example, several tutorial screens for Microsoft Excel 2.2 on the Macintosh use the Excel emblem as a backdrop for text and graphics. The graphics cover so much of the emblem that all the viewer sees of it are isolated, amputated shapes—distracting and meaningless.

This is primary: Single out one object

We cannot see or even think of something unless we identify it as separate from all other things. To show something, we must contrast it with everything else or make it stand out from the background and from other objects. To do so we must give it different graphical characteristics from objects nearby.

Design illustrations to draw attention to the essential information, especially if it is unfamiliar to the reader or differs from what the reader expects (323). Techniques to call attention to the subject include:

- ☐ **Display the object in higher contrast** with its background (26). If the background is light, make it the darkest object in the scene. If the background is dark, make it the lightest.

- ☐ **Paint the object in a bright, saturated, warm color** (314). Use brighter, warmer, and higher-contrast colors for emphasis. Warm colors (red and yellow) tend to emphasize, while cool colors (green and blue) tend to deemphasize.

Characteristics of background and object (11; 12; 24; 91; 97; 111; 154; 179; 206; 309)

Background	Object
Large	Small
Unbounded	Bounded
Unbordered	Bordered
Continuous	Discrete
Dark, dim	Light, bright
Farther	Nearer
Peripheral	Central
Cool colors	Warm colors
Unsaturated colors	Saturated colors
Concave	Convex
Static	Dynamic
Untextured or unfeatured	Textured or featured
Upper area	Lower area
Diagonal	Vertical or horizontal
Asymmetrical	Symmetrical
Complex shape	Simple shape
Abstract	Realistic

Object on background

Add contrast

Enlarge the object

Point to the object

Frame the object

Isolate the object

Present object in front

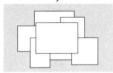

Show just the subject

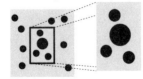

☐ **Make the object larger**. Larger objects appear more important. For objects next to one another, a 5 percent difference is noticeable. If objects are in separate parts of the display, a 30 percent difference may be required.

☐ **Point to the object**. Use elements in the graphic to direct the viewer's eyes to one particular graphical object (159):

- Include arrows pointing to the object.

- Compose the scene so that lines naturally converge on the object.

- If the graphic includes people, have them looking or pointing at the object.

☐ **Frame the object**. Use objects in the scene to form a halo, border, or box around the subject (168; 180).

☐ **Isolate the object**. Surround the object with blank space (11). This halo of blank space is especially effective in an otherwise crowded graphic.

☐ **Show the object in front of other objects**. Immediacy gives weight and importance to graphical objects (11). Things that are nearby are more useful or more threatening. To emphasize one object, let it overlap other objects in the graphic.

☐ **Show the object in motion**. People pay longer and deeper attention to objects shown in action than to ones in a static pose (45). Blinking or moving objects always take priority in our attention. However, only one object should be shown moving or blinking. Urgency can be suggested by the rate of movement or blinking, but don't expect viewers to be able to distinguish more than 2 or 3 different rates.

☐ **Show fewer objects or just the important part of the subject.** To focus attention on part of the screen, show a partial view (256).

☐ **Increase detail in the object.** Detail is lively texture that draws the eye and rewards it with new information (125; 191). Our eyes gravitate to detailed sections of the graphic and spend more time there.

☐ **Focus on the subject**. Ensure that the subject is in crisp focus or drawn with sharp lines. Let other objects fall out of focus. When photographing moving objects, let the camera move to follow a moving object and use a moderate shutter speed. Doing so will blur the background while leaving the moving subject in clear focus (2; 91).

☐ **Give graphics, especially photographs, a clear center of interest,** a single object that draws the viewer's eye to one spot (168).

☐ **Give the object a distinctive shape**. Jagged, irregular shapes are more eye-catching than smooth, regular ones (11).

Use a distinctive shape

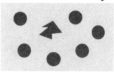

☐ **Position the subject at a hot spot**. Certain locations in a graphic are more likely to draw attention than others. By placing the subject at one of these hot spots, we ensure the viewer notices it. Hot spots include the center, the upper-left corner (in left-to-right reading cultures), and the points one-third and two-thirds of the way from top to bottom and left to right.

Put in hot spot

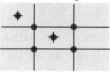

All emphasis depends on contrast. In a graphic filled with large, red, diagonal objects, a single small, blue, horizontal object will dominate. This principle is the visual equivalent of whispering to be heard in a noisy room. The goal is to make the emphasized object visibly unique (233; 309).

In pure graphics, there is no baseline of neutral emphasis—all graphical characteristics vie against one another. On the page, however, body text is the baseline or ground against which all other elements are measured (198). You emphasize objects by making them more prominent than body text and subdue them by making them less prominent.

Limit the amount you emphasize. Any emphasis device loses its effectiveness if overused (33). Highlight no more than 10 percent of the items in a graphic (337).

These are a group: Establish a family of objects

In many graphics, the essential message is the relationship among separate objects in the scene. How can we show that separate objects are similar?

Cluster objects

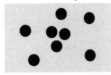

Box objects

Align objects

Use similar graphical characteristics

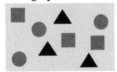

Connect objects with lines

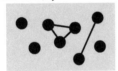

Separate with space

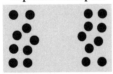

Separate with lines

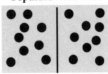

☐ **Cluster the objects together**. Proximity links the objects to each other and blank space distinguishes them from unrelated objects.

☐ **Draw a box or border** around the group of related objects.

☐ **Arrange the objects in a simple geometrical pattern**, such as a circle, a row, or a column.

☐ **Use similar graphical characteristics**. Display related objects using similar visual characteristics, such as color, texture, shape, or orientation. Color is especially effective in showing relationships between distant objects.

☐ **Connect the objects**. The eye naturally follows thin lines and will shuttle between two objects connected with a line. A simple line expresses a reciprocal relationship, while an arrow indicates a one-way relationship.

☐ **Show objects in sequence**. To imply a causal connection between two events, show them one after the other. Such temporal proximity strongly implies that the first caused the latter (129).

These are different: Show contrast

Often we must tell the viewer that two objects are similar—but not quite the same. Without contradicting the similarity of the objects, we must nevertheless help the user see the essential differences.

☐ **Separate by blank space**. Just as proximity associates two things, distance separates. In page design, typographers often use white space to separate different pieces of information.

☐ **Separate with rules and lines**. Rules and lines provide fences for the wandering eye to keep it from inadvertently straying into unrelated information.

☐ **Juxtapose opposites**. One way to highlight differences is to place them side by side so they are obvious in a single glance. For instance, the light-dark extremes of this figure are more obvious when the shades are rearranged so the most different ones are juxtaposed, without the insulation of intervening objects or space.

☐ **Increase the apparent gradient**. Select a scaling function that emphasizes differences like turning up the contrast on your TV.

☐ **Expand scale**. Another way to increase the apparent gradient is to expand the scale against which the change is measured or displayed.

Increase apparent gradient

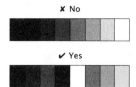

Expand scale

change this: to this:

What order: Show rankings

To show the order of ranked or graded items, represent them with graphical characteristics with a corresponding range of distinctive values.

Characteristic	Number of steps recognizable	Step size
Position	Many, almost infinite	Limited by visual acuity or display resolution
Value	20	30 percent
Size	20	30 percent
Warm–cool color scale	4	Red, yellow, green, blue
Light–dark color scale	5	Two ranges possible: yellow to red and blue to yellow

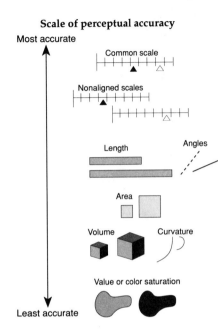

Scale of perceptual accuracy

How much: Show quantity

To display quantitative values, we represent them with continuous graphical characteristics with a wide range (ratio of highest to lowest) values. From most to least accurate, perceptual judgments are (63):

1. Position along a common scale

2. Positions on identical but nonaligned scales

3. Length, direction, angle

4. Area

5. Volume, curvature

6. Value, color saturation

Although a gradual transition between values of characteristics may more accurately represent the data, human perception cannot judge absolute values accurately enough to make use of such subtleties. Divide the range into a few segments and represent each distinctly. Weather maps, for instance, show temperature by bands of distinct colors (one for each 10 degrees F), not continuous shading. Contour maps show elevation at specifically regular intervals, not continuously.

Remember this: Ensure ideas are remembered

Some things are remembered longer and more accurately than others. If the purpose of your graphic is to present information that the viewer must recall later, try these psychologically proven techniques for making it memorable. We tend to remember objects that possess the following characteristics (13; 123; 271; 339):

• Repeated, especially if repeated in a different form

• Emphasized or exaggerated

• Unusual or even bizarre

• Single, vivid images

• Active or interactive

• New and interesting

• Concrete, rather than abstract

- Labeled and grouped by the characteristic to be recalled

Keep this list in mind next time you watch a television commercial. Advertisers want their products to be remembered and they use these techniques liberally. Those who explain computer systems can use them too—perhaps not so blatantly.

PLANNING GRAPHICS

4

Successful graphics require careful thought and a clear plan. Before you put pencil to paper, think about who will view the graphic, what you want the graphic to accomplish, and what type of information it must convey. Considering these issues will help you plan and execute the graphic.

Good technical graphics do not erupt in a mad rush of adrenalin, but are the result of patient and deliberate planning. Creativity enters not as a paroxysm but is diffused throughout every phase of the endeavor. Once created, the graphic must then be tested and revised, perhaps several times.

The process for planning and creating successful graphics can be outlined in seven steps:

1. Set clear performance objectives.

2. Select the messages, factual and emotional, you must communicate to meet these objectives.

3. Specify the graphical format that best fits your messages and objectives.

4. Consider which media you are using to communicate the message.s

5. Create the graphic or a draft of it.

6. Evaluate the graphic to see how well it meets your objectives. Until it does, repeat the preceding steps.

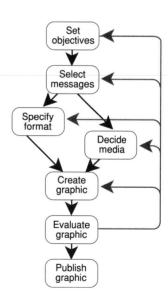

7.   Publish the graphic.

These same steps can be used to produce effective text or entire documents. Also, do not take the division into steps and phases too literally: the activities are highly interdependent.

SET A CLEAR OBJECTIVE

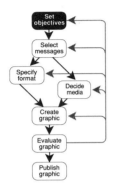

The first step is to set goals for the graphic. These goals should be:

- Clear and unambiguous so everyone works toward the same objective.

- Concrete, specific, measurable. Otherwise how do you know if the graphic succeeds?

- Complete and thorough, taking into account how and where the graphic will be used.

The best way to state such goals is to write a performance objective. A performance objective has four parts:

Viewer	Result	Conditions	Success
Who uses the graphic?	What does the graphic cause the viewer to do?	Under what conditions is the graphic used?	To what degree does the graphic accomplish its objective?

Viewer: Who will use the graphic?

Writers, illustrators, user-interface designers, sales representatives, and others need to know who uses the product. You can save time by combining your information-gathering efforts with those of others who need the same information.

It is impossible to know too much about the viewer of a graphic. It is hard, indeed, to know enough. More than any other factors, the user and the user's situation affect the performance of a graphical format (345). To make illustrations comprehensible, we must follow conventions of the viewer's culture and include familiar objects and environments (349).

By employing questionnaires for a broad statistical glimpse, using phone surveys for more focused follow up, and directing interviews for in-depth knowledge, we can learn what we need to know about viewers to prepare effective graphics for them.

The reader's job role, experience, language, and culture all affect how we must tailor graphics.

Job role

Most computers are used on the job. To understand the needs of the computer user, we must understand their job and what information they need to perform it (209). Some questions to ask include:

- **What decisions must the users make?** Do they decide whether to do a piece of work, which tools to use, and how to use them? Or is the work spelled out in great detail, leaving little room for decision? It is pointless to show people how to make decisions they do not make.

- **How well do they understand the subject of the graphic?** Are they learning to use your product at the same time they are learning their job? Must you communicate fundamental job skills or simply provide instructions on how to use your product?

- **How are users motivated?** Do they view their jobs as an exciting challenge or a stultifying drudge? How might these attitudes apply to your documents? Must your graphic seduce reluctant or hostile readers? Can your graphic help motivate users to do their jobs better?

We must also consider the technical specialization of the user. Is the graphic for the general public, for a technician, or for a technical professional?

User	Type of information	Amount of detail	Choice of symbology
General public	Nontechnical or semitechnical	Low	Only obvious symbols
Technician, repair person, mechanic	Semitechnical, usually job-related	Moderate	Simple symbols
Professional engineer, scientist, or programmer	Technical	Moderate to high (if well designed)	Specialized symbology OK if explained

Visual literacy

What visual formats does the user understand and expect? Complex, unusual graphics may fail totally for an audience unaccustomed to them (317; 341). A schematic diagram of the logic circuits of a computer would be incomprehensible to a secretary who just wants to type a memo. The same schematic diagram may be perfectly clear, however, to an electrical engineer considering modifying the circuits of the computer.

 To learn what graphical forms are well established in a field:

- Ask practitioners in the field.
- Review professional journals and trade magazines.
- Consult professional organizations.
- Check standards-making bodies, such as the International Standards Organization, the National Institute for Standards and Technology, and the American National Standards Institute.

Every field of endeavor has its own conventions and expectations for graphical formats, visual symbols, color codes, and diagrams. By using the forms viewers are already familiar with, you can take advantage of the viewer's prior learning (112). Unless you are aware of these forms you run the risk of using graphical objects and characteristics in ways that thwart the viewer's expectations. Not only do you have to teach viewers new conventions and meanings, you must convince them to forget or ignore the ones they already know and believe.

Language and culture

Unless the viewer's first language and culture are the same as yours, carefully consider the language skills and cultural associations of your viewer. Not all graphics are universal and few get by without at least some labels, captions, and annotations. For more on designing for viewers with different languages and cultures, see Chapter 12.

Learning style

Viewers learn best from graphics that fit their particular learning style (70). You can classify the learning style of most viewers along the following scales:

Holistic   **Serial**

Holistic learners insist on seeing the big picture first. Give them an overview before diving into details.

Serial learners prefer to consider every item in sequence. They are methodical. Give serial learners a simple path that takes them through all the details.

Teacher-directed learning   **Self-directed learning**

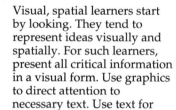

Teacher-directed learners are told exactly what to do. They resent theoretical and conceptual information and prefer step-by-step procedures.

The self-directed learner likes to learn by doing. Such a learner resents rigid procedures and prefers instead to find his or her own way. For self-directed learners, provide enough theory to get started and a road map to show alternatives.

Visual, spatial   **Verbal**

Visual, spatial learners start by looking. They tend to represent ideas visually and spatially. For such learners, present all critical information in a visual form. Use graphics to direct attention to necessary text. Use text for secondary information and details.

The verbal learner starts by reading. Verbal learners tend to analyze by representing ideas in words. To help verbal learners, present all information verbally. Use graphics to recap and summarize text.

Results: What will viewers achieve?

What effect does the graphic have on the viewer? What action or thought does it evoke? What change does the graphic produce? What do you want the viewer to do?

- Buy a product

- Perform an action

- Carry out a procedure

- Understand a concept

- Make a decision

- Experience an emotion

 For more ideas on writing objectives for computer documentation, see *Creating Technical Manuals* by Gerald Cohen and Donald Cunningham (66).

In how-to documentation, the purpose is almost always to perform an action or series of actions. The action may be performed immediately after viewing the graphic (*viewing to do*), after a lapse of time (*viewing to learn*), or continually while glancing at the graphic (*viewing while doing*).

When viewed relative to task	Examples	Design guidelines
Time elapses between viewing graphic and performing task	Conceptual diagram	Establish a memorable visual pattern Focus attention on the parts to be memorized
Graphic viewed once, information extracted and applied immediately	Reference table, decision table	Funnel attention to just a few simple facts or ideas
Viewer alternates between viewing graphic and applying information	Flowchart, diagnostic flowchart	Establish visual place holders Make the visual path through the graphic simple to follow

Conditions: How is graphic used?

In setting objectives, we must clearly state the context in which the graphic is used. We must say when, where, and how often it is used. We must also spell out any assumptions about other resources available to the viewer.

Environmental conditions

The viewer's environment consists of factors such as noise, temperature, space, and lighting. Consider how the design of the document is affected by the following environmental factors:

Condition	Design issues
Noise	Concentration is difficult to maintain so keep graphics simple with few layers of detail.
Heat	Perspiration can cause printing to run and paper to curl. Use laminated paper.
Cold	User may be wearing gloves. Avoide thin paper.
High humidity	Paper may curl. Print on heavier paper or coated paper.
Rain, moisture	Ink may run and paper will curl or dissolve. Use laminated paper.
Intense light	Glare makes reading hard. Lower foreground/background contrast and print on matte paper.
Low lighting	Reading is difficult. Maximize foreground/background contrast. Enlarge text and graphics, say 20 percent. Avoid fine details. Forego color, which is not perceived by night vision.
Cramped quarters	Make document and graphic smaller. Let viewer unfold graphic like a road map. Design graphic so user can mount it on equipment or wall surface.
Dust and dirt	Print document on dirt-resistant paper, or laminate.

Resources

What other tools and sources of information does your viewer have available? In setting your objectives, try to be specific about the following resources:

- Tools and equipment
- Other documents
- Prior training and experience

How often is the graphic used?

Another consideration is how often the viewer consults the graphic. Frequent use will tend to make even a difficult graphic familiar, but a rarely used graphic must be learned anew each time it is encountered.

How frequently does the user refer to the graphic?	How to design the graphic
Once only	Make organization and use of the graphic immediately obvious.
	Avoid deep layers of detail that yield only to repeated study.
Sporadically	Make graphic approachable with a clear organization.
	Make the organization clear so the user learns it as he uses the graphic.
Regularly, frequently	Make graphic learnable.
	Include multiple layers of detail.
	Print and bind the document for durability.
	Make graphic easy to find within the document.
Never	Eliminate it and use the resources elsewhere.
	Or, make the graphic beautiful so the viewer sees it holistically as a painting rather than studying it for detail.

Success: How well must it work?

 When you test graphics to ensure they meet objectives, also pay attention to the user's subjective reactions. Does the user smile, frown, shrug, scowl, or knit his brow when viewing the graphic? Is the reaction what you expected?

To make the objective precise and measurable (You do plan to test it, don't you?), clearly specify the degree of success you expect. Some measures of success include:

- **Speed**. How quickly does the viewer perform the action? How long does it take to master a concept or process?

- **Accuracy.** How exact must the results be? Is there some margin for error?

- **Quantity accomplished.** How much must the viewer accomplish? How many items will the user process or produce?

- **Error rate**. Must all attempts succeed or may some fraction fail?

- **Satisfaction**. Will the graphic satisfy viewers? If asked, what percentage of users will rate the graphic acceptable?

You may also want to state what proportion of viewers will meet these standards of success. A success rate of 100 percent is not realistic; 80 percent to 85 percent is more reasonable. Consider that your audience probably includes visually and mentally impaired individuals, and people who are tired ... or have not yet had their morning coffee.

DECIDE MESSAGES TO CONVEY

Once you know what the graphic must accomplish—and only then—can you decide what messages the graphic must convey.

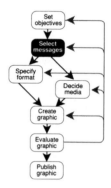

Primary factual message	Secondary factual messages	Emotional message
What is the most important question for this graphic to answer?	What additional questions can it answer? List four to seven secondary questions.	How should the graphic make the viewer feel?

Start with questions the graphic should answer, and classify the questions by importance and immediacy. Design the graphic so that the most important, immediate question can be answered in a glance; secondary questions can then be answered after some reading and study. The amount of effort to answer the question should be inversely proportional to the importance of the question.

Finally consider the viewer's emotional state before and after reading the graphic. Address the viewer's anxiety, impatience, and curiosity. For tips, see Chapter 11.

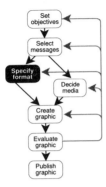

SELECT THE GRAPHICAL FORMAT

With your objectives and messages in mind, choose an appropriate graphical format. Before you concoct an entirely new form, remember the difficulties avant garde artists have in making their works communicate to the general public. Innovate if you must, but first consider whether a familiar format will do the job as well.

Chapter 2 includes guidelines on selecting graphical forms for communicating general categories of information. This section gives more specific recommendations for the types of graphics appropriate in various kinds of computer documentation. It is organized by the task the graphic enables the user to perform with, about, or for the computer.

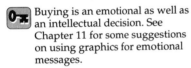 Buying is an emotional as well as an intellectual decision. See Chapter 11 for some suggestions on using graphics for emotional messages.

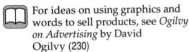 For ideas on using graphics and words to sell products, see *Ogilvy on Advertising* by David Ogilvy (230)

Decide and purchase the product

Before users can install, operate, or repair the computer, they must know the computer exists, understand its advantages, and decide to buy it.

Task the user performs	Type of graphic to help with that task
Realize need for product	Dramatic photograph or drawing showing problem and solution offered by the product; picture of results possible with product
Learn what products are available	Eye-catching photograph in advertisement
Eliminate inadequate or incompatible products	List of benefits and features of the product; table of specifications of the product; diagram of interdependencies and compatibilities with related products
Select best product	Tables or charts comparing performance of comparable products; tables comparing features of comparable products
Become motivated to buy	Attractive pictures of the product, of results from using it, or of users

Install the product

The user has bought the product. How do we get it out of the box and into service?

Task the user performs	Type graphic to help with that task
Unpack the product	Exploded part diagram showing how product is packed in the box; wordless instructions for unpacking
Identify and verify all components	Checklist of components; picture of all components, with closeup views of critical details necessary to identify components
Prepare components	Table of switch settings
Assemble components	Exploded parts diagram, phantom view, or translucent view showing assembly; numbered list of required actions; sequence of pictures showing how to open cabinet, insert circuit boards, connect cables
Configure and customize	Decision table for selecting configuration options; pictures of inserting disk; picture of sample screen showing dialog with user
Test and verify operation	Troubleshooting tree, table, or flowchart

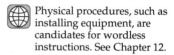 Remember that users who are installing their own equipment are often nervous and excited. They are prone to skip steps or to ignore instructions altogether. Use clean, distinct graphics to seduce them into follwoing instructions carefully.

Physical procedures, such as installing equipment, are candidates for wordless instructions. See Chapter 12.

Learn the user-interface and operating system

Before users can run application programs, they must learn the operating system and its user interface.

Task the user performs	Type graphic to help with that task
Operate keyboard	Picture of keyboard highlighting special keys; pictures showing how to use modifier keys like Shift, Option, Alternate, Command, and Control; visual symbols for special keys and key combinations
Operate mouse, trackball, or other pointing device	Sequence of pictures or animation showing how to move the pointer and how to click, drag, and double-click
Enter commands	Syntax diagrams for commands; decision table for selecting commands
Manipulate windows	Sequence of pictures or animations showing how to create, move, resize, uncover, and delete windows; visual symbols for mouse and keyboard actions
Select commands from menus	Pictures showing example of selecting from menus
Enter data on menus	Sequences of pictures or animations showing how to select gadgets, enter data into slots, and activate screen buttons
Understand file system	Tree diagram of file system, using visual symbols or analogs

Run application programs

For productive work, users must learn to start and operate application programs.

One of the best ways to clarify a task and motivate the user is to show a vivid picture of the goal of the procedure.

Task the user performs	Type graphic to help with that task
Become motivated	Attractive photo or drawing on cover and at start of each chapter; before and after pictures that clearly show the results of each command
Understand what the product can do	List of benefits, capabilities
Understand how the product is organized	Tree diagram of capabilities; map of menus
Navigate sequence of actions necessary for a task	Visual symbols for tasks and commands; flowchart of procedure; map of menus; numbered list of steps; sequence of screen snapshots for confirming location in procedure
Select command or option to perform action	Decision table or tree relating goal to command or option
Locate command in menu system	Map of menus; table relating commands to location in menus; picture of menu with command highlighted
Construct and type in commands	Syntax diagram; list of available keywords and symbols
Evaluate results	Annotated pictures of typical results; checklist or table for evaluating results
Avoid errors	Icons and color to highlight warnings and cautions
Correct errors	Diagnostic troubleshooting flowchart, table, or tree diagram; table of common problems and their solutions
Streamline procedures	Visual symbols for flagging tips and shortcuts
	Visual symbols for keyboard shortcuts and accelerator keys
	(For suggestions for programming macros and writing scripts, see the next section.)

Chapters 7 and 8 present
graphical techniques you can use
to show how programs work and
how they are structured.

Program the product

Writing programs, as opposed to running them, requires
abstract knowledge and skills. Programming is not restricted
to writing programs from scratch in assembly language or in a
high-level programming language. Today many word
processors, databases, spreadsheets, and other general-
purpose applications allow end users to write macros or
scripts. These users need much of the same information that
developers of applications need.

Task the user performs	Type graphic to help with that task
Plan program structure	Structure tree diagram; bracket diagram; architecture diagrams
Design and understand data structures and objects	Box diagrams
Design and understand algorithms, methods, and routines	Bracket diagram; logic box; structured English or pseudocode
Write syntactically correct commands	List of available commands and keywords; syntax diagram
Document program listings	Typewriter graphics embedded as comments
Debug	Troubleshooting table, tree, or flowchart; table of common problems and their solutions

Repair the product

Someday something in the computer will break or wear out and someone must know how to fix or replace it.

Task the user performs	Type graphic to help with that task
Diagnose the problem	Troubleshooting table, tree, or flowchart relating problem to cause to solution
Follow safety procedures	Visual symbol and color to flag safety warnings and cautions; checklist of precautions
Remove and replace defective component	Checklist of required tools, including pictures or visual symbols for tools; picture sequence or animation showing how to locate defective component, remove it, and install replacement—this will require images of circuit boards, cables, switches, knobs, dials, and so forth

CONSIDER THE MEDIA

Design graphics to take advantage of the features of the medium in which they are displayed and to respect the limitations of that medium. Consider the primary medium and any derivative media. For instance, a diagram might appear first in a paper manual and then later be used in an online version of the document or in a training videotape. Knowing ahead of time how a graphic is going to be used lets you design and budget for later conversions.

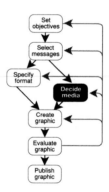

Medium	Characteristic	Special consideration
Book or manual	Read at leisure	Much detail possible
	Color	Because of expense, avoid nonfunctional use of color
	High resolution	Minimum text size six to eight points (ten points if reproduction is poor or lighting is dim)
Computer screen	Color	Use functionally
	Low resolution	Only simple graphics
	Limited text sizes	Simple typefaces
TV	Color	Use color
	Low resolution	Only very simple graphics
	Lay audience	Only common types of graphics
	3 x 4 aspect ratio	Size accordingly
	Low resolution	Minimum text size equals 1/20 height of graphic
Slide	Shown in dark room	Light subject on dark background
	Color common	Use color
	Paced by presenter	Keep simple; show only main ideas
	Medium resolution	Minimum text size equals 1/50 height of graphic
	2 x 3 aspect ratio	Size accordingly
Viewgraph, overhead transparency	Shown in lighted room	Dark subject on light background
	Medium resolution	Minimum text size equals 1/50 height of chart
	Paced by presenter	Keep simple, show only main ideas
	3 x 5 or 5 x 3 aspect ratio	Size accordingly

EVALUATE GRAPHICS

Quality is not a phase, an activity, a box on a flow chart. Nor is quality control something that is applied when the graphic is complete. Rather, the concern for quality must infuse the entire production process.

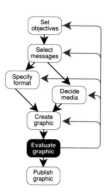

Quality begins with a clear understanding of the characteristics of good graphics and requires continual evaluation and reevaluation. Quality results from many trips around the conceive-create-critique cycle.

In this section we consider three ways to evaluate graphics: analyzing effort required, usability testing, and checklists.

Analyzing effort required

To quickly evaluate a graphic, you can simply total the physical and mental effort required to use the graphic.

1. List three to six typical questions someone would use the graphic to answer.

2. Count the eye movements and decisions necessary to answer these typical questions.

3. Identify any that are unnecessary.

Reducing the number of eye movements allows the reader to find information more quickly. Reducing the number of decisions makes it easier for the reader to learn and use the information.

Usability testing

Usability testing involves testing the graphic with typical readers to ensure that it has the intended effect.

- Test with actual viewers in the environment in which the document will be used (349).

- Test whole documents and systems, not individual graphics.

- Start early. Test sketches, rather than wait for finished drawings.

"In the absence of clearly delineated principles concerning the interpretation of pictographic material, direct empirical tests are more appropriate than even the most inspired guesswork." (17, p. 66)

- Keep testing informal and inexpensive. It is more important to test frequently and early than to rigorously gather reams of statistics.

- Search for problems, flaws, errors, and anything else you can improve. The purpose of usability testing is to improve the graphic, not to prove to management, colleagues, and customers that the graphic works.

To estimate the value of a graphic, you should know the cost of:

- One second of your user's time

- Correcting an error

- Each call to your customer-support hotline

To quickly estimate whether a change is worthwhile, conduct a simple, "quick-and-dirty" experiment. First create old and new versions of the display. Then test them with a couple of volunteers who resemble potential viewers. Measure the difference in performance with the two displays. You can then calculate whether the performance improvement justifies the cost (160).

"Pictorial standards should never be lower than those for text, especially when one realizes that pictorial communication receives more attention." (245)

Checklist

Once the graphic is complete, you must check it against your plan to ensure that it will indeed accomplish its purpose. No checklist is ever complete, but you can check for the most common errors. Points to check include:

☐ Is the main point immediately obvious?

☐ Do the details reinforce the main point?

☐ Is every dot, line, symbol, and word necessary?

☐ Does the data stand out from the annotation and background?

☐ Is it legible under actual reading conditions?

☐ Is it the best type of graphic (table, diagram, drawing)?

☐ Can it be reproduced reliably and economically?

☐ Does it follow the conventions and expectations of readers?

☐ Is it consistent with the rest of the publication?

☐ Will skeptical readers believe it?

☐ Is it pleasing to the eye?

WHO DOES WHAT?

When using sketches to make suggestions to illustrators, writers should not expect to see their ideas carried out literally (42). In many publications departments there is a controversy about whether writers or illustrators are responsible for graphics.

Here's how **not** to produce good graphics (and how to produce **bad** graphics):

1. Writer writes the words.

2. Writer describes in words to the illustrator what illustrations are needed.

3. The illustrator creates the illustrations.

4. A graphic designer puts the text and pictures together into pages.

Rather than talk about the conflicting role of the writer and the illustrator, it is better to think of three roles: the writer who is responsible for words, the illustrator who actually creates the visual image, and the document designer who decides what words and pictures are needed in the first place. Keep in mind that these are roles, not people. One person may serve in one, two, or three of these roles. Responsibility may vary from graphic to graphic or from document to document.

Here's how to produce effective graphics and documents:

Document designer	Sets objectives for the document as a whole.
	Plans the sequence of messages necessary to meet these objectives.
	Decides which messages require text, which require graphics, and which require both. Develops objectives for these components.
Document designer, writer, and illustrator	Meet, review, and understand objectives for all components.
Writer	Writes text.
Illustrator	Creates graphics.
Document designer	Merges text and graphics and evaluates the results against objectives.

"The artist and the writer need to work together on a one-to-one basis and learn to communicate the necessary information to each other." (42, p. 13)

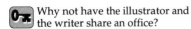 Why not have the illustrator and the writer share an office?

To produce effective graphics, writers and illustrators must work closely. Each must understand what the other does and each must keep the other informed, especially of any changes of plan or approach (159).

The illustrator must know

What is the primary purpose of the graphic? Is it to decorate, motivate, inform, or record?

What image do you want to project of your organization: conservative, flamboyant, precise, friendly, dignified, playful, creative?

How will the graphic be reproduced? At what size and orientation? On what paper? What printing method?

Is the subject or the context more important?

Are the subjects machines, people, people using machines, or something else?

Is movement important? Is color critical?

What are the approved names for all of the objects the graphic is to show?

The writer must know

Do graphics merely summarize and recap information found in text or do they include original information?

Do graphics support text or does text support graphics?

Will readers study graphics before reading the text?

How will related text and graphics be arranged on the page?

Will readers learn terms from labels in graphics or from definitions in text?

GOOD GRAPHICS

5

In this chapter we consider the characteristics common to all effective graphics no matter what the form. The information here is organized as an extended checklist of what to do and how to do it.

TRUTHFUL

Graphics should never lie, mislead, or confuse. Yet many graphics do—some intentionally, but most through ignorance and sloppiness. Though these distortions are most common in the sort of statistical graphics we find in political advertisements, annual reports, and government propaganda, computer documentation is not immune to them. As honest communicators, we must take care to eliminate them from our works.

"Some of this may be no more than sloppy draftsmanship. But it is rather like being shortchanged. When all the mistakes are in the cashier's favor, you can't help wondering." (144, p. 71)

Compare like items

To avoid misleading your viewers express all information in common units. Dollars are not dollars, unless you first compensate for inflation, for instance. Other factors that can change the basis of measurement include population growth

"For many people the first word that comes to mind when they think about statistical charts is 'lie.'" (315, p. 53)

and decline, changes in foreign exchange rates, and shifts in the book value of certain assets.

Beware of deceptive before-and-after photographs that compare more than they pretend to. Typically, the "before" is a tiny black-and-white snapshot. In the middle of a cluttered office, a wrinkled worker slouches at the end of the day. The "after" is in color, of course. In a redesigned office, the same worker, fresh from an early morning makeup session, looks perky and productive (144).

Other deceptive comparisons include:

- Comparing only selected items, such as your best product and your competitor's worst
- Comparing only over a selected range of values
- Comparing unequal ranges, spans, or units
- Failing to distinguish between missing data and data with a numeric value of zero (24)

"At the core of the preoccupation with deceptive graphics was the assumption that data graphics were mainly devices for showing the obvious to the ignorant." (315, p. 53)

Deceptive selection

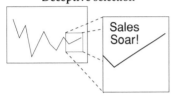

Represent information directly and simply

Graphical lies frequently happen if the method of representing meaning is not simple and understandable. This situation occurs when the size of the graphic is not a clear, visually obvious multiple of the number it represents. For instance, in a bar chart composed of cubes whose edges represent the value of a variable, a tripling of the value results in a 27-fold increase in the volume of the cube.

Graphical exaggeration

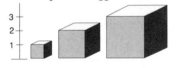

Label and annotate

Labels, annotations, and posted values cannot eliminate graphical ambiguity or distortion. They can, however, compensate for any graphic fuzziness by clarifying apparent contradictions, pointing out special cases, explaining exceptions, qualifying conclusions, and designating optional features.

Annotation clarifies feature

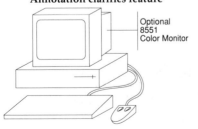

Optional
8551
Color Monitor

EFFICIENT TO USE

Efficient graphics should require little effort from users, enabling them to answer questions in a single glance instead of in repeated examinations, measurings, searches, and countings.

Immediately obvious

A graphic should be simple and visually obvious so that the reader can immediately grasp the main idea. Graphics must be understood within the "thinking time" available to the viewer. For traffic and emergency signs, that means immediately. For impatient users of computer systems, it means right now (97).

Focused on the subject

Sometimes you cannot fill the graphic with the subject. You may need to show the subject in its surroundings. However, there is a danger that the user may not pay adequate attention to the subject of the graphic. In designing the graphic, you may need to take special steps such as to direct the viewer's attention to the subject of the graphic and to ensure that the subject dominates the graphic.

Point out the subject

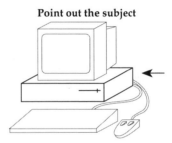

Zoomable

To fully understand a complex idea, we must see its structure. Graphics can reveal that structure (282) and helps the viewer identify the critical units of information (196; 270). Graphics that make the structure of information clear serve as advance organizers. They allow learners to add new information onto the structure (340).

Show structure and details

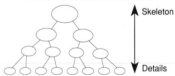

Skeleton

Details

Effective graphics combine an overview with several levels of detail. The viewer immediately sees how the information is organized and understands the main point of the graphic before focusing attention on interesting details. In other words, the viewer starts with a wide view and then zooms in on details.

Some examples of how to apply this principle include:

☐ Maps can serve as tables of contents or menus for access to information organized by geography, location, or logical relationship (223).

"In the functionally oriented maintenance manual, we want to maximize communication efficiency by providing a concept of visibility that, for lack of a better name, we refer to as scan-zoom…. What we need is a technique that will allow a person to scan the whole system, then zoom in on the level of detail he needs at the moment while being able to zoom back out and maintain his system perspective." (190, p. 8)

Point to related text

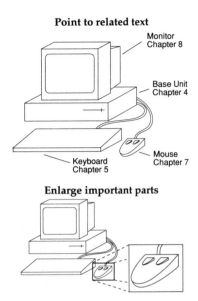

Enlarge important parts

□ To guide a user in selecting what parts of a hardware manual to read, annotate a picture of the product with the numbers or names of chapters that describe parts of the product (253).

□ Rather than producing a single complex drawing, present an overview followed by more detailed drawings of various sections of the object (256).

□ For overview and closeup, draw a box on the main view to show the enlarged area. Make the shape, color, and proportions of the enlargement the same as the box on the overview that shows what area is enlarged.

□ Combine both overview and details in the same graphic. Make the lines and areas of the details much smaller and finer than those of the overview. Thus when viewing the overview, the viewer sees the details as little more than a pleasant texture and when viewing the details, the overview appears as broad lines and geometric shapes. This way the viewer can rapidly switch back and forth between broad and detailed viewing.

Apply the 30-3-30 rule. Design the graphic so it can be read in 30 seconds, in 3 minutes, and in 30 minutes (115).

For the 30-second reading, the viewer will look at the main picture, read the significant statements in its title and caption, and scan the rest of the display, picking up perhaps the main words of headings. The viewer should get the main idea and know what other information is available.

In the 3-minute read, the viewer returns and studies the complete captions and titles, a few labeled parts of a drawing, a few items in a table, a few data points in a graph, the first few list items, and all the headings. This expands the viewer's understanding and confidence in the material presented.

The 30-minute study is for the few very curious or seriously compelled individuals who consider every fact on the page. This time the viewer reads every word—even the footnotes—and compares and cross-references the information.

Easily viewed and scanned

Well-designed graphics deliver information quickly; the best convey meaning in a glance. Poorly designed graphics require irregular scanning, backtracking, and repeated assaults to decipher (24).

Although most authorities agree that we start scanning a graphic in the upper-left corner, they disagree as to where we go from there (100; 129). In practice, the order depends on the placement of text and graphics and on the viewing habits of the individual viewer (228).

Though we cannot absolutely control the order in which the viewer scans the graphic, we can design the graphic to promote more efficient scanning (340).

☐ Arrange objects and categories in a grid so that the eye can readily discern equivalent objects (24).

☐ Locate items in a display by sequence of use, giving the user a continuous visual path from the upper left of the display (49).

☐ If viewers have only a short time to view a graphic, make it larger than it would be if they could inspect it at length (45).

☐ Place items close together if they are frequently compared or contrasted or if the user must examine them in sequence (49).

☐ Make clear whether they are all part of the same scene (111). Group or frame the objects to make relationships clear.

☐ Place the most important items in the most conspicuous and most easily viewed area of the display. Place less important and less frequently viewed items around the periphery (49). The most conspicuous points are the upper-left (100), the one-third points within the rectangular frame (304), and the optical center about 5 percent above the geometric center (223).

☐ Use distinct marks to direct the eye to the next item in sequence. Although detailed reading is possible in only a narrow angle, we can recognize large, simple shapes in an area up to 40 degrees (about 30 cm or 12 in.). Such peripheral vision helps select the next fixation point for the eye (152).

☐ To ensure people recognize and process a group of objects at a glance, place them within the area of one eye fixation— about 2 to 4 degrees of visual angle (about 15 to 30 mm or

Arrange objects for easy scanning

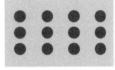

Design a visual path

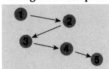

Put critical information at hot spots

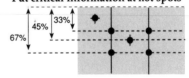

 People who read right to left will look at the upper-right rather than upper-left.

Remember that online documents are read at a different distance than paper documents. Typically the reader is 50 percent farther away.

0.5 to 1.0 in.). Objects within this zone are seen as a group and processed as a unit (248).

☐ Place repeated items in predictable locations within the graphic (327).

Consistent

> "As our eye moves from one image to the next, this constancy in design allows viewers to focus on changes in information rather than changes in graphical composition. A steady canvas makes for a clearer picture." (314, p. 29)

Graphics must be consistent internally and externally. Use graphical objects and characteristics consistently within an individual graphic and among all the graphics of a series. Characteristics to standardize include:

☐ **Conventions**. If different conventions are necessary within a graphic, visibly separate the two zones and clearly inform the viewer of the change (24).

☐ **Color**. Use the same color scheme and color codes on all pages of a document (319).

☐ **Style**. Don't change stylistic features, such as mechanical versus hand-drawn formats or the use of frames versus drop shadows. Make all the illustrations of a series consistent in format, size, viewpoint, scale, symbology, and labeling. This is essential for figures on the same page (8).

☐ **Type size**. Take into account any enlargement or reduction as part of the publications process (259).

Encouraging exploration

Some richly detailed graphics are intended to be consumed gradually, rather than at a glance. Posters, museum exhibits, and summarizing displays fall into this category. But how do we package enough detail into the graphic to make it interesting without making it appear cluttered or intimidating?

☐ **Establish a clear visual hierarchy**, emphasizing primary information and providing layered access to more levels of detail as necessary.

☐ **Design a clear visual starting point** from which viewers can proceed into the graphic. This starting point can also serve as a home base should they get lost.

☐ **Design viewing trails**. Pick a series of related objects and arrange them so that the viewer's eyes naturally flow from one to the next. Provide enough trails so that the viewer has adequate choices to keep the exploration fresh and exciting.

VISUALLY LAYERED

Well-designed graphics reward continued study with multiple layers of meaning. They employ a technique called *layering* to combine—in a single graphic—distinct levels of detail, abstraction, and generality. This form of coding and sequencing lets users handle more information without reducing performance (160). Some examples of the principle of layering include:

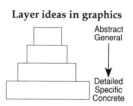

Layer ideas in graphics

Abstract General

Detailed Specific Concrete

☐ Display information over a larger area with specific zones for different types of information (160).

☐ Superimpose information in distinct colors, values, sizes, or symbols (24).

☐ Introduce new features gradually and only as viewers see the need for them. This technique is called *progressive disclosure* (100).

 Some online documentation systems let the user control the order in which segments of information are displayed. This is called *selective call-up.*

☐ Rather than a single complex drawing, present an overview followed by more detailed drawings of various sections of the object (8; 256).

Design a simple visual hierarchy

Graphics must immediately and automatically make the most important point, then present secondary points, and with study reveal details (224). They must organize information into a clear visual hierarchy.

A visual hierarchy assigns elements of the graphic to various levels of conspicuity. It lets the eye explore the graphic in an orderly way without being overwhelmed with detail. Before composing the graphic, plan its visual hierarchy, assigning various parts of the graphic to definite levels of conspicuousness (197).

1. Start by identifying the most important information in the graphic. This is what you want the viewer to notice first. Allow no more than three to seven objects at this top level. Ideally, identify a single object to dominate the graphic.

Design a visual hierarchy of concepts

 Typical assignments for a four-level hierarchy:

Level	Used for
1	Primary scanning targets, such as the title of the graphic, its main object, and safety warnings
2	Secondary scanning targets and emphasized content, such as important graphical objects
3	Primary content
4	Secondary reference information, such as notes and labels

2. Next, identify objects at the second level of importance. These will appear at the next level of conspicuousness.

3. Repeat for the third, and possibly fourth level.

4. Review your choices of objects for each level of the hierarchy. The hierarchy should have a pyramid shape with a few objects at the top level, more at the second level, and more still at each additional level.

Create distinct levels of emphasis

Design the graphic with distinct levels of emphasis, rather than a smooth spectrum of emphasis. Maintain a clearly recognizable difference in conspicuousness between adjacent levels in the hierarchy. Make at least a 30 percent difference in emphasis between levels of information (118). You can create this difference by varying a single graphical characteristic; for instance, you can make upper level objects 30 percent larger. Or you can combine graphical characteristics, such as making the higher-level object brighter, more colorful, and positioning it more prominently.

Verify with the squint test

To test the visual hierarchy of a graphic, apply the squint test. The test is simple, requires no special equipment, and is highly revealing.

1. With the graphic in front of you, close your eyes.

2. Slowly open your eyes. The first thing you notice or recognize is the most conspicuous item in the graphic. It is the top of the hierarchy.

3. Continue opening your eyes. The next group of objects you notice are next in the hierarchy.

4. Continue until you can recognize the entire graphic.

A well-designed graphic will have distinct levels of recognition in its visual hierarchy and will have no more than four or five levels in the hierarchy from the most conspicuous object to the smallest annotation or note.

SIMPLE

The principle of economy guides us to minimize the number of graphical elements used to convey a message. Doing so reduces decoration and noise so the user naturally focuses on the essence of the graphic (331).

Any time a graphic seems too complex, consider whether it offers too much information or too many types or levels of information. Pictures that are too complex can require too much study, and learners may lose interest before getting the message of the graphic (45). If many different symbols or pieces of information are displayed at the same time, searching for information will be slow, tiring, and error prone (160). In such a complex graphic, viewers have trouble discerning individual objects, they cannot tell what to attend to, and they must exert excessive mental effort to understand the graphic (273).

Show the complex simply, not the simple complexly.

Coherent

Each graphic should be a single visual entity, not a mere collection of points, lines, shapes, numbers, and words. It must demonstrate coherent relationships among the information. Design graphics to focus on the values and variations in the information. This means that the design elements of the graphic must be stable and subdued. They must not vie with the information for attention; they are merely the vehicle for organizing and presenting the information to the reader (180).

Easy to process

Understanding a graphic should not require complex thought processes. Minimize the number and difficulty of decisions required to extract information from a graphic (345).

☐ **Organize for top-down processing**. Move from general to specific and make the most important information the most prominent and conspicuous (155).

☐ **Pose questions as positive comparisons**. Negative questions are harder to answer than positive ones. *More than* decisions are easier to make than *less than* decisions (345).

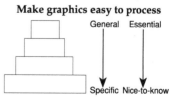

Make graphics easy to process

General   Essential

Specific   Nice-to-know

Which of these two questions is easier to answer:

Is 5 more than 3?

Is 3 not less than 5?

☐ **Put objects in expected locations.** Arranging objects in unexpected or unlikely positions increases errors and slows processing time (152).

Clearly organized

It's not the heat, it's the humidity. It's not the density, it's the entropy (disorder). That is, it is seldom simply the amount of information in a graphic that makes it difficult to understand. We can comprehend large, detailed, dense graphics—provided they are well organized. Organizing information lets the viewer grasp the main idea instantly and understand secondary ideas with minimal effort. Organization also makes graphics more memorable (166).

Organize objects

☐ Reclassify and reorder objects to produce simpler, clearer images (24; 100).

☐ Average, generalize, and consolidate closely related items while preserving distinctions essential to the meaning of the graphic (201).

Reduce unimportant differences

☐ Order quantitative information by value to simplify the overall pattern. This is called *diagonalization* (24).

Diagonalize data

☐ Retouch graphics to eliminate clutter, to remove irrelevant objects, to subdue the background, and to juxtapose related objects (138).

☐ Don't make graphical distinctions that are not important to your viewer or to your purpose. Use the simplest of the many variations possible for an object (11).

Simplify to generalize

COMPLETE

Selecting what to put in and what to leave out is one of the toughest decisions facing the designer. We want to make the graphic complete and interesting while keeping it uncluttered and clear. This decision must be made at two levels: content and details. On the first level—content—we must select the concepts and objects to be depicted in the graphic. On the other level—details—we must decide how much information to provide about each item.

This section considers content; the next, details.

Make graphics self-explanatory

Create quotable graphics. Design graphics to be complete and self-contained. The essential meaning of the graphic should be clear, even if it is presented without the surrounding text. The reader should never have to search through the text to understand what the graphic means (51).

Each graphic should answer these questions: What is this? What is most important about it? How do I use this graphic? How is it related to the rest of the document, especially to other illustrations and to the text I have already read? (8; 45)

"If you have to explain the purpose of the artwork, it is probably unnecessary." (98, p. 87)

Don't overwhelm the viewer

Our ability to perceive, process, and remember information is severely limited. We can perceive up to about six dots without counting. We can remember about eight digits, seven letters, or six syllables given at random. This limit has been called the "magic number 7 ± 2" and appears an effective guideline for the number of symbols we can deal with at once.

These limits apply to adults under laboratory conditions. They will be less for children, learners of low ability, and people under stress (as when using a balky computer). Remember that this limit refers to the number of symbols we can handle, not the amount of information those symbols can express (210; 340).

"The binding fact of mental life in child and adult alike is that there is a limited capacity for processing information—our span, as it is called, can comprise six or seven unrelated items simultaneously. Go beyond that and there is overload, confusion, forgetting." (48)

"The key to journalistic and general artistic impact is selectivity—not comprehensiveness. Select the detail that explodes with meaning; eliminate the parts that simply lie there as clutter or background." (245)

To reduce the content of graphics without reducing meaning:

- [ ] Do not patronize the reader by showing the obvious. Show what needs illustrating, not what is easy to illustrate.

- [ ] Crop or retouch the picture to remove or subdue irrelevant items (138).

- [ ] Eliminate repetitive information within reason. Allow redundancy if it provides a context, organizes information, simplifies comparison across categories, or aesthetically balances the display. Do not, however, repeat information without good reason (223).

- [ ] Display only selected groups of objects or ranges of values (24).

- [ ] Use color, value, size, and other graphical characteristics to clearly separate primary and secondary information.

Subdue irrelevant components

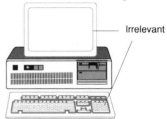

Irrelevant

APPROPRIATELY DETAILED

Once you have decided what to include in the graphic, you must achieve the appropriate level of detail. Since real-world tasks and information are rich with detail, oversimplified descriptions and instructions may seem patronizing to users (290). Also, detail draws attention to individual items, making it easier for users to recognize and remember them (129; 166). However, detail makes it difficult to see the overall pattern of relationships between the items (339).

The visual image one creates depends on the subject and audience. Electrical engineers, aerospace engineers, civil engineers, and computer scientists often deal with schematic diagrams of abstract relationships rather than realistic drawings of physical objects (329).

The rule is simple: Include only the details necessary for the graphic to accomplish its purpose (112). Applying this rule requires taking into account the user, the task being performed, and the purpose of the graphic.

For instance, in working with block diagrams for networks or multicomponent systems, technicians and novices performed better when they used realistic drawings of actual equipment than when they used abstract symbols (339). However, electrical engineers designing a circuit may work better with a simple schematic diagram that focuses attention on abstract concepts than they would with a realistic drawing (339).

Use the right degree of detail

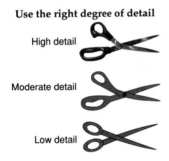

High detail

Moderate detail

Low detail

Include more relevant detail in these circumstances	Reduce detail for these circumstances
For technicians, novices, and the general public (96; 201)	For scientists, engineers, programmers, experts (201)
For tasks involving recollection and recall (166; 339)	For showing the big picture, conveying relationships and similarities (340)
For engaging the viewer (45; 129)	
For tasks involving discriminating among similar concepts (340)	For more accurate learning of concepts and abstractions, such as the organization and operation of systems (191; 339)
In drawing attention to one object within the graphic (339)	When graphic is small or viewing time is short (191)

Reducing unnecessary detail simply requires removing graphical objects and characteristics that contribute more noise than meaning to the graphic:

☐ Avoid complex coding schemes of color, shading, or symbols. Likewise, avoid the *look-what-my-computer-can-do syndrome*. For example, in graphs, unnessary bars, boxes, and drop shadows add no new information and can overwhelm the message with visual noise.

☐ Keep the same number of objects but reduce the amount of detail displayed for each. Let the viewer selectively request more detail on individual items (160).

☐ Do not label more items than are discussed on the same page or a facing page (26).

☐ Explain exceptions and special cases in footnotes or body text. Excessive detail often springs from a perfectionist tendency to continually interject, "Yes, but ...." (46).

☐ Show details for only a few of the items duplicated many times in a scene (125). By the *etc. principle*, viewers will complete redundant details (111). Give them the corners, they will sketch in the lines. Show the beginning and end of a series and they will fill in the middle.

☐ Rearrange items to avoid crossing or dog-legged lines (201).

"Oversimplification is less likely to give trouble in drawing than when it occurs in either language or mathematics." (223, p. 91)

Feature the data

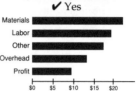

Eliminate needless duplicates

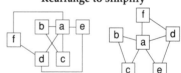

Rearrange to simplify

VISUALLY HARMONIOUS AND BALANCED

Of course graphics must depict information accurately and adapt to the form of the object shown. But rarely does content dictate exactly how the graphic will appear. Designers, thus, have considerable flexibility in giving the graphic balance and proportion.

Balance

Balance concerns the way objects are distributed about the visual center of the graphic. This visual center is usually defined by the intersection of the horizontal and vertical axes of the primary objects in the scene. The closer this visual center corresponds to the geometric center of the frame, the more formal and static the appearance of the graphic (159).

Objects suggest visual center

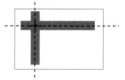

Frame suggests visual center

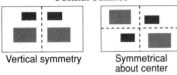

Formal balance

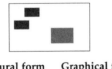

Vertical symmetry   Symmetrical about center

Informal balance

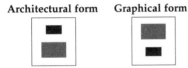

Architectural form   Graphical form

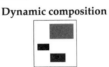

Dynamic composition

Proportions of graphics

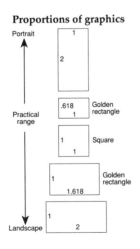

Lacking predominant objects, the graphic's visual center will tend to be about 5 percent above the geometric center (223). This is why book designers leave wider margins at the bottom than at the top and why picture framers make mattes 15 to 20 percent wider at the bottom than at top and sides (11).

For a formal, static balance, distribute equally prominent objects symmetrically about the center or the vertical axis.

For a more informal balance, balance large central objects with smaller peripheral ones. Graphical objects have leverage. The visual weight of an object increases with its distance from the center (11). A small object in the corner will balance a large one near the center (11).

Stability

To control the stability of the graphic, raise or lower the center of attention. For a stable display, create a bottom-heavy image by putting prominent objects in the lower half of the display (223). This bottom-heavy format is called *architectural form*.

For a less stable display use *graphical form,* which places the more prominent objects in the top of the display (19).

For a more dynamic composition, place the center of interest off center, away from the center point (159).

Proportion

The shape of the graphic should be practical and appealing. To ensure that graphics are easily scanned, make the graphic a rectangle with width:height ratio of from 1:2 to 2:1.

The proportions should be visually attractive. One especially favored proportion is the golden mean—1:1.618 or 1:0.618.

Consider the margins too. If the graphic appears within a frame, make the top margins less than the bottom. Leaving more space at the bottom makes the graphic appear stable. Common proportions are 7 units for the top margin, 6 for the sides, and 11 for the bottom (223).

Landscape (horizontal), as opposed to portrait (vertical), orientations are easier to work with. They better match the shape of the human field of vision. Also labels fit better. Horizontal rectangles are easily scanned from left to right.

Consider the margins

SOCIALLY RESPONSIBLE

All documents, even computer documents, are read in the larger context of work and society and thus must conform to the values, norms, and laws of those societies.

Egalitarian

Graphics must reflect appropriate corporate and social values. They must avoid stereotyping or demeaning groups or individuals. We need not indulge in fiction or revisionist history in order to avoid racial and sexual stereotypes in graphics: the unemployed black; the blue-collar Hispanic; the gum-smacking secretary; the husband unable to cook dinner (147). To avoid racial and sexual stereotyping:

☐ Simplify drawings of people. Such drawings use cartoon-like representations of people and line drawings of unisex hands (143). Even quite realistic drawings can minimize racial and sexual characteristics.

☐ Show people as they are, not as stereotypes portray them. Chinese do not have yellow skin, Native Americans are not "redskins," white people are generally tan and pink, and black people come in innumerable shades and hues (147).

☐ Especially avoid what sportscasters refer to as the "honey shot," the pretty girl whose sole function is decorative (143).

☐ Attend to the messages of body language. Showing one person seated and another standing implies unequal status (147). Show people working side by side in comparable positions.

In avoiding racial, ethnic, and sexual stereotypes, you must walk a fine line between what is and what should be. If your management team for a particular project is all white males, you can't ethically hide the fact. You could, however, substitute a photograph of the whole development team in a way that emphasizes the contributions of all members without denying the makeup of your management team.

"The landscape is not teeming with barbarians just waiting for the chance to put women into demeaning illustrations. There is a danger, however, that we will by not thinking perpetuate old stereotypes—the helping/nurturing woman, the subordinate woman, the sexually decorative woman, or even the nonexistent woman." (143, p. W-192)

Simplify pictures of people

Show people as equals

✗ No

✔ Yes

Legal

Graphics must obey the letter and the spirit of the law. Designers must take care to avoid infringing on the rights of others and involving themselves and their organizations in protracted and expensive legal disputes. Talk to your lawyer about the legal issues raised by the graphics you create. Consider these potential problems:

 Remember that the legal requirements of graphics vary from one legal system to another. What is acceptable practice in one jurisdiction may be a flagrant violation in another. See your lawyer or solicitor.

Issue	Concerns	Possible protection
Libel	Does it hold the subject up to undeserved criticism or ridicule?	Check and double check your facts.
Copyright and libel	Are you reproducing an image owned by someone else?	Obtain permission. Restrict use to "fair-use" exceptions to copyright protection. Making slight modifications is not sufficient.
Privacy	Does it violate someone's right to privacy?	Have the subject sign a model release. Such a release may be part of an explicit employment contract or may be included in the standard terms of employment.
Obscenity	Will it offend deeply held values of propriety?	Consider the viewers' sensibilities, especially viewers of other cultures.

FOLLOW PROVEN CONVENTIONS

If a graphical form is widely practiced or well established in a field and your readers are familiar with it, think twice before you tinker with it. Unless your improvement is vast and obvious, it will confuse readers and probably be rejected by those comfortable with the familiar form (80). If you do create a new graphical form, remember to explain how to view it. One of the advantages of standard forms is that you seldom have to explain how to decode them.

"In every well-established artistic, literary, scientific, and engineering field or specialty there has evolved among experienced, knowledgeable, and proficient practitioners a genuine consensus of values and standards that serve as guideposts in judging what is 'good' and 'bad' or 'acceptable' and 'unacceptable.'" (276, p. 10)

 For information on preparing some of these specialized graphical forms see *Diagramming Techniques for Analysts and Programmers* by James Martin and Carma McClure (196).

Standardized computer graphic forms include:

- Microprocessor signal diagrams
- CPU and memory cycle timing diagrams
- State-transition diagrams
- Logic diagrams
- Structure diagrams

SHOWING WHAT THINGS LOOK LIKE

6

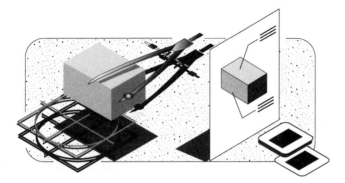

When the task involves locating, recognizing, or just imagining something, a clear visual likeness can help. But providing the most effective likeness requires careful choices of format and technique.

SHOW NECESSARY DETAIL

No graphic is an exact likeness—all simplify, abstract, or reduce the original scene to make it more comprehensible and meaningful. A fundamental design decision is how much detail is necessary. The answer, as always, depends on the purpose and viewer of the graphic. Any details that do not serve the purpose of the graphic and do not communicate to the audience are just noise.

Photograph of a gadget

Detailed drawing of the gadget

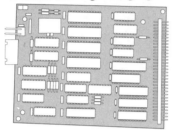

Simplified drawing of the gadget

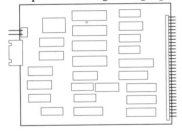

Detailed pictures convey more information than simplified or stylized drawings (240). Realistic pictures are especially helpful when viewers must identify objects by outward appearances rather than by internal features (223; 340). Details are certainly essential when the viewer is required to distinguish between similar objects. If controls look similar—for example, DB-9 and DB-15 connectors or male and female connectors—you must show them in enough detail that the viewer can see the differences.

However, richly detailed pictures, which require effort and time to understand, may overload viewers (273). Use highly detailed pictures only when viewing time is controlled by the reader. Where viewing time is short, use simplified line drawings (84). Simple line drawings are perceived and recognized as quickly and accurately as detailed color photographs (28). For some instructional tasks, users perform better with simplified line drawings than with detailed photographs (84).

The best strategy is to use detail selectively. Increase detail where it is needed to identify critical items, to distinguish easily confused alternatives, and to focus interest. Reduce detail everywhere else. For instance, you could show the subject of the picture in great detail while rendering the background information sketchily. Or for similar items, you could detail only the first and refer to it in the following items (201).

SELECT A REVEALING VIEWPOINT

Traditional viewpoint

Typically, solid objects are drawn from a viewpoint above, in front of, and slightly to one side of the object. By convention, the primary illumination comes from above and to the left and behind.

This viewpoint represents a compromise between making the object recognizable and displaying it without distortion. This is the position a curious person might assume when first inspecting the object. Variations of this viewpoint allow us to design graphics for specific purposes.

Viewing angle

The angle at which we view an object determines how well we recognize the object and its details. When deciding on the angle of view, here are some considerations:

- To help someone conceptualize an object, show a three-dimensional view of it.

- Use angled views to make something recognizable and to help viewers identify parts of a solid object.

- To show one side of a three-dimensional object, draw it with that side facing the viewer (91).

- Avoid side or top views in publications for novices who may not recognize the flat images (211).

- Show an object from a viewpoint high enough to see its top and far enough to the side to reveal its edges (223). An overhead view of a washing machine confused consumers who were accustomed to off-axis views (17).

- Remember that form is difficult to recognize if the object is centered symmetrically on the vanishing point (97).

- Use straight-on views when giving dimensions. Such viewpoints provide the least measure of depth but minimize perspective distortion.

The horizon line strongly affects how people interpret a scene (91):

Angled views reveal solid objects

Straight-on views lack depth

Unusual views may baffle users

Use straight-on views for dimensions

Horizon line	Example	Meaning
Low		Draws attention to sky and highlights abstract and spiritual values
High		Focuses attention on foreground and emphasizes concrete, immediate issues
Straight		Suggests stability, peace, permanence, and balance
Diagonal		Creates a feeling of instability, suggesting change and motion
Jagged		Suggests dynamism, change, and violence

Closeup view

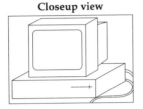

Distant view

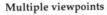

Apparent distance

The apparent distance of the object controls the balance between context and detail, between intimacy and detachment. The most common view shows solid objects as if viewed through a window with a 45-degree to 60-degree field of vision (69; 179). The amount enclosed in that field depends on whether the view is a closeup or a distant view. Vary the distance as shown here (91; 277):

Use more distant views to ...	Use closer views to ...
Distance the viewer from the subject and foster passive observation.	Give a sense of direct contact and involvement with the subject.
Show the whole subject and how it relates to its environment.	Let the viewer "put himself in the picture."
	Enhance textures and patterns.
Orient and prepare the viewer for more detailed views to follow.	Make important parts large enough to show necessary details.

Multiple viewpoints

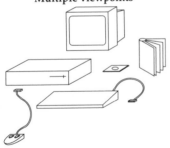

Multiple viewpoints?

When showing separate physical objects—in a visual checklist, for instance—it may not be possible to draw them from a single viewpoint without greatly reducing the size of the far items. In this case, draw them as if from the same distance but position them as they would appear spread out in space. Group them into logical arrangements, such as manuals with associated disks, all cables together, monitor above main unit and keyboard in front.

Beware of mixing spatial metaphors and perspective viewpoints in diagrams that use three-dimensional objects. Examples include:

- Network diagrams that show front views of computers superimposed on an overhead view of an office—as if computers were lying flat on desks and tables

- Three-dimensional boxes representing storage locations on flat magnetic disk or tape

- Mixing three-dimensional and flat drawings of objects in a single diagram

CLEARLY INDICATE SCALE AND VIEWPOINT

Graphics can be bewildering if viewers are unsure what they are looking at. Such confusion often occurs when we do not provide adequate clues as to the size of the subject and the direction from which we are viewing it. To orient the viewer:

☐ **Put a familiar object in the scene**. For the user to grasp the size of an object, the scene must contain a familiar object of known size, against which the size of the unknown object is gauged (91). For example, to show the size of a semiconductor chip, you might include a coin or even a human hair. To show a massive power plant, you might include one of the operators. For objects on a human scale, the best device for showing scale is the human body or hand, simply drawn (125).

☐ **Show the object from a familiar vantage point**. Show an object the way it would appear to an observer under normal conditions. Avoid artistic shots that rely on unusual camera angles or positions. For example, show interior views of equipment from the viewpoint of a technician making repairs.

☐ **Explain in a caption**. If the scale or viewpoint is not obvious, include a brief caption to orient the viewer. The caption can be a brief phrase ("Looking into the cabinet from the bottom") or even a drawing or other graphic showing the viewpoint.

Use familiar object for scale

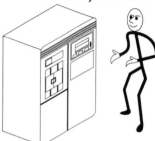

Overhead view may confuse

Show from familiar viewpoint

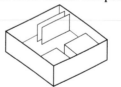

Explain viewpoint

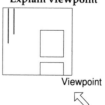

Viewpoint

PHOTOGRAPHS VERSUS LINE DRAWINGS

In most cases you can use either a photograph or a drawing to show what something looks like. Your need for detail in the picture may make the choice for you. Simply put, use photographs to show great detail throughout the scene; use drawings to reduce the amount of detail or to show details selectively.

If the level of detail needed does not decide the issue, consult the following guidelines:

Use photographs ...	Use drawings ...
To show exactly what something looks like (340).	To selectively emphasize small details.
When all textures and small details are important.	For things that do not exist.
To show parts in exact positions and perspective.	If printing or photocopying will not reproduce photographs with adequate detail (28) or contrast (273).
To prove that something exists (230).	If small, frequent revisions are expected.
To interest the viewer in the subject (230).	If the subject is impossible to illuminate properly or foreground objects block view of subject (211), as in a tightly packed cabinet.
When time is short or no illustrator is available.	When no professional photographer is available and the shot is too difficult for an amateur.
	When photographs are not adequate for reproduction but can be traced.

LINE DRAWINGS

Line drawings simplify objects to only essential outlines, ignoring surfaces and interior elements (97). Experiments have shown that such line drawings of familiar objects are readily recognized even by children and monkeys (11) and are effective in teaching and guiding technical tasks (28; 84).

The best drawing is the easiest to understand, which is usually the simplest drawing possible for the purpose at hand. Because many of the general guidelines and suggestions elsewhere in this book apply to line drawings, this section covers a few issues especially important for line drawings.

Particular versus general

Focus on the essential characteristics

Design the drawing to draw attention to important aspects of the subject. Do not overemphasize details not important to the reader of the drawing. For most objects, these essential details are the boundaries and edges of the objects. In visual scenes, these lines transmit the most information (191).

If the purpose of the graphic is to illustrate a common concept, generalize it by removing personal characteristics and identifying details that do not matter (112). If, however, the purpose is to show an individual instance, concentrate on individual characteristics and omit common, general traits.

Omit extraneous details

Until the twentieth century, technical drawings tended to be extremely detailed and literal. Today, scientific and technical illustrations are usually simpler, concentrating on the most important aspects of an object.

Since every line and every dot should be meaningful to the viewer, eliminate any details that do not communicate. Be especially watchful of mechanical drafting conventions significant only to the producer of the document, such as boxes and borders, approval signatures, and identity blocks and symbols.

Make primary edges heavier

Vary the weight of lines to suggest different levels of importance for edges and outlines. Use the lightest lines for interior edges and the heavier lines for interior outlines. Reserve the heaviest line for the outline of the entire scene. Use dashed or dotted lines for aspects not visible from a particular viewpoint, for hidden or imaginary lines, and for lines with special meaning (118). Emphasize contours of projected parts and hollows (223).

Surround objects with white space

To more clearly show overlapping objects, draw objects as if surrounded by a thin aura of white. Thus, the lines of overlapped objects do not intersect those of nearer objects. This separates overlapping objects and helps us perceive depth in the otherwise flat display (142).

Avoid impossible-scene drawings

Just because you can show things that do not really exist does not mean you should. Deliberate fraud is seldom a problem as it is too easily detected. However, inadvertent over-simplification is a problem. Some examples:

Literal illustration

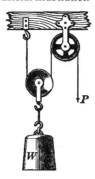

Simplified illustration

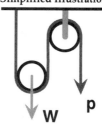

Make primary edges heavier

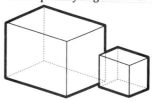

Surround with blank space

- The levitating printer shown conveniently hovering in mid-air as paper effortlessly feeds itself into the printer from underneath
- Pictures of desktop computers that omit cables and connectors
- Cable-routing diagrams that omit intervening obstacles

PHOTOGRAPHS

For more on photography, see:

- Ansel Adams's series of books on photography (1-5)
- *Total Picture Control* by Andreas Feininger (91)

Photographs, though not frequently used in computer documentation, deserve closer study. With automatic cameras anyone can make a properly exposed photograph (though not necessarily an effective one). Electronic publishing tools let us edit photographs to eliminate flaws and enhance depiction before dropping the images onto electronic pages.

Even publications that include no photographs can use photographs as a basis for line drawings. Photographs can be traced manually or electronically. For some subjects, photographs are the only way to capture a great amount of realistic detail quickly.

"Technology has made it easier than ever for you to make bad photographs." (82, p. VC-42)

The best advice for preparing photographs is simple: Hire a professional technical photographer.

This section assumes you are not a professional photographer. It won't substitute for a pro or make your photographs award winners, but it will fend off many common photographic disasters. It will help the occasional photographer improve photographs. It will also help the writer and editor to commission photographs and to select from available photographs.

Use "safe" techniques

If you are not a professional photographer, take a safe, conservative approach. Your photographs may not be exciting, but they can be clear. Some tips from the professionals include:

☐ **Start with the standard viewpoint**. For an emotionally neutral, totally objective, and probably boring photograph, set up the shot as follows: Use a lens with a moderate focal length at a distance sufficient to show all of the object. Set the camera at eye-level and pointed horizontally. Center the subject in the frame. Light the scene to eliminate all deep shadows (159). After setting this up, if you don't like what you see through the viewfinder, move. Move closer or farther, zoom in or out, change the viewpoint, change the f-stop for a different depth of field, or change the focal length of the lens to alter perspective (287).

☐ **Use a tripod**. Next to the camera and lens, the tripod is the most important piece of equipment in photography. It holds the camera steady and level, lets you attend to the scene without losing your viewpoint, and encourages deliberate images rather than machine-gun snapshots (1; 3).

☐ **Light the scene well.** Avoid black shadows that hide parts of objects and cut across the contours of other objects (11). Avoid an on-camera flash, which produces glowing, red eyes and pitch-black shadows on the wall behind the subjects. Either use natural light or bounce the flash off a ceiling or wall (82).

☐ **Leave room for error.** "Bracket" your standard shots. Rely on your meters and handbooks to set your basic shots. Then systematically vary the f-stop, shutter speed, focal length, and other variables. For color, use color negative film instead of color slide film. With negative film, more sins can be corrected in processing and post processing.

☐ **Try, try again.** Take lots of shots. If your photographs don't look as good as those in *National Geographic*, there is a reason. Each year when *National Geographic's* 18 staff, 10 contract, and 35 freelance photographers take to the field, they take their pick from 900 cameras and 3000 lenses. They shoot 35,000 rolls of film a year or over 90,000 photographs per issue (202). And these are professionals.

Photograph of computer from standard viewpoint

Light the scene well
✗ No

✔ Yes

"Of course, no photographer of worth shoots roll upon roll of pictures in the hope that one of his shots may 'turn out all right.' No, each of his many shots is carefully timed for in each there was a reason to shoot. This method provides the only way to be sure not to miss the decisive moment." (91, p. 342)

Simplify the photograph

The first requirement of technical photography is simply to let the viewer concentrate on the subject of the photograph.

See what the camera sees

"The eye sees subjectively, focusing only on what interests us and what we wish to see, overlooking everything else. The uncontrolled lens, however, "sees" indiscriminately, rendering both the important and the unimportant in a photograph." (91, p. 82)

Often what we think we see through the viewfinder is not what we get on the negative. Photographs with distracting clutter result from our tendency to pay attention to just what is important to us and to ignore the rest. The camera, alas, is not so selective (11). Photographs must be edited as they are created, since it is difficult to alter a photograph once it has been taken (287). Thus, before you press the button, examine the composition in the viewfinder critically and thoroughly.

Feature the subject

Feature the subject and simplify the scene

✔ Yes

Because photographs show everything in equal detail, you must take special measures to direct attention to the subject and let it dominate the photograph (168). Showing too many objects at one time can confuse the viewer, so select a subject and let it fill the space of your photograph. Do this by zooming in on the subject or by cropping off irrelevant details from the print. Larger objects in a photograph will seem more important; closeup images will reveal more details.

Use a plain background

To direct attention to the subject, keep the background simple. Many photographers isolate and suspend an object in space, or in television parlance, in *limbo* (138). To accomplish this, shoot the object against a plain black or white backdrop. Black is more dramatic but may require special care in printing to preserve deep tones. Shoot small objects on ground glass a few inches above a white surface (91).

In color photographs, avoid brightly colored backgrounds; use black, dark blue, pastel, or off-white.

Avoid venetian blinds, plants that seem to grow out of someone's head, and boldly patterned wallpaper (159).

Remove distracting details

Before taking the photograph, remove distracting objects from the scene: Styrofoam coffee cups, flashy jewelry, notes taped to walls, pocket protectors, badges (unless required for security), untidy stacks of papers, and dead plants (159).

Keep photographs honest and credible

Readers expect photographs to show exactly what something looks like. Photographs offer great credibility, but that credibility can be lost if the viewer suspects that things are not as shown in the photograph. In advertising photography, some license is permitted; but with technical publications, any obvious distortion can provoke angry disbelief.

☐ **Avoid obviously posed photographs**. Such photographs give themselves away by showing fastidiously neat desks and people posed in unnatural positions.

☐ **If you use models, make sure they look the part**. Nothing looks sillier than someone operating a drill press while wearing a three-piece suit—unless, of course, it is an office worker in an evening gown. Pay attention to more than dress, however; someone unfamiliar with a piece of equipment may hold or touch it in an unrealistic or inappropriate way.

"Not only do many models look obviously like models, they may not be able to give the impression of functioning in the role in which they are posing." (143, p. W-190)

☐ **Own up to deliberate distortions**. If you have edited the photograph—only to make it clearer, of course—then admit to the fact and explain it ("Units photographed separately and juxtaposed for easier comparison").

Avoid photographic clichés

Consider these images from your typical color brochure for a hotel: a well-dressed couple is served a flaming entrée by a white-hatted chef; jolly revellers crowd in the bar; and a contented businessman talks into a telephone while punching up substantial profits on the calculator. Such photographs are so common, they are clichés. As such, they communicate little.

"Passive photos, like passive sentences, are boring. The 'head shot,' straight out of your high school yearbook days does nothing except tell you what the person looks like." (287, p. G-55)

Clichés also occur in technical documents, including these stale images:

- **Computer operators pointing at computer screen**. Only in photographs do two people take part in the strange bonding ritual of both touching their index fingers to the surface of a video display tube. In the real world all the fingerprints would smear the screen.

- **The firing-squad pose**. This shows a group of people standing in rows blandly facing the viewer. It may be a graduating class, the company softball team, or the last view of the condemned prisoner facing the firing squad. Instead of lining the people up in a deadly array, why not show them in action? Limit group photos to three to five persons (168).

- **The grip-and-grin presentation**. One person hands a rectangular piece of walnut to another, and nobody cares. Instead of such a stilted pose, show the person doing what he did to win the award (168).

- **Person with lockjaw**. There she stands for all the world to see, with her mouth wide open and one eye half closed. Take several shots and throw away the ones that show people in embarrassing positions or frozen in the middle of some motion.

"One of the most difficult things to time correctly is a smile. Everybody has seen the toothy grins shot by commercial photographers at the command 'Say cheese'; there is no real pleasure or joy in them, they are clichés, meaningless and embarrassing." (91, p. 76)

Photographs for tracing

If instead of printing the photograph directly, you will trace it to produce a line drawing, design the photograph to clearly depict the features you will trace:

☐ Use a light, untextured background and eliminate unnecessary elements from the scene (322).

☐ Light the scene to enhance contrast across edges to be traced. Do not use diffuse, frontal lighting. Instead light the object from an oblique angle to highlight edges. Use fill lighting from the opposite side to reveal detail in deep shadows.

☐ Pick typical or even stereotypical versions of objects to be recognized after tracing. For people, pick individuals of average stature and physique.

☐ Ensure a simple, clear profile and outer edge of the object. For people, use models with close-fitting clothes and close-cropped hair.

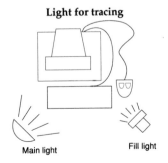

Light for tracing

Main light   Fill light

Color or black and white?

Should you use color photographs or stick with black and white? The decision depends on your purposes and your resources.

Use color when ...

Aesthetic values are primary.

Color is part of the message, as in instructions on how to specify color in desktop publishing programs.

The photograph must draw attention, as in a cover illustration.

Use black and white when ...

Your budget will not support the cost of color photography, color separations, and color printing.

The photograph may later be copied in black and white.

Color would be distracting—for instance, if the subject is surrounded by brightly colored, but irrelevant distractions.

Tonal contrast is most important, as in medical X-rays.

Conditions do not permit lighting the subject adequately for realistic color photographs.

 See Chapter 13 for more information on color.

Keep in mind that realistic color photographs will require 5 to 25 times the memory and storage space as black and white photographs, and they will display considerably slower.

Special-purpose photographs

Special photographic techniques and equipment let us go beyond the limits of human perception. Consult the references to see what equipment is required and how to apply the techniques.

To show ...	Use this technique ...
Objects that move too quickly or change too rapidly for the eye to follow	Stop-action or freeze-frame photography can show one isolated instant (71). Stroboscopic photographs can show intervals as short as a millionth of a second (91; 162).
Path of motion of an object through space	Multiple exposure photographs superimpose images separated by intervals of time to produce a composite clearly depicting the course of motion by the object (91; 162).
Tiny objects	Macrophotography uses special "macro" lenses to enlarge objects as small as 1 cm in size. Microphotography combines camera and microscope for even smaller objects (163).
Wide vistas and cramped quarters	Cylindrical and spherical perspectives, as rendered by special wide-angle lenses reveal a panorama in a single view (91). They seem strange at first, but viewers quickly learn to understand such views.

SHOWING HOW TO DO SOMETHING

To help users perform a task, make sure they can visualize performing the task. Include graphics to show the position and action required for every key, button, control, switch, and dial.

Do not overload the picture or the viewer

Detailed for novice

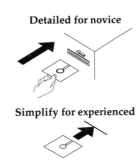

Simplify for experienced

How many illustrations do you need to show a procedure? Opinions vary from three pictures per step (101) to one picture for three steps (255). The range reflects differences in the way the procedure is broken into steps and in the needs of different users.

Start with very concrete, realistic pictures of each atomic action when introducing a procedure, especially if users have little experience or ability. Shift toward simpler, more abstract visuals as users learn and consolidate actions and steps (37). If locating a physical object is at all difficult, make locating the object a separate instructional step from operating the object (173). Show only details relevant to the step being performed. Indicate repetitions, for instance, by multiple arrows, in a single picture (139).

Show where to act

"Terms like forward, backward, over, and under seem quite simple, but may be interpreted several ways when users work on equipment and when they place their bodies in unusual positions." (173, pp. 66-67)

Before the user can press a button or point with a mouse, he or she must see where to act.

First of all, design the graphic to show the entire piece of equipment—not just the part the user interacts with—so that users can properly orient themselves (17; 193; 323).

For solid objects, use photographs or three-dimensional drawings rather than flat engineering drawings or straight-on views (209; 323).

To show where something is, identify its location relative to known fixed objects (138). Pick reference points that are close enough to each other to be in the same view, that are always present when the user searches for the object, and that are recognizable by the reader.

Be consistent. Snapshots of computer screens can be confusing when the order of items varies from one use of the system to another.

If the part the user interacts with is small, include two pictures: one to show where the part is and a closeup to show how to manipulate the part. In switch-flipping illustrations, you may need to highlight the hand, if it is small in the illustration. One way to do this is to position the hand so that its curved profile diagonally interrupts the straight lines of the equipment. When showing hands in action, show the side applying the force. Do not hide the part that applies force or guides a motion.

Enlarge small features

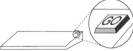

Show people in action

To convert a single procedural step to pictures, first identify the parts of the instruction and create a pictorial form of each (322):

Part	Description	Words	Pictures
Who?	Human who is doing something; normally this is the reader	You (implied)	Picture of hand from user's viewpoint
Does what?	Action being performed	Insert	Arrow showing path of motion
To what, with what?	The object of the action, the thing altered or manipulated	The diskette	Drawing of diskette in user's hand
How, where?	Manner in which the action is performed	Into the slot of the upper drive	Arrow extending into slot

"I have found through testing that people relate more quickly and with more accuracy to pictures showing people in action poses rather than in static pictures that show a picture of the product with a callout to the parts where some action is to be performed." (322, p. VC-25)

Showing motion

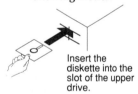

Insert the diskette into the slot of the upper drive.

Make change and motion visible

In procedures, users must understand the direction and nature of required movements (263). Animation and video can provide this information naturally, but with a little cleverness, we can show change and motion on the static page or display.

With arrows

Show with arrows the pattern of movements required to perform an action. Making the pattern visible helps the viewer learn it (37).

Action   **Emphasis**

Draw arrows in perspective

Use a sequence to show action

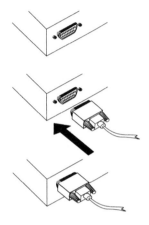

To experience persistence of vision, hold your hand up in front of your face with your fingers spread apart. Slowly start to wave the hand back and forth. Gradually increase the speed of waving until you can see everything behind your fingers as if your fingers had become transparent.

Speed lines suggest motion

Shake lines suggest vibration

Distinguish action arrows from attention-directing arrows. Use solid arrows for actions and shaded arrows for emphasis (139; 322).

Never point to something not clearly visible; for instance, a switch on the back or side of the computer away from the viewer.

Draw arrows in perspective to show the true direction, speed, length, and acceleration of motion.

With sequence of images

Use a sequence of still pictures to show a single, steady change in a familiar scene or object. This technique works best when change takes place against a fixed background or from a fixed viewpoint (315).

As a minimum, show the action and then the result. For instance, to tell how to make a connection, show the equipment before the connection is made, as the connection is being made, and after the connection is made. The first and last of these may be the pictures of the preceding and following steps (101).

With trailing images

Ever see a speeding bullet? Do you notice the individual still frames of a movie or TV program? Probably not. The reason is a phenomenon called *persistence of vision*. When something moves in our field of vision, its image takes time to register and to fade. We see the moving image trailed by faint afterimages. The eye follows the trail left by a moving object, just as it does the line left by a pen, pencil, or brush. Some techniques for showing motion include:

- **Speed lines** trail behind the object like contrails from a speeding jet or the tail of a shooting star. In cartoons, speed lines imply the velocity of an object. The number, length, and direction of the lines indicate its speed.

- **Shake lines** parallel the edge of an object to suggest vibration. Use shake lines to:

    - Show that the object is vibrating

    - Make invisible sound waves visible

    - Suggest turmoil, turbulence, or agitation

    - Convey a nervous, stressful state

- **Ghost images** trail behind the rapidly moving object. Use ghost images in line drawings or cartoons to show motion along a curved, but simple, path. To use this technique the moving object must have a simple, strong outline and an uncluttered background. Show lighter outlines trailing behind its path of motion. Use no more than five to ten, and make them lighter and fainter the farther they trail the object.

Ghost images suggest movement

 To teach manual procedures, have users simulate the procedure by performing the required actions on the illustration, pressing buttons, turning knobs, selecting icons. Such activity exercises the same motor and visual skills necessary to operate the real system (37).

Show what the user sees

Show procedures from the viewpoint of the user and maintain the same viewpoint in all drawings of a series. Clearly signal a change of viewpoint (139; 209).

Include hands as long as doing so does not obscure critical parts. If hand and finger positions are not critical, you may arrange them to make switches, connectors, and plugs easier to see.

Pick examples from the reader's world of work. One notable failure from a government research laboratory was a word-processing manual that used Edgar Allen Poe's poem "The Raven" as a continuing example (44).

Keep in mind that people tend to see what they expect to see. People generally read instructions to verify their predictions about how something works. If something is contrary to common expectations, highlight it to emphasize the difference (323).

Show from user's viewpoint

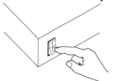

Use words too

Though wordless instructions are sometimes effective, we can generally make procedures more reliable by using words to tell the user what pictures cannot (37; 173):

- How something feels ("You will feel a firm resistance as the board begins to slide in place.")

- What it sounds like ("It beeps once.")

- How it behaves ("... blinking twice a second.")

- Force and extension required in movements ("Push hard until your thumbs come to rest against the sides of the cabinet.")

- Purpose, actions, and result of the step ("To secure the lid, close it until it snaps shut.")

 See Chapter 12 for details on developing wordless instructions for international audiences.

 Test and retest with actual users if possible. Just because you can do it does not mean they can.

SHOWING COMPUTER SCREENS

Images of computer screens are the most common form of illustration, probably because with screen-capture utilities they can be created in a few seconds. They let the user verify an action ("Press Enter and the following screen will appear ....") and learn the location of important parts of the display, such as the positions of commands on menus.

Distinguish different kinds of information

Use type to distinguish different kinds of information

labels
menu selections
user-entered data
required
optional

In screen images, distinguish labels from menu selections and from user-entered data (100) and differentiate required entries from optional ones (337). One way to make these distinctions is to use different typefaces for labels, menu selections, and user-entered data and use different styles or colors for required and optional items.

Reduce screen images

In general, display all screen images at the same reduced size—50 to 75 percent of actual size.

This is actual size but it is obviously too large. It wastes space and dominates the page to the detriment of more important information.

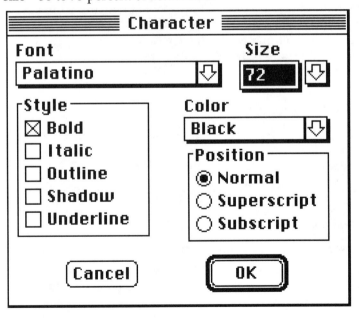

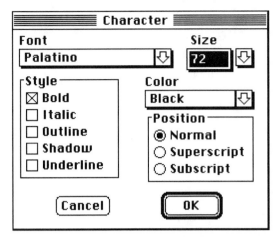

This is 75 percent actual size. It simulates what the user actually sees. Because paper pages are typically read at 75 percent the distance of computer screens, this version subtends the same visual angles as the actual menu on the screen. This size is more than adequate for even detailed reading and study.

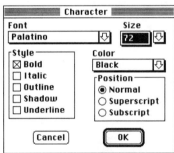

This is 50 percent actual size. Generally this is the best size for screen images. Viewers can easily locate items and read text.

This image is 25 percent actual size. It is adequate for simple recognition and for locating large objects in the display. Even at this reduction, text can be read, though not comfortably.

Scale snapshots to the resolution of the output device to avoid distortion caused by rounding off the number of pixels. Each pixel in the snapshot should scale to a whole number of pixels on the output device.

$$\text{Reduction} = n \times \frac{\text{screen resolution}}{\text{printer resolution}}$$

where n = a whole number (1, 2, 3, 4, ...)

For example, for a 72 dots/inch snapshot being printed on a 300 dots/inch laser printer, scale the display to exactly 96 percent, 72 percent, 48 percent, or 24 percent.

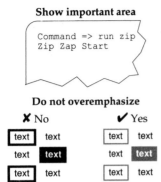

Show important area

```
Command => run zip
Zip Zap Start
```

Do not overemphasize

✘ No   ✔ Yes

Highlight what is important

If only part of the screen image is important, emphasize it:

- Show only a half or quadrant of the screen area. Use a jagged line to show that the screen continues. Use extra space for annotation.

- To call attention to a small pop-up menu, print it in black and white and the main menu in gray and white.

- Screen reverse-video areas and thick lines so they do not dominate other items on the display.

Reproduce the screen exactly

Make the picture an exact facsimile of the screen (15). One user of the Macintosh version of a product became confused by a manual that mixed screen images from the Macintosh and Microsoft Windows versions of the same program. Though the menus had the same text and screen devices in the same relative locations, differences of type style and menu borders proved distracting.

Use electronic snapshots, not photographs or drawings. Electronic snapshots avoid screen curvature and glare.

Show the most common or default configuration of the screen. Show menus in the standard colors and with no added or rearranged commands. Show the product just as it came out of the box.

SHOWING PEOPLE

People are the most difficult subject to depict well and are especially hard to use in pictures of inanimate objects. In fact, one reason the human face is used on stamps, currency, and corporate securities is that it is difficult to counterfeit (111).

Don't let the person distract from the subject

Unless the person is the subject, the human form distracts from the real subject. Showing people in illustrations can prove distracting or even offensive to some viewers. Our perceptual system treats images of human faces differently from other objects (94). From four days old to six months, infants prefer the image of a familiar human face to all other images (90; 94). Faces are so important to us that they are processed in special areas of the brain, on the underside of the occipital and temporal lobes (176).

Given this fascination with the human face, you should carefully examine the inclusion of people in your illustrations. If a scene includes a person, the viewer will notice and study the person first (127).

Therefore, if the subject is not a person, you may want to make the person small, place him to the side or in the background, deemphasize his face, or leave him out altogether.

You should also be aware that not only can showing people in illustrations prove distracting, it can be offensive to some viewers. In certain cultures, showing the human figure is forbidden and in may Arabic cultures, men and women cannot be shown working together (119).

Pose people carefully

As generations of portrait painters and photographers will attest, it is hard to show people well.

Show people from one side and from eye level or slightly higher. Avoid profile and full-face views seen on driver's licenses and police mug shots. The painter Alberto Giacometti once quipped to the subject of one of his portraits, "Full face you go to jail, and in profile you go to the asylum." (11, p. 109)

Photograph people early in the morning, before makeup begins to run and a beard regrows.

Give people something to look at. Show them looking at the viewer or at a subject of interest, not staring into space or gazing at each other. To show someone using the computer, arrange the user's face, hands, and screen in a triangular composition (168). Show the user looking at but not touching the screen.

Take care with how people sit and stand relative to the equipment and one another. Viewers often read a story from the positions and body language of people in an illustration (119).

"Don't publish photographs that make people look ridiculous. Avoid using photos that show skin between pants cuffs and socks, crotches, women's cleavages, or tongues sticking out." (168, p. 5)

Arrange face, hands, and screen in triangle

Show average (beautiful) people

When showing generic people, make them as nearly average as you can. Draw someone of average height and weight, dressed in a simple, classical style, with a simple hairdo and no facial hair.

"The most attractive people are not blessed with rare physical qualities others can only dream about. A knockout face possesses features that approximate the mathematical average of all faces in a particular population." (35, p. 298)

By *average* I do not mean unattractive or even typical. In fact, research has found that for music and human faces, what we identify as beautiful closely resembles a mathematical average of all we experience. In a test, students rated composite faces more attractive than almost any of the faces used to create the composite (35).

Avoid unnecessary detail

To produce a recognizable human face requires remarkably little detail. We can recognize faces based on just the shape of head and shoulders and hairline (127).

"One is surprisingly ready to recognize the human body in the most primitive stick figure or the most elaborate paraphrase—if only the basic axes and correspondences are respected." (11, p. 95)

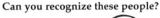

Can you recognize these people?

If you are not a skilled artist, consider using a stick figure or cartoon-style outline figure. You can even use a different geometric shape or substitute some easily drawn object as a symbol for each person (25).

Avoid distracting and soon-dated personal characteristics. Trust in the common folk and eschew the trendy, the glitzy, the odd-ball. Beware of distracting items of clothing or jewelry. In clothing, chose plain, timeless styles. Intricate folds are difficult to draw, and detailed patterns may distract the viewer (219). Avoid fashion trends that may make the photograph seem quaint in a year or two. Watch out for hairdos, dress and suit styles, beards and sideburns, makeup, loud prints and patterns, purses, and briefcases.

Don't dissect the human form

If you show a person, show all of him or her. Or at least show enough so that there is no question that the person is whole. It is OK to show just the face or the upper body, but avoid slicing off an arm or a leg. Never chop off part of a person's face.

PAINT WORD PICTURES

The true medium of the illustrator is not the printed page or computer screen but the imagination of the reader. Words too can evoke visual images—not as precisely or vividly as with explicit, external graphics—but well enough to provide memorable images. To help readers visualize patterns of relationships in text:

☐ Write in active voice and use action verbs (200).

☐ Use examples, scenarios, case studies (200).

☐ Describe objects in sensual terms (200). Tell what things look like, sound like, feel like, smell like, or taste like.

☐ Use concrete words that can be memorized verbally and visually (235).

☐ Create vivid images of interacting objects (166; 236).

A word picture from a master technical writer

"Some of the exposed snails were so masked with forests of algae and hydroids that they were invisible to us. We found a worm-like fixed gastropod, many bivalves, including the long peanut-shaped boring clam; little brilliant orange nudibranchs; hermit crabs; mantids; flatworms which seemed to flow over the rocks like living gelatin; sipunculids; and many limpets." (298, p. 60)

SHOWING PROCESSES AND PROCEDURES

To operate or program a computer successfully, users must understand the course of actions and decisions necessary to perform a piece of work. These may be performed by the computer in which case we *describe* a *process* or by the user in which case we *prescribe* a *procedure*.

The same graphical techniques are available for both processes and procedures. These techniques clarify the sequence of events without necessarily providing information on individual events. They tell us *what* without specifying *how*. The details of individual actions or decisions are communicated by other graphical forms described in Chapters 6, 7, and 9.

SIMPLE SEQUENCES

Step-by-step sequences are vertical lists containing items to be read and acted on in a specific, fixed order, such as the assembly instructions for a child's toy or for a nuclear power plant. Such lists are the most effective way to present several short pieces of information, especially to novice users (153). However, they work only for simple, linear procedures and processes that have a definite beginning and ending and few branches or decisions in between (101).

In instructions performed one step at a time, it is crucial that the reader be able to return to the correct place in the instructions without repeating or skipping steps. This means each step must be a single distinct action and must appear as a separate visual unit set off with blank space.

Paragraph

Example of a paragraph procedure

To move the files to a new directory, start by creating the new directory to hold the files. Next, use the COPY command to place duplicates of the files into the new directory. Finally, use the DELETE command to delete the original files.

Before considering graphics for showing processes and procedures, let's consider the textual alternative. When are graphics unnecessary and a simple paragraph more effective? When can you get away with presenting a sequence of events in a paragraph?

- The procedures are so simple and familiar that they can be memorized while reading the paragraph (23). Generally this means the procedure consists of no more than three or four steps that the user already knows how to perform. Events are a simple sequence—no nested steps, conditional steps, loops, or repeated steps.

- The procedures can be performed without looking away from the paragraph. Touch typists and users thoroughly familiar with the layout of controls may be able to act without looking at their hands or the computer display. It is very hard for readers to resume reading in the middle of a paragraph without inadvertently skipping or repeating sentences.

- The description of the process can be readily visualized by the reader.

- The overview of a procedure or process is spelled out in more detail elsewhere.

Numbered list

For simple, sequential procedures and processes, it is hard to beat a numbered list (208). The format of separate numbered paragraphs tells readers that they are looking at a step-by-step procedure without requiring them to read a single word (58). The outdented numbers stand out from the text and serve as bookmarks so that the reader returns to the right place after performing a step.

Use a numbered list when the process is a simple sequence of steps, generally no more than six or seven steps, rarely more than ten. Use a numbered list only if the reader will readily understand the individual steps, and pictures would be an unnecessary distraction.

Keep the list simple. Make individual steps parallel and include no more than one action or event per step. Don't mix instruction, description, and commentary within the list. If the reader may not understand individual steps, switch to another form or supplement the list with pictures. See the section on picture sequences later for suggestions.

Instructions on creating and formatting lists are included in Chapter 8.

Example of a simple numbered list

To change the line spacing within a paragraph:

1. Select the paragraphs you want to change.
2. Select the Character Format command.
3. On the Character Format menu, enter the desired line spacing in units of points.
4. Select the Done button to dismiss the menu.

Checklist

Checklists present a series of items the reader must complete or consider but not always in the order given (58). Examples are the agenda of a meeting or the ubiquitous to-do list. These items are often preceded with a check box so the reader can check off each item as it is completed.

Use checklists to imply that all items on the list must be done but not necessarily in the order shown. If the order is important, use a numbered list instead. Because a checklist can be used only once, you may want to use a numbered list for step-by-step procedures that are repeated.

Example of a checklist

Before beginning the repair, gather the tools you will need:

☐ Philips screwdriver

☐ Grounding strap

☐ Antistatic mat

☐ Logic probe

Example of action-response table

Action	Response
Press F10	The File menu appears. The command SAVE is highlighted.
Press the down arrow twice	The command SAVE A COPY is highlighted.
Press Return	The File menu is replaced by the SAVING COPY message. When the message disappears, the copy is complete.

 Consider showing the actions and responses as simple pictures or visual symbols.

Example of question-answer list

Do you have more than 10 computers on your network?
   If so, enter SET SIZE=LARGE

Do you have IBM PCs or compatibles on the network?
   If so, enter ADD TYPE=PC

Do you have Macintoshes on the network?
   If so, enter ADD TYPE=MAC

Do you have Unix workstations on the network?
   If so, enter ADD TYPE=UNIX

Will units share a printer on the network?
   If so, enter SET PRINT=NETWORK

Action-response table

The action-response table shows both parts of a simple, sequential human-machine dialog. One column shows what the user does and another how the computer responds. Use this form when:

- Actions and responses are simple and readily recognized by the user.

- The user needs to see the responses to know whether the previous step succeeded or when to take the next step.

Question list

A question-answer format is a proven way to guide a novice through a sequence of optional actions that are performed infrequently (23). In fact, it is this format that Henry Ford used in the owner's manual for his Model T (44). In designing question-list procedures:

☐ Keep the number of questions few, no more than 10 or 12.

☐ Phrase questions consistently. Establish a grammatical pattern and follow it.

☐ Phrase questions so a positive answer triggers the associated action (345). Especially avoid double negative questions, such as "Did you fail to omit the dual-processor option?"

☐ Phrase comparisons in terms of "more" rather than "less" because people make such comparisons more quickly and accurately (346).

☐ Graphically distinguish questions from answers. Put them in a different type style, indent answers, or put them in separate columns.

Whenever you find yourself using a question list, consider having the computer present the list as a menu or a series of prompts.

Sequence of pictures

As an alternative to text lists, we can present step-by-step information as a sequence of pictures. These pictures may be extensively annotated or may contain no words at all.

Begin a procedure with an attractive picture to capture the user's attention and provide orientation cues (139). Remember, photographs of completed dishes consistently draw more readers than photographs of the raw ingredients (230). In other words, this picture can be simplified and abstract, provided it clearly communicates the benefits of the procedure.

For each step, include a picture of a person performing the step along with a verbal summary of the purpose, actions, and result of the step (37).

End the sequence with a detailed picture of the results. Unlike the opening picture, this one should show results realistically and precisely enough that the user can analyze the results in detail.

Except for the first attention-grabbing, orienting overview, make all drawings of a procedure a uniform sequence. Make them the same size, style, and scale (139).

Typical picture sequence

Pictures	Text
Attractive, stylized picture of potential results	Goals of the procedure
Overview and orientation	Where procedure is performed
Step being performed	Summary of purpose, activities, and results
Step being performed	Summary of purpose, activities, and results
Step being performed	Summary of purpose, activities, and results
Detailed results	How to interpret and evaluate results

 For information on how to show the individual actions, see Chapter 6. To see how to prepare wordless instructions, turn to Chapter 12.

MULTIAGENT PROCEDURES

Complex systems and difficult tasks require teamwork and cooperation. In such cases we need graphics that have more than one active agent. We may be setting forth a multiperson procedure, describing a human-computer dialog, or describing the protocol of a communications channel.

For a sequence of events we must distinguish those performed by one person, department, or device from those performed by another. Such formats help users in such procedures answer the following questions:

• What do I do (as distinct from what others do)?

• When do I do it? What event tells me when to act?

• From whom do I pick up the work in progress?

• To whom do I hand off the work in progress?

Example of playscript

Manager	Create new record in program-module database.
	Assign it a title, description, and analyst.
Analyst	Add performance objective.
	Assign programmer and tester.
Programmer	Write and document module.
	Check it into program library.
Tester	Verify the module meets performance objective.
Analyst	Verify documentation.
Manager	Authorize release of the module.

Playscript

The technique of playscript is aptly named. It looks like the script of a Broadway play except that the speeches of the actors have been replaced with actions. Playscript is especially appropriate in shepherding a team of users through an unfamiliar procedure or one they perform only occasionally (23; 44). The procedure must be strictly sequential: it cannot have conditional steps or simultaneous actions. If the procedure is not this simple, you may still want to use playscript for an overview and supplement it with more flexible formats to provide details.

Process diagram

Process diagrams are based on process charts widely used in industrial engineering to plan manufacturing processes. Such diagrams consist of a table with actions listed in the left column and marks in subsequent columns to show which actor performs each step.

Example of a process diagram

Action	Manager	Analyst	Programmer	Tester
Create new record in program-module database. Assign it a title, description, and analyst.	✔			
Add performance objective. Assign programmer and tester.		✔		
Write and document module. Check it into program library.			✔	
Verify the module meets performance objective.				✔
Verify documentation.		✔		
Authorize release of the module.	✔			

The process diagram has several advantages:

- It is especially helpful to users familiar with traditional process charts.

- It can show different types of action as well as different agents.

- It can show individual actions performed by more than one person.

- It features a pattern of interchange that suggests ways the process or procedure can be more efficient.

STRUCTURED PROCESSES AND PROCEDURES

Structured processes and procedures involve a well defined hierarchy of nested substeps, conditional steps, and loops. Such procedures are the result of decades of research and development in software engineering aimed at making computer programs more comprehensible and reliable. This research has shown that all procedures can be represented by linear sequences, binary branches, and repetition. For efficiency, these basic structures are usually supplemented with case structures for multiple branches, repetition with decision before and after the action, and repetition with an abnormal exit from the loop of repeated actions (208).

Graphical techniques with conventions for representing these patterns can thus show both the organization and the sequence of steps in any structured procedure. They encourage familiar top-down reading patterns. These graphical techniques use branching and indentation to show subordination and subdivision.

Structured English and pseudocode

Structured English and pseudocode, which both use an indented outline format to show the organization of a procedure or process, are quite similar. A specification might start in structured English, which a nonprogrammer can easily understand, and gradually be refined into pseudocode, which more closely resembles the statements in a programming language (196).

Example of structured English
For each **order**:
    For each **item**:
        Identify the item.
        Check to see that it is **in stock**.
          If so, **pack** it.
          If not, **backorder** it.

Scale of structure

Narrative paragraph — Unstructured and unconstrained

Indented list

Structured English

Pseudocode — Totally constrained and structured

Computer program

Form for action structures

Sequence:
> operation
> operation
> operation

Alternative
> If condition
> > then
> > > action 1
> > else
> > > action 2

Case
> select appropriate case:
> > description 1: action 1
> > description 2: action 2
> > description 3: action 3
> > description 4: action 4

While-do
> while condition do
> > action

Repeat-until
> repeat until condition
> > action
> for condition
> > action

Abnormal exit
> begin repeated section
> > action 1
> > if condition
> > > then exit repeated section
> > action 2
> end repeated section

You can think of structured English and pseudocode as points along a spectrum running from unstructured, unconstrained paragraphs to the totally constrained structure of a complete computer program. In structured English, statements correspond to logical constructs but use English phrases. Pseudocode tends to replace English terms with equivalent keywords from the programming language used on the project.

An example of pseudocode is:

> IF account is from another branch
> > THEN enter Branch ID
>
> END IF
> Enter account number
> REPEAT UNTIL all transactions complete
> > Enter transaction code
> > Enter amount
> > SELECT transaction type
> > > withdrawal: verify balance
> > > deposit: verify balance
> > > conversion: revise inventory totals
> >
> > END SELECT
> END REPEAT
> Print transaction summary

Sequence is shown vertically and subordination horizontally. In pseudocode procedural constructs are shown by prominent keywords, such as IF, THEN, ELSE, REPEAT WHILE, REPEAT UNTIL, REPEAT FOR, and EXIT. Logical constructs are likewise signaled with keywords like AND, OR, EQUALS, GREATER THAN, LESS THAN. Comments and labels are clearly set off from program constructs. The extent of control structures is communicated by indention and by ending flags like END IF, END REPEAT, and EXIT (196).

Structured English and pseudocode are most useful for planning and explaining the structure and logic of computer programs. At the detail level, it is hard to beat the compactness of pseudocode or structured English. A flowchart may be three or four times larger than pseudocode for the same program (196). Programmers will find both forms familiar, and with modest training, so will most others.

 The term *structured English* does not imply that this technique is limited to the English language. This technique works for any language that uses indentation for subordination.

Bracket diagrams

Bracket diagrams use brackets and indented lines of text to show the overall structure and details of a process or procedure (196). For example:

```
+-- If account is from another branch
|        Enter Branch ID
+---
Enter account number
=== Repeat for all transactions
|    Enter transaction code
|    Enter amount
| +-- If transaction is withdrawal
| |       Verify balance
| +-- If transaction is deposit
| |       Verify balance
| +-- If transaction is conversion
| |       Revise inventory totals
| +---
+---
Print transaction summary
```

Bracket diagrams are designed to be simple to create and maintain. As the example shows, they can be created from standard alphanumeric characters. Brackets surround structural units while nesting shows the hierarchy of units. To indicate repetition, the top bar of the bracket is doubled. To show the inputs and outputs of processes, bracket diagrams are extended by expanding brackets to form boxes and posting the inputs at the upper-right corner and outputs at the lower-right corner.

Standard logical structures in bracket diagrams

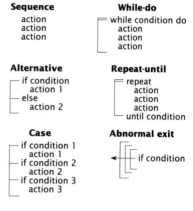

Example showing input and output

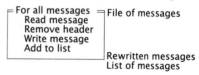

Standard logic structures in logic-box diagrams

Sequence

action
action
action

Alternatives

question	
answer 1	answer 2
action 1	action 2

Case

question		
choice 1	choice 2	choice 3
action 1	action 2	action 3

While-do

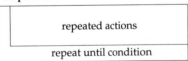

repeat while condition
repeated actions

Repeat-until

repeated actions
repeat until condition

Logic-box diagrams

Logic boxes, Chapin charts, and Nassi-Shneiderman diagrams graphically present detailed program flow and logic in a subdivided box (196; 221). They can also be used for sequences of decisions. They are limited to about 15 to 20 options and actions and are not useful for showing overall structure.

Is account from another branch?		
Yes		No
Enter Branch ID		
Enter account number		
Repeat for all transactions		
	Enter transaction code	
	Enter amount	
	What type of transaction?	
	Withdrawal	Deposit	Conversion
	Verify balance		Revise inventory totals
Print transaction summary		

FREE-FORM PROCESSES AND PROCEDURES

Flowcharts, logic maps, state-transition diagrams, and fence diagrams all fulfill the same purpose: to show all the possible paths through a complex interrelated system. A logic map may help the end user figure out how to get there from here. Flowcharts let the viewer chart the flow of data or control in a program. State-transition diagrams let the designer analyze transitions between parts of a program.

Flowchart and logic map

Flowcharts show the sequence, cycle, or flow of a series of activities, procedures, tasks, operations, ideas, or events. They can show causal connections among concepts, the flow of people or data through a process, or the sequence of activities in a procedure (180).

Data-flow diagrams show the free-form flow of information, files of data, or paperwork through a process. Flowcharts are especially useful to show how tangible data, such as forms or documents, flow through a complex, multiperson procedure and how events in one part of the procedure trigger other events (196).

Computer programming flowcharts use a well-defined, formal set of symbols for various computational activities. Other types of flowcharts use less precisely defined symbols or invent symbols for the purpose at hand.

In one test, when flowcharts of control logic supplemented program listings, the flow was simplified and debugging easier (47). In another test where flowcharts replaced narrative instructions, errors were reduced by two-thirds (124).

When to use a flowchart

Flowcharts are best for directing users through procedures when the number of variables affecting the decisions is moderate but the possible combinations of those variables is large (29). For unstructured programs, flowcharts are the only visual way to depict the logic and flow of control within the program (196).

Flowcharts are not especially effective, however, for aiding learning or memorization (29). Nor do flowcharts show the part-whole relationship among the steps of a procedure (208); these relationships are best described as structured processes (284). Also, traditional computer program flowcharts have slipped into disfavor because they foster unstructured design filled with dreaded GOTOs (196). Such flowcharts lost favor because "the typical reader couldn't handle them" (109, p. 172). In other words, traditional flowcharts require too much training for use by novices and occasional users.

How to design flowcharts

If flowcharts are to be effective, they must be streamlined for easy reading, even by those who are not computer programmers.

☐ **Above all else, keep the flowchart simple**. Subdivide complex procedures into multiple simple flowcharts. Otherwise, they will appear as a vast tangle of activities and relationships.

Data-flow diagram

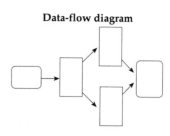

Example of a computer flowchart

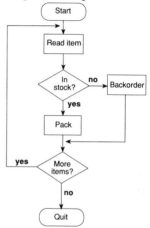

Make flow easy to follow

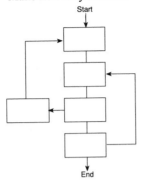

Simplify for nonprogrammers

Simplify the main path

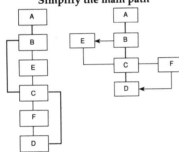

☐ **Minimize the number of decisions** in a procedure. Complexity depends on the number of decisions in a procedure. The number of paths through the procedure grows geometrically as the number of branches increases (208).

☐ **Make the flow easy to follow**. Make clear where the flowchart begins. The assumed direction of flow is from top to bottom and left to right (340). Links that move in these directions may omit arrowheads. Links that move counter to these directions must include arrowheads.

☐ **Pick symbols to suit your purpose**. For initial learning, use realistic pictures or visual symbols (339). For reminders and for more abstract subjects, use simpler and more geometric symbols. The value of the diamond shape for decision points is questionable, however. It is an awkward shape for enclosing text and the phrasing of the text makes clear that a question is being asked (346).

☐ **Style it as a map**. For general audiences, avoid computer flowchart symbology. Though many nonprogrammers think programmers love flowcharts, experience and research have told me that almost no one likes formal computer flowcharts. Almost everyone, however, loves a simple map. So call it a map, and for nontechnical audiences, round the corners and soften the edges. For a more informal look, draw it free hand.

☐ **Simplify the main path.** Make the simplest path the default case, the most common situation, the recommended path, or the one you want to emphasize. Make it a vertical or horizontal sequence or a circular loop (180). However, if your purpose is to encourage users to consider many alternatives, you may reverse this strategy (346).

State-transition diagrams

State-transition diagrams show possible movements among the states of a system. States are represented as bubbles and transitions by arrows between bubbles. Such diagrams are best for simple systems with few states and only a few transitions per state. Typically they are used to show:

Example of a state-transition diagram

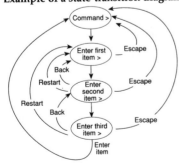

- Data-communication protocols
- Possible actions and responses in the user interface of a program
- Navigational pathways within a complex system

Fence diagrams

Fence diagrams are useful for the same purposes as state-transition diagrams. Fence diagrams work best for many transitions among few states. They make it easier to show symmetries and other patterns of action. They do, however, require some training.

Each state is represented by a vertical line. Transitions are shown by arrows from one vertical line to another. To keep the fence diagram simple, group related transitions and emphasize the most common ones.

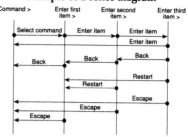

Example of a fence diagram

MAKING DECISIONS

Much of the difficulty in using computers comes from the many decisions we must make. Graphics can help us make those decisions quickly, accurately, and confidently. Procedures consisting mainly of decisions and a few actions are best represented by a selection table, decision table, or decision tree (208).

If-then selection table

Selection tables guide us in choosing one action based on a combination of a few, simple conditions (208; 346). You can use selection tables to help users navigate a system of menus, troubleshoot hardware or software, select commands, and decide on entries for prompts or fields (106).

Example of a selection table

If Status says...	and Online says ...	and Process says ...	then you ...
IPL	Y	READY	Press RESET and resume normal operations
		HOLD	Turn the power off and then back on
	N (or blank)	--	Press ONLINE once
DCL	--	READY	Press RESET and resume normal operations
		HOLD	Replace device at once

Or would you rather have this information in paragraph form?

First check the status indicator of the malfunctioning device. It will read "IPL" or "DCL." If it reads IPL, check the ONLINE indicator. If the online indicator is Y and the process indicator is READY, press the RESET button and resume normal operation. If the online indicator is Y but the process indicator is HOLD, turn the power off and then back on again. If the online indicator is N or is blank, press the ONLINE button once. If the status indicator reads "DCL," check the process indicator. If it says READY, press the RESET button and resume normal operation; if it says HOLD, replace the device immediately.

Selection tables are sometimes called if-then tables because they consist of columns of conditions (the *if* part) that lead to a choice of action (the *then* part).

In selection tables, write column headings as the beginning of a sentence that can be completed by any of the entries (95) or as "If ..." statements or as yes/no questions (106). To guide action, phrase all responses as instructions for the user to act— for instance, "Press the Return key." To aid in making decisions, phrase responses as descriptions or explanations (106).

Decision table

The decision table extends the concept of the selection table to guide users in appropriate responses for various conditions or for a combination of events (106; 208; 214).

Decision tables can also map inputs to outputs without specifying the exact relationship. As such, they are useful in representing entire programs for those not involved with the internal logic and structure (182).

Do not use decision tables, however, when users need detailed step-by-step instructions or an overview of a procedure or process (106).

Because it is a bit more complex than the selection table, the decision table requires some training to read:

- The table is divided into quadrants. The user starts in the upper-left quadrant with the possible conditions.

- Columns in the upper-right quadrant contain dots or check marks to show various combinations of conditions. The user scans the columns in the upper-right quadrant to find the combination that describes his or her circumstances.

- The user then looks down that column to the lower-right column where marks flag the actions to take in response to these conditions. If the order of the actions is important, it is shown by numbers rather than by dots or check marks (106).

- If no response is possible for a condition, the user is directed to a detailed explanation of why and what to do, or such a column is omitted entirely from the decision table (106).

Example of a decision table

Conditions				
New account	■	■		
Withdrawal			■	
Deposit		■		■
Actions				
Process application	■	1		
Check balance			1	
Enter transaction		2	2	■

Decision tree

Like selection tables, decision trees guide us through a series of decisions to a single conclusion or answer. Decision trees work well when the number of conditions is more than two or three (346).

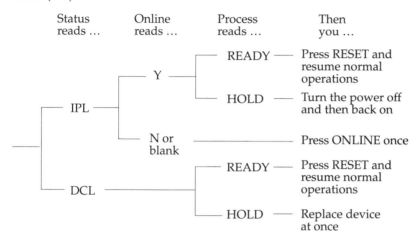

| Status reads ... | Online reads ... | Process reads ... | Then you ... |

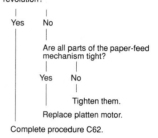

Fragment of a decision tree

(C57) Does pressing RETURN 10 times cause the platten to make one complete revolution?

Make decision sequences as short as possible. This reduces the chance for error and the number of decisions the user must make. A long series of binary decisions may cause more errors and prove more tiring than a single one-from-many decision (346).

SHOWING ORGANIZATION

8

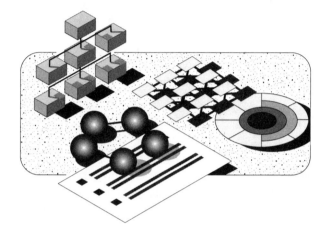

Whether we are talking about the circuits of the computer, the steps of a procedure, or the reasons for buying a product, understanding depends on seeing how ideas are related and how parts fit together.

Thus, we need a clear, graphic organization that lets a user deal in concrete images rather than emphemeral abstractions (340). Such a visual organization provides a framework into which details can be readily assimilated (341) and makes information easier to understand and to remember (123; 340).

The techniques discussed in this chapter use horizontal and vertical position, proximity, borders, lines, marks, and labels to express relationships of sequence, control, causality, physical and electrical connection, and ranking.

PATTERNS OF LINKAGES

To make organization clear you must have a clear organization—a simple, familiar pattern of relationships

 To see the importance of making relationships clear, compare the difficulty of memorizing these two lists of words:

ash banyan buttercup chestnut
conifers daisy dandelion
deciduous delphinium elm
flowers garden lupin mango
palm pansy pine plants redwood
rose spruce trees tropical violet
wild willow

minerals	stones	masonry	limestone granite marble
		precious	sapphire emerald diamond ruby
	metals	alloys	bronze steel brass
		common	aluminum copper lead iron
		rare	platinum silver gold

among the parts of a system. Sometimes that pattern is determined by the design of the system. In certain systems one pattern or another may predominate or be the only pattern permitted. In other systems, especially ones that are conceptual rather than physical, it is up to you to fit information into a simple, logical pattern for the viewer. In most cases you must compromise between the patterns suggested by the subject, those most efficient for the task, and those easiest for the user to comprehend. Although no complex system has a single, pure, and simple structure, most can be described as combinations of a few simple models.

Chain

Chain

The simplest is the sequence. Item follows item. The reader has two choices: to go forward or to go backward. Though monotonously predictable, the chain is perfectly reliable. Because it is so safe and sane, the chain is the backbone of most textual documents; it is also implicit in processes and procedures.

Grid

Grid

The grid or orthogonal structure organizes and presents information along two logical dimensions. The reader can read down the columns or can skim along the row to compare various items. The ubiquitous grid is a permanent and familiar part of our psyche; we see it embodied in spreadsheets, tables, game boards, street plans, marching bands, and the rank and file of the workplace. This familiarity makes it a popular way of adding another dimension to structure without great loss of predictability.

Tree

Tree

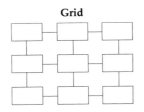

The same familiarity is also true for the tree structure. The simple hierarchy is the basis for classification and management. The Vatican, the Kremlin, the Pentagon, and General Motors all have hierarchical management structures. We see the tree structure in the 3.4.5 style of numbered headings common in technical manuals.

Web

The web structure is the ultimate in flexibility. Anything can be linked to anything else; associations are not bound to strict rules as for the other structures. The power of the web structure is that with it the designer can construct the other simpler structures, as well as special ad hoc structures, such as cycles, stars, and diamonds. The danger, however, with the web structure is that it quickly grows complex, resembling nothing so much as a bowl of spaghetti.

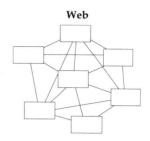

Web

TEXT LISTS

Whether probing the limits of machine intelligence or making a shopping list, we rely on the simple organizing principle of the list. The list is fundamental to our language, even our experience of life. We progress through a succession of days, reason through a chain of events, pursue a train of thoughts, solve a string of crimes. Lists help regulate our lives and jog our memories. Who has not relied on laundry lists, shopping lists, wish lists, or to-do lists?

What are text lists?

The most common kinds of lists are display text lists. These all display a series of short text segments in a vertical stack with each item preceded by a visual marker. The marker is a symbol that provides an easy scanning target so the eye can reliably "fast-forward" to the next item in the series without reading through all the previous items. It provides a conspicuous flag of the beginning of the next item.

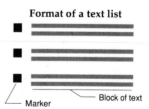

Format of a text list

Marker — — Block of text

Why use text lists?

You might question including lists in a book on graphics. After all, lists, especially word lists, are hardly graphics at all. Yet they are quite important in a book like this for several reasons:

- Lists are the simplest of graphical forms. They are the easiest to understand and create.

- Lists occur as components of other graphics, such as column and row heads of tables and as the scales of graphs and charts.

"Lists help readers find information quickly and easily because readers can scan lists more quickly than they can scan paragraphs. Readers can also extract information more easily from lists than paragraphs." (58, p. 218)

- Lists can be used in word-only documents where no other graphical form is possible.

- Text lists are the most effective way to present several short pieces of information, especially to novice users (153). They are understood more quickly and remembered better than the same information in body text.

How text lists work

The list format tells the reader at a glance that it is a list, what type of list it is, how many items it contains, and how long the items are (58). Transitions and organization are signaled by blank space and indentation rather than by words or punctuation (167). Each item is usually preceded by a visual marker. These visual markers:

- Help the eye to quickly find the beginning of the next item

- Signal the type of list: bullet, numbered, checklist

- Show how many items are in the list, especially if the items are closely spaced

- Convey information about each item, for instance, its order in sequence or ranking

Avoid run-on lists

✘ No   ✘ No

■ xxx xxxx xxx   ■ xxx xxxx xxx
xx xxxx xxx   xx xxxx xxx
■ xxxx xxx xxxx   ■ xxxx xxx
xxx xx xxxx   xxxx xxx xx xxxx
■ xxx xxxx xxx   ■ xxx xxxx xxx
xxxx xxx xx xxxx   xxxx xxx xx xxxx
■ xxx xxxx xxx   ■ xxx xxxx xxx
xxxx xxx   xxxx xxx
■ xx xxxx xxx   ■ xx xxxx xxx
xxxx   xxxx

✔ OK, if space is tight

■ xxx xxxx xxx xx
xxxx xxx ■ xxxx
xxx xxxx xxx xx
xxxx ■ xxx xxxx
xxx xxxx xxx xx
xxxx ■ xxx xxxx
xxx xxxx xxx ■ xx
xxxx xxx xxxx

Format of text lists

Popular style guides and experts are either evasive or contradictory on the subject of text lists (246). The following suggestions, though not universally accepted, seem to represent an intelligent compromise among common practice, common sense, and expert opinion (58; 246; 335; 337).

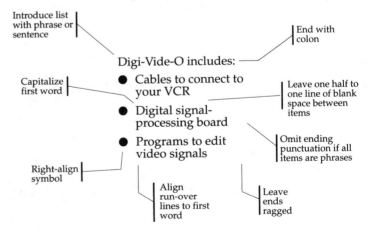

Do not indent the marker into the body of the list item as is often done with flush and run-on lists. If space is tight you may run list items together in a paragraph format, while making the marker bolder so it stands out from the text. Keep the marker small, no larger than a capital M, but make it prominent enough that the eye can easily find the beginning of each item.

Don't interrupt lists with graphics or make subordinate information more prominent than the list items. Doing so splits the list and makes it harder to scan.

The marker signifies the type of list and how the items are related.

Don't split lists

✘ No   ✔ Yes

Marker	Used for...	Notes
(None)	Very simple equivalent items	If all items are less than a line, you may omit the symbol (335).
Bullet ●	Equivalent items without sequence, ranking, or ordering (58; 246)	Instead of the standard bullet markers, you can substitute a simple visual symbol that conveys more information about the list item. For instance a list of office activities might include: ✍ ✂ ☎ ✆ ✉
Number 7.	Step-by-step procedure or set of ratings (58; 208)	Use letters if the list items are numbers (58). For short lists you can precede each step with an increasing number of bullets (180): • Step one •• Step two ••• Step three
Check box ☐	Lists where the reader must consider all items (58)	Because a checklist can be used only once, you may want to use a numbered list for step-by-step procedures that are repeated.
Word	Definitions of terms	Position and align terms to speed scanning.

Multilevel indented lists

We can extend the format of text lists beyond the limits of the simple chain to include tree structures as well. Such multilevel lists use indentation to show multiple levels of abstraction, inclusion, or detail.

Consider sublists for lists over five items (58). Multilevel lists let people find individual items quicker. The reader finds it easier to read an indented list than to scan a table. A hierarchical search involves only one point of attention. For quicker scanning, make subordinate heads complete, even if this requires some redundancy with higher-level heads (346).

In general, limit lists to no more than three or four levels. Use en-dashes (–) or hyphens (-) to label the second level in a bullet list. In a numbered list use these symbols: 1., A., (1), and (a).

Multilevel bullet list

- First level
  - Second level
  - Second level
- First level
  - Second level
  - Second level
  - Second level

Multilevel numbered list

1. First level
   a. Second level
      (1) Third level
          (a) Fourth level

Make list items consistent

List logically comparable items and format them similarly.

Present items of the same type. Do not mix logical categories within the items of a list. Violation of this rule can produce confusion ... or humor, as in Mark Twain's classic summary of his life:

> I have been in turn reporter, editor, publisher, lawyer, burglar. I have worked my way up and wish to continue to do so.

Or Groucho Marx's definition of an ordinary fellow:

> 42 around the chest, 42 around the waist, 96 around the golf course and a nuisance around the house.

Present items in the same grammatical and pictorial style. Remember that lists are scanned more than read and any elegant variation may obscure the meaningful differences the viewer depends on to distinguish similar items (246).

Complete the list

Often careless or lazy writers test our intelligence and patience by asking us to interpret statements such as:

> The control panel contains knobs, etc.

This is like trying to geometrically define a straight line by giving only one point. The line can go in any direction. And so will the reader's imagination, unless clearly pointed in the correct direction. Almost as ambiguous is a statement such as:

> The repair kit contains 100-ohm resistors, screwdrivers, a log book, and so forth.

Keep the list short

Lists work best for sequences of three to nine items. Fewer than that, and there is little advantage over the paragraph format. More than that, and the list looks intimidating and is hard to remember (210). If the series is longer than nine items, consider rearranging it as a multilevel list of sublists or else presenting it in alphabetical or numerical order to simplify finding individual items.

Order the list meaningfully

Order items in the list to accomplish your most important point. Arbitrary order or no order is do-it-yourself order. If the order is not apparent, the reader will impose an order on the list. The order the reader imagines may not be the one you intended. Pick a clear strategy for ordering the list and make the order clear.

For this purpose ...	Present items in this order ...
Teach location of controls on a panel or display	Spatially, left to right, top to bottom, or clockwise as in the user's field of vision
Teach use of controls	Chronologically by order of use in most common procedures
Describe a process	Chronologically from beginning to end; logically from cause to effect
Spell out a procedure	Chronologically from first step to last—save the flashbacks and time travel for your science fiction novel
Convince or persuade	Climactic from least to most convincing; "clincher" order, that is, from more to less convincing, but saving the strongest item for last
Sell a product	Logically from general feature to specific benefit
Have information remembered after some delay	From most to least important
Have information applied immediately	From least to most important

Enable user to scan and find items in a long list	Indexed order, arranged alphabetically or numerically. Use alphabetical lists only as a last resort. Users find information more quickly when arranged by familiar categories (346).
Compare and contrast items	Ranked from best to worst
Explain a puzzling phenomenon, such as an error message	Logically from effect to cause

If the order is not readily apparent, explain it in the introduction to the list.

TABLES

For over 5,500 years people have used tables to organize complex information into neat rows and columns. The basic grid structure of the table permeates technological civilizations which march by rank and file and lay out their cities into a grid of blocks. No wonder, then, that tables are a natural way to organize many separate pieces of information needed by computer users.

How tables work

Searching a table

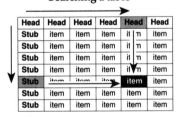

Tables ingeniously let the impatient reader zip right to the single nugget of information while bypassing everything else. By merely scanning two lists of headings—one horizontal and one vertical—the reader locates the information sought at the intersection of a row and a column. Likewise from row and column position, viewers can infer qualities of table entries and can accurately interrelate many concepts at a time (106).

When to use tables

Whenever items can be arranged by two characteristics, you can organize them into a grid and present them in a table. Tables work well for both small and large sets of data. They can summarize a few data items or provide reference to thousands. Use tables to:

- Present a large amount of detailed information in a small space (315).

- Facilitate detailed, item-to-item comparisons (223).

- Show individual data values precisely (149).

- Simplify access to individual data values (50).

Design headings for scanning

Place in the column and row headings information that is unique to the row or column and that applies to all its members. If information is too long or detailed to go in the heading, put it into a table note and cite the note in the heading.

Tables can include multiple levels of column and row headings. If the table contains more than one level of column headings, let the main heading span subheadings. Include a line under the main heading. Extend the underline from the beginning of the first column to the end of the last column covered. Always leave visible space between the underlines of adjacent columns (81). Indent subordinate row headings. Indent them more than continued lines of headings (192).

Place an ellipsis (...) after any header continued in other headings or in the body of the table.

Design tables so that all columns, including the leftmost, have headings. The leftmost column heading labels the row headings below it, not the other column headings to its right (81; 118).

If table headings are boxed, center them vertically. If unboxed, center them flush bottom near the start of the columns they label (81).

Two-level column heads

Column head		Column head	
Subhead	Subhead	Subhead	Subhead

Two-level row heads

Row head
    Subhead
    Subhead
Row head
that is
continued
    Subhead
    Subhead

Areas of a table

Column heads	
Row heads	Body

✗ Seldom necessary

Column head	Column head	Column head	Column head
Row head	Item	Item	Item
Row head	Item	Item	Item
Row head	Item	Item	Item
Row head	Item	Item	Item

✔ Often sufficient

Column head	Column head	Column head	Column head
Row head	Item	Item	Item
Row head	Item	Item	Item
Row head	Item	Item	Item
Row head	Item	Item	Item

Minimize lines

Avoid the fish-net school of table design. Excessive lines make a table harder, not easier, to read (118). So do without them if you can; use thin lines if you must (314).

Since space is usually adequate to show functional groupings in a table, lines are seldom required. Add lines only as they seem necessary:

- To separate title, heads, body, and notes
- To show the extent of a heading spanning multiple columns
- To show logical groupings
- To separate closely spaced columns
- To guide the eye.

Make tables accessible

To find information in a table, the user must formulate a question in terms of the table's row and column heads. Success, then, depends on how well the table's organization anticipates the user's questions (346).

Arrange rows and columns to make finding an individual item in the table simple and natural (86). Order rows and columns by a clear, logical scheme that the reader can readily grasp and use to quickly locate the appropriate column and row headings.

In tables, group similar items so viewers can compare them and see logical relationships (346). Make items in a row or column parallel in form and logical category (138). Information may vary by column or by row—but not both at the same time. Especially avoid unnecessary changes of units: for example, switching from inches to centimeters. Use chronological order for information recorded in sequence or by date or time. Put more important and more frequently accessed items toward the top and left so they are found more quickly. Arrange major and subordinate items in order from whole to parts. Group together items of the same type or size. Place items that will be compared close together. Put comparable numbers in a column so they can be compared or summed digit by digit. Put pictures and words side by side (51).

Style for scanning

Never space out the columns of a table merely to fill out a text column. Space columns for legibility and either center or left-justify the table within the text column (335). Gaps between columns should be no more than three to five times the distance between lines. To achieve this ratio, stack column heads, run them vertically, or use a moderately condensed typeface. If you cannot closely space columns, increase the space between rows.

If the layout of a table is awkward, consider switching rows and columns (161). If a table has too many headings and subheads, consider breaking it into two or more tables (192). If a table is too wide, try converting columns to rows (335).

In tables that are scanned, such as tables of error messages, emphasize the differences between individual headings and entries so users can locate the sought after item quickly. In such tables, show items with only two or three possible values graphically rather than as separate columns for each alternative.

Unless obvious, flag and explain missing data. Indicate missing data with words such as "none" or "not applicable" or with a symbol such as a dash (81; 223).

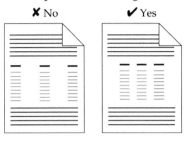

Keep columns close together

✘ No   ✔ Yes

Emphasize the differences

✘ No

Model	Good	Better	Best
3841	■		
3851		■	
3861			■

✔ Yes

Model	Quality
3841	■
3851	■■
3861	■■■

Common types of tables

The remainder of this segment considers the design of specific types of tables.

Look-up-a-value tables

Most tables are designed to let the reader quickly find one single value. In such tables the reader scans the row and column headings for those that describe the target item. The desired information is then located at the intersection of the row and column bearing these headings.

For such tables, design column and row headings for scanning. Make them distinctive and keep them short. Use column and row headings and subheadings to express a hierarchy of choices. Use blank space or lines to guide the eye horizontally and vertically about the table. Consistency of formats and

Example of look-up-a-value table

Switch settings

Model	Memory		
	640K	2Mb	8Mb
2860	1	2	3
3860	4	5	6
4860	7	8	9

alignment within columns and rows help guide the reader's eye and emphasize the logic and organization of the table.

Decision and selection tables

Decision tables guide the reader in making complex decisions. They simplify selecting one alternative from many possibilities. They summarize if-then conditions in a way that the reader can quickly and reliably identify the current situation and decide how to proceed. Such tables can thus summarize long, complex sets of instructions. They are ideal for quick reference or summary. (Decision and selection tables are described in Chapter 7).

Example of a selection table

File format	Color?	Option
.PDX	No	PX
	Yes	PCOLOR
.QDZ	No	QZ
	Yes	QCOLOR

Matrix tables

Matrix charts are grids in which the row and column headers are uniformly spaced scales or categories and each cell presents information about the combination of values represented by the cell. The periodic table of the elements is an example of a matrix table. In addition to looking up a value, the viewer can read the table from inside out. The viewer locates a familiar item in the matrix and then deduces its characteristics by its row and column and by its neighbors.

Any diagram can be represented as a matrix with one row and one column for each object and their relationship posted at the intersection (24). If every item is related to every other one, use the matrix table. If interrelationships are sparse, use a diagram (223).

In matrix tables that show reciprocal relationships, you can usually omit half the table and rearrange the rows and columns to simplify reading (81).

Example of a matrix table

Cambricomp System Boards

CPU	Speed		
	20MHz	30MHz	40MHz
68020	202C	230C	240C
68030	302C	330C	340C
68040	402C	430C	440C

Matrix shows interrelationships

From	To				
	A	B	C	D	E
A	-	●	●		
B	●	-	●	●	●
C	●	●	-	●	
D		●	●	-	●
E		●		●	-

Simplify matrix

	E	D	C	B
A			●	●
B	●	●	●	
C			●	
D	●			

DIAGRAMS

Diagrams show how pieces work together. Since they express relationships, they are especially suited to showing how various components of a system interact. Diagrams connect items in recognizable patterns or topologies, such as chains, rings, trees, and webs.

Diagrams used alongside text help reveal the structure of information. Displaying relationships two-dimensionally this way helps users understand complex relationships more easily (178; 340) and classify ideas more reliably (340).

Diagrams also enable designers to exchange ideas and plan massive projects. And because diagrams promote clear thinking, they can speed the work and improve the quality of a design.

Symbol-link diagrams

Symbol-link diagrams are the most versatile way for showing any pattern of conceptual relationships. They are widely used in technical documents and readers are well acquainted with their conventions. They are especially appropriate when many concepts are tied together by a sparse network of relationships. If every concept is related to every other, consider a matrix table instead (223).

How symbol-link diagrams work

Symbol-link diagrams consist of symbols, which represent the objects of the system, and links, which represent the relationships among them. Symbols may be pictures, icons, dots, boxes, and words; links are lines and arrows.

Create recognizable symbols

Symbols represent the objects or key concepts of a system. They can be a combination of:

- Detailed pictures
- Silhouettes or icons of familiar objects
- Solid or outlined geometric shapes
- Words
- Points

"The essential purpose of a diagram is to analyze or break down an object or event into its parts, rather than merely describing it verbally or representing it photographically. The complete picture is therefore either stylized, cut up, or dissected, so that a construction, a mechanism, or a function can be explained." (97, p. 229)

Block diagram of a computer

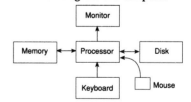

Simplify symbols when showing patterns

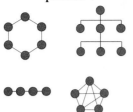

Label symbols

Use realistic, detailed drawings for symbols in diagrams to highlight critical characteristics and to aid low-verbal learners (201; 340). If a diagram mixes hardware and software or concrete and abstract, use more detailed, realistic, three-dimensional symbols for concrete and tangible objects and use simple, geometric shapes for abstract concepts and software constructs. If only the pattern of relationships among objects is important, use only dots or squares for the objects and make the illustration quite small.

Use larger symbols for more important objects in a diagram. Do not use so many symbols that the reader cannot easily learn and remember the meaning of the symbols. More than five or six basic symbols is too many.

Label all symbols. The more abstract or schematic the diagram, the more it relies on text labels for explanation (97). Put labels next to or within the visual image they label. Put labels inside hollow shapes unless they will not fit. If space does not permit a complete label, place a short label in or near the shape and use a footnote to provide more information.

Draw links to show relationships

Links connect symbols. Each symbol should be connected to at least one other symbol. Links express the relationships of the system. The pattern of linkages among symbols is the message of the diagram. Each link is like a sentence expressing a relationship between two items of the system. Links can show relationships in one direction, in both directions, or in no particular direction. Links are represented by lines and optional terminal symbols and labels.

Various types of connections can be shown by using different types of lines. You can vary or restrict the following:

- **Weight or width of the line**. Use heavier lines for more powerful or important relationships.

- **Number of lines**. Use double lines for primary relationships and single lines for secondary relationships.

- **Style of line**. Use solid lines for primary and concrete relationships. Use dashed and dotted lines for secondary or abstract relationships. Use the line pattern to distinguish between a few different types of relationships.

- **Curvature or direction of the line**. Straight lines suggest directness; jagged lines, excitement; fluid curves, smooth transition. You may also vary direction and curvature to make lines easier to distinguish and to follow.

If the diagram contains different types of lines, label them (201). Keep the labels horizontal if possible. Place the label next to the link. Do not use arrows to connect labels to links. In some cases, however, it may be necessary to run the text along the link. Avoid curving text. Rotate the entire label, not its individual letters.

The shapes of the ends of bars and lines can reveal the nature of the link symbolized by the line. Terminators are small symbols at the ends of lines that further qualify relationships; for example, arrow heads show direction of a relationship.

Arrange symbols for meaning

In arranging symbols in the diagram, use position and proximity to express or reinforce relationships among objects (340; 341).

☐ Arrange objects with respect to their analogous real-world positions, orientations, and directions. Pay special attention to objects that are typically above or below the viewer's horizon.

☐ Arrange objects in diagrams by the "semantic distance" between them. Put similar and closely related items close together. Put more distant concepts farther apart.

☐ Put more general or powerful concepts "over" more specific or less powerful concepts.

☐ Put central concepts in the center. This will draw attention to them first and then let the eye explore related concepts.

☐ Arrange sequential concepts in a line and cyclical ones in a loop.

☐ If in doubt about placement of objects, follow the natural word order of the language.

Simplify and clarify the display

Free-form diagrams are often called "can-of-worms" diagrams or "COW" diagrams for short. The lines between symbols seem to meander like the trails of cattle (196). They are difficult to understand, to maintain, and to revise (109). But these difficulties are not necessary. Without changing the meaning of the diagram, we can often simplify and clarify its display.

Show direction of relationships

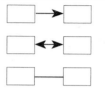

"For English speakers, as for speakers of many other languages, sequences of ideas are expected to run from left to right and from top to bottom over the page. Thus simply arranging elements in this configuration, even without using lines or arrows, is an effective device for illustrating sequential processes." (340, p. 302)

Emphasize the primary pattern

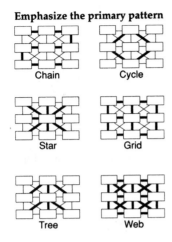

Chain   Cycle

Star   Grid

Tree   Web

"Sometimes the advocates or owners of a particular diagramming technique defend it more like pagan priests defending a religion than like computer scientists seeking to advance their methods." (196, p. 4)

☐ Emphasize the primary pattern of relationships in a diagram (340).

☐ Group or consolidate similar lines or closely related objects (201). If a diagram involves more than about 30 components, try grouping some of the components and showing them on a supplementary diagram (223).

☐ Simplify all lines and other paths the eye must follow (345). Make the paths between resting points smooth, short, and simple. In decision trees and flowcharts, consistently position yes and no answers.

☐ Make the natural flow through a diagram from top to bottom and left to right. Minimize the backward flows and clearly label them (340).

☐ If objects are highly interrelated, arrange them in a circle so all interrelationships can be shown by straight lines (24).

Follow conventions, if any

Most technical disciplines, such as computer science and architecture, have formal diagraming techniques. These techniques are standardized and well codified. If such a system exists, you should follow it scrupulously. Failing to do so can result in miscommunication or even worse. Architectural house plans, for instance, are part of a legal contract. When using a standardized diagrammatic form—such as logic circuits, Warnier-Orr diagrams, or electronic schematic diagrams—draw the diagram in the simplest, most unadorned style possible. Any attempt at decoration will make the standardized symbols harder to recognize.

Box-border diagram

Like symbol-link diagrams, box-border diagrams arrange symbols to show relationships and to represent concepts. With box-border diagrams, concepts are represented by blocks or areas. Relationships are represented, not by lines, but by borders between adjacent objects.

Stacked-block diagrams represent conceptual relationships through the familiar metaphor of stacked blocks. They use vertical position or gravity to represent support and dependency and use common borders to represent connections. They are visually attractive, and the analogy to familiar, three-dimensional objects ensures they are easily understood (340). Each layer provides an additional type of service by drawing on services provided by lower levels.

Three-dimensional blocks also offer another dimension of relationships as blocks can be drawn beside as well as on top of one another. Because three-dimensional blocks look more like concrete objects, they further enhance the solid-blocks metaphor. Our experience with solid objects and with gravity provides a strong, familiar metaphor to make the supporting role of lower blocks obvious and understandable.

Example of box-border diagrams

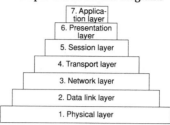

Inclusion diagram

Inclusion diagrams use borders and areas to show relationships of inclusion, overlap, and exclusion. A box reduces the semantic distances between the objects it contains and increases the distance between objects inside and outside the box. Use boxing to emphasize similarities of the objects within the box (341).

Chinese-box diagram

Chinese-box diagrams use boxes within boxes to show a hierarchy of inclusions. In such diagrams, place subordinate concepts within the boundaries of encompassing concepts (340).

Example of a Chinese-box diagram

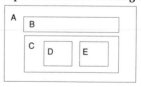

Onion diagram

To emphasize the inclusive nature of layers and to reinforce a shell or onion metaphor, draw a hierarchy as a shell or onion diagram. Such a diagram emphasizes the equality of parts and the fact that the core can be reached only through the outer layers.

Example of an onion diagram

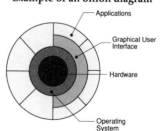

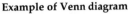

Example of Venn diagram

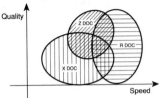

Venn diagram

Venn diagrams use bordered areas to represent conceptual categories. Such diagrams can show which concepts include or exclude other concepts. They can also show concepts that overlap—something that the other diagramming forms cannot.

WHICH FORM SHOULD I USE?

The general-purpose techniques described in this chapter are both flexible and familiar. Because they are flexible, you can use them for various subject matters: hardware and software, concrete and abstract. Several of them, especially symbol-link diagrams, can describe various structures and their variants and hybrids. They are familiar to readers of technical publications. Their many incarnations are well established and readily understood by readers of scientific and technical documents.

The following table lists the main graphical forms and the structures they can represent.

	For this pattern of relationships …			
Graphic	Chain	Grid	Tree	Web
Text list	■			
Indented list	☐		■	
Table		■		☐
Symbol-link diagram	☐	☐	■	■
Stacked-block diagram	■	☐	☐	
Inclusion diagram	☐		☐	

■ = Primary use   ☐ = Secondary use

SPECIFIC APPLICATIONS

Now let's look at some established formats for showing how specific kinds of systems are organized.

Organization charts

Organization charts are symbol-link diagrams that display the interrelationships within a hierarchical organization. Organization charts thus show the makeup (or breakdown, depending on viewpoint) of a system. That system may be the divisions, departments, and work groups of a corporation; the assemblies, subassemblies, and components of equipment; or the modules, routines, and subroutines of a computer program.

Organization charts can be drawn vertically as a pyramid, vertically as a tree, horizontally, or circularly. On a multilevel organization chart, the biggest problem is usually running out of space for boxes. Solutions include starting in the center and branching outward or turning the chart on the page (180). The drop-down tree diagram emphasizes sequence at the expense of hierarchical level.

Organization charts should be balanced, like a well-developed tree: not too many branches on one side or another. An unbalanced organization chart will draw attention to the imbalance in the organization (180).

In an organization chart, use solid lines to show official command and control relationships. Use dashed lines to show coordination, communication, and temporary relationships. To show relative importance, use larger boxes, bolder borders, and higher (or leftward) positions for more important items.

Example of an organization chart

Example of a drop-down tree diagram

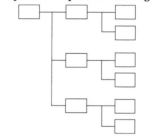

Interior views

Showing physical organization requires looking inside to see how things are put together. Such interior views help us understand, appreciate, and repair equipment.

Internal views are not a new invention of twentieth-century technology. Australian aborigines include internal organs in drawings of kangaroos. Children often draw the baby inside the mother's abdomen (11). Cutaways, skeletal views, and phantom views provide a familiar frame of reference for the viewer and give us X-ray vision (8; 125).

Cross-section

A cross-section shows an imaginary slice through an object. It reveals the location of ordinarily hidden components.

Cross-sections work better for more technical viewers. Engineers prefer cross-sections for showing how something is designed or constructed. Repairmen prefer simple exploded parts diagrams to show how it is assembled.

Cross-section

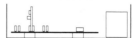

A broken section removes a surface from an external view to reveal a cross-section of an important component (223).

Sometimes the most revealing cross-section is not one that cuts along a straight slice but one that zigzags or even circles through the features of most interest.

To help viewers understand cross-sections, include a separate graphic showing the cutting plane line. In this view, show the object 90 degrees from the cross-section view. Use a heavy dotted line to show the cutting plane line. For symmetrical objects, you can draw a half-section showing the surface of one-half of the object and the interior of the matching half.

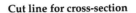
Cut line for cross-section

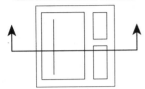

Cutaway view

Cutaway views show a small part of the interior of an object through a break in its exterior surface (223). They show both the construction of the object and its exterior. For untrained viewers, the cutaway provides better orientation than a cross-section.

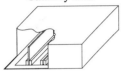
Cutaway view

Phantom view

To clearly show hidden parts, draw them in full and superimpose an outline of the edges of surrounding objects. Such a drawing is called a phantom view (223).

Phantom view

Exploded view

Exploded views show a complex device separated into its components to reveal how the parts fit together and to make clear internal relationships that are invisible on the assembled unit (138). Exploded views are excellent for showing technicians and laymen how to take something apart and how to put it back together again.

If assembly is not along a single straight line, use a dotted center line to show the direction along which parts are collapsed. Use branching lines to show alternative assemblies (223).

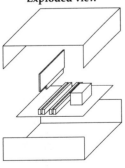
Exploded view

Menu maps

Menu maps combine techniques of flowcharts and state transition diagrams to give users a road map of the screens or menus they go through to perform a task. Such menu maps help users navigate a complex interactive system. Showing a command's position in menus answers two important questions: Where does this fit in the scheme? And, how do I select it?

Make the main menu larger, higher, and to the left of subordinate menus. Show which keys or commands are used to go from screen to screen (256).

 Put such a road map at the beginning as an overview or at the end as a summary. Or put it on a foldout page so users can refer to it throughout.

Syntax diagram

A syntax diagram shows the parameters and values that can be specified for a statement or command in a programming language. Probably the earliest form of syntax diagram is the infamous Reed-Kellogg diagram used to show grammatical relationships among the words of a sentence (223). Syntax statements for computer programming and macro languages benefit from a similar approach (136).

Reed-Kellogg diagram

Why use syntax diagrams?

Syntax diagrams, sometimes called railroad diagrams, can guide the way users conceive of and learn a language (136). Users with diagrams scored 90 percent correct compared with just 55 percent for Backus-Naur Form (BNF) (39). According to a survey of the programmers using Tandem's *TACL Programmer's Guide*, 77 percent found railroad diagrams easy to understand and 70 percent found them easy to use. Over half recommended replacing BNF diagrams with railroad diagrams (39). Diagrams, however, do take up 50 percent more space than textual statements.

Definition in Backus-Naur Form (BNF):

```
<simple type> ::=  <type identifier> |
<scalar type> | <subrange type>
<type identifier> ::= <identifier>
<scalar type> ::= ( <identifier> {,
<identifier> } )
<subrange type> ::= <constant>..
<constant>
```

Definition as syntax diagram:

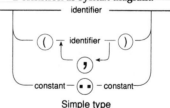

Simple type

How to design syntax diagrams

In syntax diagrams, show construction directly (9; 39):

☐ Eliminate pseudocharacters, such as braces and brackets, which are not actually entered but are used to show relationships among parameters and to define the syntax.

☐ Use branching lines to show alternatives.

☐ Use sequences to show dependencies.

☐ Use looping lines and numbers to show repetitions.

☐ Use heavier lines to indicate the path through defaults. Separate required from optional parameters.

☐ Vertically align alternatives.

☐ Use subdiagrams to show components repeated through the main structure or to expand components in greater detail than can be shown on the main diagram.

LABELING WITH ICONS AND VISUAL SYMBOLS

9

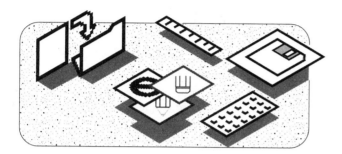

Visual symbols are simple, sometimes abstract, visual representations of objects, actions, and concepts. The wordless signs you see in airports and on the dashboard of your car are examples. So are religious and political symbols. Trademarks, too.

Icons are the pictorial symbols used on computer menus, windows, and screens. They represent certain capabilities of the system and can be animated to bring forth those capabilities for use by the operator. In the computer industry, the term *icon* is often used as a synonym for visual symbol.

For hundreds of examples of international symbols from various fields of endeavor, look at *Symbol Sourcebook* by Henry Dreyfuss (79).

WHERE TO USE VISUAL SYMBOLS

We can use visual symbols wherever we use word labels. They can be used on covers, in the table of contents, on tabs, and and in headings. We can use icons for the commands and objects of interactive computer programs. We can use them to supplement words or sometimes to replace words. Consider using symbols for any of these reasons:

Visual symbols have distinctive shapes

☐ Square

◯ Circle

△ Triangle

Widely recognized symbol

Symbols for geometric concepts

△ Equilateral triangle

◯ Rounded rectangle

☐ Define rectangle by corner points

- **To speed search.** Visual symbols each have a distinct shape that we can recognize instantly, even on a crowded page. Word labels, however, all have a basically rectangular shape and must often be read to be understood.

- **For immediate recognition.** The skull and cross bones on a bottle means poison to three-year-olds to whom the word poison in a thousand languages would mean nothing (79). The unique shape of a visual symbol ensures that once it is learned, it is retained reliably and recognized immediately. This makes visual symbols especially valuable in systems containing a large number of items that the viewer must recognize instantly.

- **For better recall.** Visual symbols are easily learned (325). They can be more memorable than words because they are more visually distinctive from one another (134). Visual symbols are also better retained because we tend to apply a name to the symbol, even if one is not supplied. Where the name is appropriate, it is remembered along with the visual image. Thus familiar visual symbols are stored in visual and verbal memory while labels are stored only verbally. On the other hand, if we cannot reliably name unfamiliar or unrecognizable symbols, they may not be remembered at all (339).

- **To save space.** Carefully crafted visual symbols can say much in a little space. Often a compact visual symbol can say more than an equally conspicuous word label or heading. Visual symbols require less space than equivalent words (263). Like monograms and trademarks, they provide a more compact, squarish alternative to strung-out text (97). Visual symbols fit conveniently and legibly on computer menus, keys, buttons, and knobs where words would not (79).

- **For graphic or spatial concepts.** Describing graphical concepts, spatial concepts, or physical operations in word labels is indirect and unnatural. Graphical ideas need graphical labels.

- **For visual appeal.** Visual symbols add visual appeal to a document. A visually attractive product is easier to sell. It is also more pleasant to use day in and day out. Attention to aesthetics demonstrates a genuine concern for the attitude of the user.

- **For international audiences.** Visual symbols, because they do not depend on any single natural language, can be understood more widely than words in a single language. For centuries merchants in Europe have hung three-dimensional symbols outside their shops to indicate the nature of their business: a fish for a fishmonger, boots for a shoemaker, eyeglasses for an optometrist, a key for a locksmith, or a clock for a watchmaker. Such signs were useful in times past when illiteracy was common and are useful today when tourists are common (79). The international symbols for first aid, mail, no smoking, and no entry are more widely understood than any words in any language (213). Using visual symbols saves having to translate every time the product is marketed in another country and clearly gives a product an international character.

International symbols

Use visual symbols where you would use a word or phrase as a label. Better still, use visual symbols to reinforce word labels (141).

QUALITIES OF GOOD SYMBOLS

In designing visual symbols, consider and balance the requirements and limitations imposed by the communication task, the needs and experience of the viewer, and the characteristics of the display medium.

Immediately obvious

Strive for symbols that are universally recognized (6). To be recognizable, a visual symbol must spontaneously suggest in the mind of the viewer the concept represented. If the user has to look up the meaning of a visual symbol in a manual, half the advantage of using it has been lost. The viewer should naturally associate the icon with what it represents (119). If not, you must label the symbol and teach its meaning.

For immediate recognition, select or design symbols strongly associated with the meaning you wish to convey. Use a direct association, such as physical resemblance or analogy, or select one that the viewer has previously learned.

"If, then, we are looking for a type of visual that conveys the most meaning with as little training as possible, it must be one that has a degree of realism but also contains abstract qualities as well. The ideal pictorial symbol ... possesses degrees of both concreteness and abstraction, is recognizable and does not rely too much on memory, and lastly, implies a degree of figurative thinking." (336, p. VC-20)

Simplify symbols

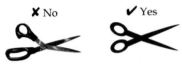

Attractive

A visually appealing symbol rewards the viewer's glances and demonstrates a solid concern for the aesthetics of the product or manual. It makes the product easier to promote and sell. Of course, prescribing beauty is impossible, even in simple visual symbols. However, some commonsense guidelines can help:

☐ Keep visual symbols simple. Avoid extraneous detail. Make every pixel or every speck of ink count.

☐ Avoid ragged edges and lines.

☐ Proportion the symbol to fit the available space.

Stylize unpleasant objects

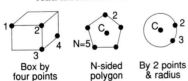

Simple

Visual symbols are not pictures. They are not intended to be pictorially accurate portrayals of the things they represent (263). In fact, they work best when they do not include too much detail (194). Each visual symbol should abstract the essence of just one idea and make that idea visible.

Refine and simplify visual symbols and illustrations, especially those of unpleasant subjects, such as bugs. A stylish scarab will find wider acceptance than a realistic cockroach.

Add informative details

Informative

A good visual symbol is a good label. A great visual symbol is more. It can contain additional information beyond the identity of the thing represented. Visual symbols can convey simple instructions (75). For example, icons for commands in Intergraph's I/EMS system for creating mechanical designs included information about the command:

• Shape created by the command

• Type inputs (position, text, numbers) required

• Number of the inputs

• Order of the inputs

Balance the need for additional information against potential complexity (263).

Distinct

One of the most common uses of a visual symbol is to help the user select one alternative from another; for instance, to pick one section of a manual to read or to activate a particular command in a computer program. Thus, the visual symbol must clearly distinguish one choice from others.

This means the visual symbol must be distinct from those representing other alternatives. It can gain this distinction by highlighting the single characteristic that separates its alternative from others. The visual symbol does not have to fully represent all characteristics, only the one that is unique. The visual symbol does not have to distinguish its referent from all others in the document or in the system, either. It merely has to distinguish its referent from other items the reader considers at the same time.

Emphasize critical differences

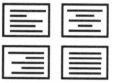

Ways of justifying type

Concrete

Where possible, use simplified images of concrete objects as symbols. Concrete objects are recognized more quickly, learned easier, and recalled more reliably than abstract forms (142; 300). Even abstract subjects are better depicted as concrete objects being used than by arbitrary, abstract shapes (263). If you must use abstract shapes, label them and teach their meanings.

"Specifically, the icon sets with the most direct mapping (i.e. those depicting concrete objects operated on) were found to have the highest number of correct matches, with over 85 percent of the icons being correctly identified." (263, p. 586)

Show operations on objects

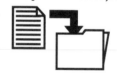

Familiar

Pick images already familiar to the viewer (59; 80; 338). For general purpose symbols, consider fields of broad interest and experience: household objects, tools, and sports (141). For symbols encountered on the job, base icons on objects from the user's world of work so they can apply what they know about the real objects in guessing how the icons operate (27). For example, symbols for petroleum geologists showed storage using oil drums rather than disk drive cylinders. For engineers, transferring data was indicated by a pump. But make sure you know your audience: What is familiar to one group of users may seem strange to another.

Pick familiar images

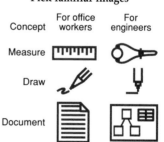

Legible

The effectiveness of a visual symbol often depends on how it is displayed. Preview the symbol in the actual display colors. Symbols that look crisp when drawn white on a black background or plotted black on white paper often look timid when displayed on a gray background. Sketch the symbol in the actual display colors so you see right away how it will appear in use.

Simplify symbols that must be read at reduced sizes or at great distances (97). Also display them in high contrast with their backgrounds.

Few

Although there is no practical limit to the number of symbols a user can learn with prolonged study, do not force viewers to memorize unjustified numbers of symbols. For documents and products used without training, limit the number of symbols to between 12 and 20 (100). For more complex systems, build large symbol sets from a smaller vocabulary of elementary symbols.

PICKING SYMBOLS

Whether communicating visually or verbally, we express ideas by exposing the reader to symbols that represent our ideas. We pick a sequence of symbols that most reliably and most quickly evoke the desired meaning in the viewer's consciousness. For this sequence to work, the association between each symbol and its meaning must be direct and strong—in the viewer's mind, not just in the designer's mind. The association must be perceptually apparent through a physical resemblance or must have been learned.

In picking or designing symbols, strive for images directly and naturally associated with the meaning you want to convey. Symbols that physically resemble their referents are easiest to learn and understand. Others relying on analogy require some examination and thought, but are usually understandable with little effort. Symbols based on abstract signs require outright learning (97).

Mimicry

Mimetic shapes avoid the problem of having to look outside the graphic to decode the symbol. Visual symbols derived from physical objects, perhaps by including the silhouette of the object, are readily and reliably understood. Whenever the symbol refers to an actual physical object, make the symbol a simplified picture of the object. The symbol need not be detailed. In fact, a simple profile may be sufficient provided the object has a distinctive outline shape.

"There is no universal shape signification. The meaning of a symbol becomes familiar to us only by habit; through the repetition of a similar situation." (24, p. 95)

Physical analogy

Another relatively direct way to symbolize concepts is through analogy with familiar physical objects. This method is widely used in creating icons for computer systems. The formula is simple:

Physical object = Software concept

Physical analogy is the basis for the desktop metaphor and other direct manipulation schemes. Some examples include:

Physical object (icon)	Software concept
Page of paper	File of data
File folder	Directory of files
Trash can	Deletion of files
Index cards	Records in a database
Mail box	Electronic-mail message

This technique is not limited to desktop publishing. A collection of programming modules is represented by a toolbox. The on-screen menu of controls for editing videotapes uses buttons that precisely resemble those on the control panel of an editing console.

Control-panel analogy

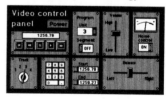

Associated object

When we cannot show an object or concept directly, we can still signify it with a closely associated object.

Show tool used for operation

Cut   Create   Change   Affix

Show resulting object

Use antiquated objects

Data   Electronic mail

Oil pressure   Key concept

Factory whistle or skyrocket?

Tool

Many computer programs automate manual processes. Many of these manual processes were performed with physical tools and devices. Such tools and devices often make effective symbols for the commands that effect the same results. Desktop publishing systems typically use a pencil point as an icon for drawing a line and an eraser for making a change. Drawing and painting programs represent commands with images of pens, paint brushes, and spray cans.

Result

To represent a process or action, we can show its tangible goal or result (134). Accounting programs use symbols of reports for commands that generate these reports. Drawing programs use geometric shapes for commands used to create such shapes.

Antiquated objects

For a visual symbol, show not what something actually looks like but a simplified version of what people think or remember it looks like. Often this is an earlier, simpler version. Use this strategy when the current versions of an object are too diverse or have immediate associations that interfere with your use. A skeleton key is often used to represent "key" facts. For one project a deck of punched cards proved the best symbol for raw data more than a decade after punched cards were discontinued. One of the most common symbols for the oil pressure indicator in automobiles is a long-spouted oil can found only in antique shops. The most common icon for electronic mail is the rural mailbox, seldom seen in cities where most users live (194). Before using antiquated objects, make sure your users recognize the object. In one case, a majority of viewers mistook a factory whistle for a skyrocket.

Visual figures of speech

Poetry, and other forms of figurative language, use figures of speech to express what cannot be said literally. We can use visual equivalents for some of these techniques when we cannot show the idea directly.

Established visual metaphors

With metaphor we communicate a characteristic by selecting a familiar object closely associated with that characteristic. A tenacious person is referred to as a bulldog and a courageous one as a lion. Many common objects have metaphorical meaning. The following table lists some common objects and their symbolic associations.

Object	Symbol	Association
Sun		Warmth, day, daily cycles, yearly cycles
Moon		Night, dark, month, monthly cycles
Fire, flame		Heat, fire, energy, ardor
Earth		Global issues, environment
Mountain		Loftiness, height, mass
Chain		Limitation, confinement, oppression
Bird		Flying, freedom, escape, spirituality
House		Home, lodging, home base

Synecdoche—part stands for the whole

In the figure of speech called *synecdoche*, we use a single, familiar part to stand for the whole object. This technique is widely used in road signs where a gas pump signifies a service station; a tent, an entire campground; a knife and fork, a restaurant; and a bed, a hotel. We see this technique in the tendency to represent entire cities or even countries by a single prominent building, such as the Eiffel Tower for Paris, Big Ben for London, and the Space Needle for Seattle.

Let part stand for the whole

Exaggerate crucial concept

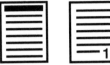

Page header   Page number

Negate the opposite

Keep cool   Keep dry

Use texture to suggest an object

Keyboard   Water   Brick

Text   Rock

Hyperbole—exaggeration

If the object or concept we must symbolize is a small part of a whole, we may use *hyperbole* or exaggeration to make it more prominent. This technique is valuable when you must clearly distinguish among otherwise similar objects or concepts. To highlight a small part, we can make it larger, point to it, or give it a distinctive graphical characteristic such as color or brightness.

Litotes—double negative

When you cannot find a direct symbol for a concept, consider whether you can show it by the negation of its opposite; for example, broken shackles can suggest freedom or liberty. Such double negatives work better graphically than verbally. To show negation or denial:

☐ Show a broken or distorted form of the object.

☐ Mark through it with an X.

☐ Superimpose the standard circle with a diagonal slash.

☐ Show an object used to block or defend against the concept.

Metony—quality represents object

In a metaphor, an object stands for a characteristic. In *metony*, a characteristic stands for an object. For example, IBM is frequently referred to as "Big Blue" after the color of its logo. The building that houses U.S. military headquarters is referred to as "The Pentagon" because of its shape. In geology, the symbols for various types of rock resemble the pattern of actual rocks. Tire treads can represent tires, rubber, and adhesion. For a symbol, consider all the graphical characteristics, especially shape, color, pattern, and texture.

Established and conventional symbols

Another source of already learned symbols is all around us, on doors and walls, along highways, and in books and magazines we read.

Technical symbols

Many technical symbols have found their way into common usage. These include the arrow to indicate direction, force, or movement; the cross-hair to indicate an exact location; or a thermometer to indicate temperature or the degree of some variable (97).

Use established technical symbols

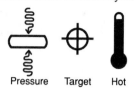

Pressure   Target   Hot

Public signs

Signs in public buildings and along roadways have given us a vocabulary of shapes with definite, well-known meanings. For example:

Sign	Example	Meaning
Slashed circle		Prohibition
Open circle		Permission
Triangle		Caution
Octagon		Stop
Human form		Activity performed by person

Mathematical symbols

Common mathematical symbols are widely understood, especially in technical disciplines throughout the world. Even the general public understands the plus, minus, and equal signs. However, avoid using X for the multiplication sign or / for division unless the context makes absolutely clear that they are to be interpreted as mathematical signs.

Use math symbols

$$+$$
$$-$$
$$=$$

Punctuation marks

Though not as universal as mathematical symbols, punctuation symbols can be used for audiences whose written languages contain the symbols. For English and the Romance languages, the question mark and exclamation mark are safe when used in their conventional meanings. Avoid using periods, colons, and semicolons as they are too small, easily confused with other symbols, or not universally understood.

Use recognizable punctuation marks

Remember that industrial tools and procedures vary around the world. The file folder, so common in American offices and desktop metaphors, is not so familiar in India, Japan, Africa, and parts of Europe, where documents are stored in open cardboard boxes (194).

Industrial symbols

Almost all technical disciplines have evolved their own system of visual symbols. In designing documents for these disciplines you should use these symbols, which are already familiar to the reader. At the start of a project, collect all the symbols you can find relating to the subject (141). Sources of such symbols include textbooks, handbooks, and trade journals from the discipline for which you are designing.

Abstract shape

Because abstract shapes have few natural associations, they are difficult to use for specific meanings and are best used for general and abstract concepts where the association between symbol and concept must be taught (79; 111; 263).

Use simple shapes for abstract concepts

- For abstract concepts, use simple shapes, such as squares, rectangles, circles, and ovals. More complex shapes will carry more associations.

- Respect, but do not absolutely depend on, common associations, such as those assigned to traffic signs.

- Remember that closed signs tend to be seen as objects, open signs as abstract qualities (97). Consider the use of boxes and lines in diagrams.

Forms to avoid or use with caution

Some objects and shapes are best avoided or used sparingly, especially in works for an international or multicultural audience.

Letters and other shapes

Avoid signs that inadvertently resemble familiar symbols like letters or numbers. Viewers will have trouble seeing them as anything else (97). Letters have strong meanings. The letter *A* is a good grade in school, the "Scarlet Letter" of adultery, an indefinite article, and the first item in the alphabet.

Avoid shapes easily confused with letters

Animals

The symbolic associations for animals vary among different cultures, social groups, and religions. The owl, which is a symbol of wisdom in most Western cultures, is thought to be an especially stupid and brutal bird in parts of the Orient.

Some animals are used to stereotype nationalities, often in a deprecatory fashion: kangaroos for Australians, frogs for Frenchmen. Many animals have negative religious connotations: cattle to Hindus, pigs to Moslems and Jews.

Hand gestures

Almost all configurations of the human hand are obscene or rude gestures somewhere in the world. For instance, the thumbs-up symbol, which means OK in the United States is an obscene gesture in many Mediterranean countries.

Be careful, but not paranoid, about using hand signs as visual symbols. Their rude meaning is often dependent on a particular social context and easily overridden by the context in which you use the symbol (215).

Humorous signs

Although nothing is wrong with a light, almost whimsical touch in designing visual symbols, even a good joke gets tiresome when repeated many times, as happens with icons in computer programs or symbols in manuals.

Visual symbols should especially avoid puns, which rely on words. For instance, using a balance scale to represent the concept of rescaling or resizing may seem fresh and clever at first. But such an icon works only because the word "scale" has two meanings in English; it falls short in other languages.

Emotional associations

Avoid symbols with strong emotional associations:

- Religious or political figures or symbols, unless they are the subject

- Objects of emotional attachment, such as cats, dogs, and infants

- Politically loaded symbols, such as top hats and money bags for investors (223), hammers or muscular arms for laborers, and egg-heads for academics

DESIGN A PICTORIAL LANGUAGE

If you are designing a large number of symbols, do not design them independently but as part of a coordinated "language" of related symbols. For consistency, ease of learning, and ease of design, a large set of visual symbols should build on a simple scheme of signage. This scheme should create most unique symbols by combining simpler, more generic symbols. The generic icons are like the words of a natural language. Complex concepts can be communicated by combining familiar graphical symbols in a consistent, logical way (266).

Establish basic symbols

The first step in creating the pictorial language is to build a collection of basic visual symbols that will appear in composite symbols. These symbols must be simple so they can be joined with other basic symbols. Your vocabulary will probably require three parts of speech:

Objects

Objects are the things of the scheme. They are the nouns of the language. For a concrete noun, show a simplified form of the object itself. For an abstract noun, try an analogous or associated object. To symbolize the concept of taxes you might use a tax return. Clearly distinguish icons for objects from those for actions or the effects of actions (172).

Actions

Action symbols make visible changes that occur and forces that act on objects. Actions include movement, transformation, and creation. Actions are the verbs of the language.

Visual symbols for verbs are difficult to create (344). Consider the simple words *push* and *pull*. Equipment designers have struggled for decades through thousands of attempts to design universal, unambiguous visual symbols for these actions. They do not appear to have succeeded (79).

In the static symbol, you must show change indirectly. Some ways are:

☐ Show verbs by what they do instead of how they look (134).

☐ For state changes, show before and after. Make the direction of change clear, through an arrow or by making the after state more prominent.

Show result of action

Left justify   Align top

Show before and after

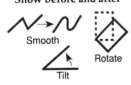

Smooth

Rotate

Tilt

☐ Show the tool with which the action is performed (264).

☐ Use graphical conventions such as ghost images or speed lines trailing behind the moving object (142).

☐ Show increase and decrease through a tapered shape or other gradient. To show acceleration, vary the rate of the taper or gradient (79).

Modifiers

Modifiers tell how, when, where, and to what degree. They are the adjectives and adverbs of the language. Use them to distinguish similar forms of a command or concept (134). Construct modifiers by altering the basic symbol, for instance, changing the length, direction, or width of lines, or attaching smaller secondary symbols (79). Some examples are:

To show ...	Use this modifier ...	
Where	Dot, cross-hair, arrow	
Order or sequence	Numbers, arrows	1, 2, 3 →
Avoidance or negation	X-mark or slashed circle	
Degree, percentage	Proportionately filled shape	

Show tool that performs action

Paint Draw Change

Use graphical conventions

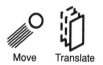

Move   Translate

Use gradients

Low   High Acceleration

Add a grammar for composite symbols

A grammar is a set of rules for combining symbols, whether the symbols are words or icons. Such a grammar ensures that basic symbols are combined in simple predictable ways that the reader finds obvious or intuitive.

The grammar of symbols is not the same as the grammar of words. Visual symbols may have different parts of speech and may be expressed by a sequence of actions, rather than subject-verb-object order of English (171). For our symbol language, we must establish and follow rules.

Let's take one famous example of a visual sentence: the peace sign, which first appeared during Easter of 1958 at a march for nuclear disarmament. Reportedly designed by Bertrand Russell, the sign superimposes a circle representing the globe

Origin of a famous symbol

Total   N   D   Peace

and lines for the semaphores for N (Nuclear) and D (Disarmament) (79).

The graphical grammar should specify:

- Which parts of speech are required and which are optional
- How elements may be combined, for instance, by composition, sequence, juxtaposition, and overlap (97)
- How components are arranged left to right and top to bottom
- How many elements may be combined before the resulting symbol is too complex
- Use of color
- When and how to include text with the symbol

In designing icons, use open-ended or outward-compatible analogies or metaphors. This way the analogy or metaphor continues to apply after the user progresses beyond using individual basic functions symbolized by icons. This open-ended strategy also makes adding new icons easier (249).

Keep the language consistent

Keep symbols consistent

Cumulative distance

Length along a curve

Keep the language both functionally and aesthetically consistent. Use the rules of the language uniformly and adopt a consistent graphical style for all symbols (194). Similar, but not identical, sets of visual symbols can confuse users (172). Don't mix metaphors, motifs, and design styles within a set of symbols (344).

Just as you want to use already established symbols where possible, you also want to reuse symbols you have already established. Besides saving time in development, reusing existing symbols promotes consistency and reduces the learning required by readers. For instance, for symbols about taking measurements, you could use a ruler along the edge being measured.

Family of symbols

... based on the same shape

Visual symbols are seldom viewed individually. They usually appear in groups or are used in related sets. Give the icons of a set a common design element, such as a texture, pattern, or line style. Choose a secondary element that does not reduce the distinctiveness of the visual symbols. Identify common characteristics to serve as themes. Such themes simplify design and make the display more cohesive.

DRAW MEANING FROM THE REST OF THE DISPLAY

Don't design visual symbols to stand alone. A visual symbol, like a word, achieves meaning only by its use in a particular context (55). Trying to make a visual symbol completely unambiguous to everyone under all possible circumstances is usually impossible. Attempting such a feat leads to overly complex designs. Instead, design the symbol so that under actual reading conditions it combines with other information in the reader's field of view and working memory to produce a clear meaning.

Symbol + Context = Meaning

Visual symbols are not complete messages, nor should they be. Visual symbols achieve unambiguous meaning only by use in a context that constrains and clarifies their possible meaning. This context includes the previous training and experience of the viewer, the position of the visual symbol and other nearby objects, and other visual symbols displayed as a set. In a rich context, a simple abstract symbol will suffice. Without the context, the symbol must be more detailed and realistic (223).

For example, notice how the following three icons achieve different meanings in different contexts:

Graphic	Context	Meaning
	Hallway door	Women's restroom
	Hospital	Gynecology
	Audiovisual catalog	Film equipment
	Computer animation program	Show animation
	Highway sign	Restaurant
	Restaurant menu	Beverages
	Grocery store	Coffee

Combine symbols and words

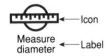

←—Icon

Measure
diameter ←—Label

Define icons in a glossary

Paint command—applies
color and pattern to object

Print command—sends
information to the printer

Quit command—exits
the program

Reverse command—moves
one unit in the opposite
direction

With icons "beginning users may make
good initial guesses of command
meanings, quickly identify which
command they are seeking, and better
recall command meanings during
subsequent use of the same
system." (171, p. 207)

COMBINE VISUAL SYMBOLS AND WORDS

Generally you should use words and visual symbols together, thereby gaining the advantages of both. Almost all research comparing the use of visual symbols and word labels has found that the combination of the two works better than either alone. In one study, users made 25 percent fewer errors when labels were added to the icons they were learning (27).

If the symbol is not obvious or known to all your readers, you must label it, at least the first time the reader encounters it. Few symbols are so unambiguous that first-time readers do not benefit from word labels (6). Include icons in your glossary. Include them in a separate column from text. Put them in alphabetical order by name.

REVISE TILL YOU GET IT RIGHT

Designing visual symbols is hard work. Even if you are an artist, do not expect to get it right the first time. The quality of a visual symbol often depends on the number of times you have revised it. Do not be satisfied with your first idea. Sketch several ideas before you draw the symbol. Test the symbol, and do not be too proud to replace it if someone else has a better idea. As a rule of thumb, five to ten revisions are necessary to get an effective visual symbol.

SYMBOLS YOU NEED

Visual symbols are especially valuable for representing computer commands in programs, actions by users in interactive applications, and as flags for parts of documents.

Computer commands

Probably the most visible use of visual symbols is on the screen as the emblem for computer commands. Unfortunately, not all icons used on the screen are understood by the user seated in front of that screen. Some authorities have (facetiously, perhaps) suggested replacing current computer icons with Chinese ideograms, whose meanings are standardized and already known by over a billion people (241).

Concrete operations on concrete objects can be shown directly using techniques discussed elsewhere in this chapter. Abstract commands and commands without visible results are more difficult. Experiments comparing different strategies found that the most effective strategy was to show operations on concrete objects (263).

For commands that require manipulating controls, pictures showing a prototypical action sequence made up of abstract symbols were most effective (264).

Mouse and keyboard actions

Computer documents continually tell the user to push this button or press that key. Repeated actions of computer operators benefit from shorthand symbols. Create a set of symbols for all common actions with the keyboard and mouse.

Use these symbols in other graphics, and in manuals. If you make them small and simple enough, you can include them inline with text.

Parts of manuals

Every publication and set of publications can use icons to label important segments of information. Candidates for icons in technical publications include:

- **The subject** of the publication. This may be an emblem or logo for the product.

- **The type of publication**. You may have different symbols for different categories of manuals (reference versus tutorial) and audience (operator, programmer, repairman). Put such icons on the covers and spines so users can quickly find the individual manual they need.

- **Chapters and sections**. Each chapter or major section may have a visual symbol. Include this symbol in the table of contents, on the first page of the chapter, and in the page header or footer—anywhere you put the chapter title or number.

- **Flags for special portions of text**, such as warnings, cautions, and notes. Limit the number of such symbols to about seven (44).

Show operation on concrete objects

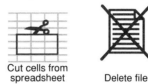

Cut cells from spreadsheet   Delete file

Show prototypical action sequence

Symbols for mouse and keyboard actions

Instead of saying ...	Show ...
Press the Return key	[Return]
Press Esc and then press G	[Esc] [G]
Hold down CTRL, press C, release CTRL	[Ctrl] [C]
Double-tap the left mouse button	
Drag with the right mouse button	
Select the Copy command from the Edit pull-down menu	

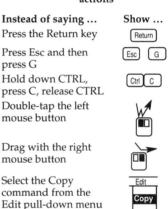

Symbols for types of manuals

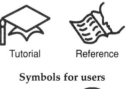

Tutorial   Reference

Symbols for users

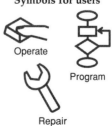

Operate

Program

Repair

DISPLAYING GRAPHICS ONLINE 10

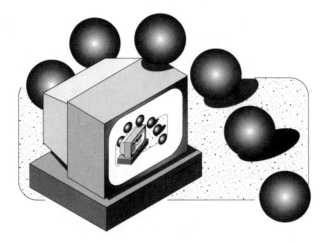

The screen is not a page and online documentation is not read as a book. Producing illustrations for online documents not only employs different tools, it requires different priorities and imposes different limitations than those for paper documents.

A SCREEN IS NOT A PAGE

The display screen differs from the printed page in both obvious and subtle ways that challenge designers of graphics and online documents.

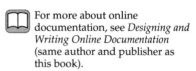

For more about online documentation, see *Designing and Writing Online Documentation* (same author and publisher as this book).

> For all the split-screen capabilities of some systems and windowing capabilities of others, the operator is still limited to viewing on-line documentation within the borders of the computer monitor. Yet, an operator can easily read and follow two full pages of printed instructions in a book as she or he works through the application on the system. An operator can more easily flip between different pages in a manual than between different help screens or on-line reference pages (67, p. ATA-65).

Online graphics are rougher

Graphic as printed

Graphic as displayed in online document

 For general information on using color in graphics, see Chapter 13.

Online pages are grainier

Resolution, the sharpness of displayed characters and lines, determines the minimum legible text size and limits the detail displayable in graphics. Resolution is usually defined as the spacing between pixels on the screen and is expressed as the number of dots per unit of distance or of area. Even the resolution of "high-resolution" computer screens is low compared to typeset paper pages or even laser printed-pages.

	Typeset paper pages	Laser-printed pages	High-resolution screen	Low-resolution screen
Dots per cm	1,000	120	40	20
Dots per inch	2,500	300	100	50
Dots per square cm	1,000,000	14,000	1,600	400
Dots per square inch	6,250,000	90,000	10,000	2,500

Remember that online graphics cannot show any feature smaller than a single pixel or any line less than 1 pixel wide. Gradations must be in whole multiples of pixels.

Online color is different

Online and paper documents may have different sets of colors available, and even when the same colors are available, these colors may appear different on screen than on paper.

Colors produced differently

Displayed colors are produced by a different process from that of printed colors. On the screen, colors are produced by adding varying amounts of three primary colors: red, green, and blue. On paper, colors are produced by subtracting various amounts of cyan, yellow, and magenta and by adding black as a fourth color.

On color monitors, small objects formed using a combination of primary colors may appear fuzzy because of misregistration, especially near the edges and corners of the screen (337).

Fewer colors?

Computer displays vary in the number of colors they can display. Although 16 or 32 colors prove more than adequate for color coding, 256 colors may be required to make colored objects recognizable. Showing subtle colors, such as facial tones, will require a palette of thousands of colors.

Even color computer displays with many colors cannot produce all possible hues. Additive colors can produce only those colors that lie between their primaries on the CIE 1931 color chart. Hues between these primaries will appear less saturated than the primaries (288).

Keep in mind that some users may not have the maximum number of colors and others may have to print out graphics on a black-and-white printer.

Available more widely?

Because of the cost of printing color, many designers may find color more readily available in online documents where it comes for free if all viewers have color monitors.

Online displays have limited colors available

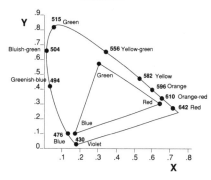

Navigation and perusal is electronic

In paper documents, the viewer moves from text to related graphic, from graphic to graphic, or within a complex graphic rapidly, automatically, and fluidly. Often these movements require only moving the eyes because much material occurs on the same two-page spread. Because online documents display less, the same movements must be accomplished electronically and activated mechanically by pressing a button or operating a mouse pointer. Such operations must be learned and can cause some delay.

COMMUNICATE MORE IN GRAPHICS

Online documentation is an inherently visual medium. The computer monitor looks a lot more like television or a videogame than a book. For online documents, you must adopt a graphocentric, not logocentric approach.

"… the screen has a closer affinity to a film than to a book." (33)

✘ No
At the "Command" prompt, type
the word "DELETE" and press
the Return Key.

✔ Yes
Command ==> DELETE

Use visuals for primary communication and not just for
summarizing or supporting text. Use text to elaborate on and
flesh in details not possible in the graphics.

Use graphics to provide:

- Visual table of contents
- Maps of the structure of the document
- Conceptual models of the information presented
- Concrete examples of procedures and processes

Whenever words would fill a screen or window, consider
whether your message could be presented as a list, table,
diagram, icon, graph, outline, flowchart, or some other
graphical form.

USE GRAPHICAL DESIGN CHARACTERISTICS OF SCREENS

Though online and paper documents share many graphical
design elements, they each possess unique characteristics. For
instance, some typographical refinements of printed pages are
not available in online documents. The following table lists
these characteristics and differences of online and paper
documents.

Graphical characteristic	How graphics on the screen differ from those on paper	Number of different levels, rates, or steps recognized (100; 195)
Dynamics	Blinking, visual transitions, and animation can be shown directly in many computer systems.	Two blinking rates
Position	Because most online displays are shaped differently from paper pages, the ratio of vertical to horizontal space is less online. Because of the lower resolution of the screen, items can be positioned less precisely.	Depends on screen size and display resolution

Value	Color and gray-scale monitors can show value directly, rather than as a halftone pattern of dots as on paper. The levels of value available depend on the number of colors or gray-scale levels.	Two or three brightness levels
Size	Online display area is usually smaller. Small sizes are limited by resolution of screen.	Three or four line lengths, two or three line widths, three sizes of objects
Color	Not all printed colors can be displayed. Availability of color may vary from user to user.	Four codes (six if displayed together)
Texture	Fine textures are limited by the resolution of the screen. Gradients of texture are limited to multiples of the screen resolution.	Depends on screen resolution
Pattern	Fine patterns are limited by the resolution of the screen.	Depends on screen resolution
Shape	Small shapes are limited by screen resolution. Edges of colored objects have fuzzy, colored fringes.	Ten geometric shapes
Orientation	Diagonal and curving lines are more jagged.	Four to eight angles

For online graphics, be aware of these differences. Respect the limitations and take advantage of them.

Everybody can use typewriter graphics

Even documents displayed on alphanumeric monitors can include pictures. You can combine standard letters, numbers, and punctuation marks to form simple but effective illustrations. I call such illustrations *typewriter graphics*. Typewriter graphics can produce vertical and horizontal lines well. Diagonals are much more difficult, especially if symmetry is important.

You can form arrows to show movement or flow, to highlight an object, or to guide the user's eye about the screen.

Typewriter graphics

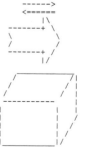

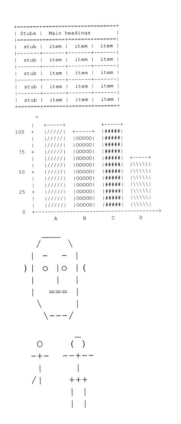

You can use typewriter graphics to draw two- and three-dimensional boxes and shapes.

Using typewriter graphics, you can create tables, complete with vertical and horizontal lines. You can also draw simple bar and column charts, scatter diagrams, area graphs, and histograms. In addition you can even create simple representations of the human figure and face.

Ensure foreground/background contrast

Computer displays typically produce less foreground/background contrast than paper documents. Legibility depends on adequate contrast between the graphic and its background (286). Accuracy and response time improve with increased contrast, and increasing contrast has been shown to make smaller text legible (49; 292).

Change colors

Select foreground and background color combinations with adequate contrast. Hue alone is not sufficient. Value or lightness contrast is required.

To enhance contrast, use *opponent* colors, such as red-green or yellow-blue. Since red-green color blindness is relatively common you may want to avoid these colors. Also, because the part of the eye that detects edges and fine details is relatively insensitive to blue, you should use pure blue as background only.

In picking colors, keep in mind that no color combination has greater contrast than black and white.

Adjust line weights

Use thicker lines for dark-on-light displays. Light lines appear to bloom outward on a dark background. Dark lines seem to shrink on a light background (305).

Adjust font stroke width

Likewise, use fonts with thicker strokes when displaying dark text on a light background (305).

Maintain foreground/background contrast

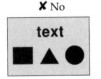 ✘ No

 ✔ Yes

Antialias to cure the jaggies

Aliasing is the technical term for what users informally call "the jaggies," the stair-step appearance of diagonal lines and curves on the computer screen. On color and gray-scale displays, we can use in-between tones to round off edges and smooth lines and curves. This process is called *antialiasing*.

One unexpected result of antialiasing is that screen fonts become more legible because their boundaries are less distinct. So-called fuzzy fonts use four to eight gray tones and hand-designed characters to smooth out the staircasing effect of angled and curving strokes (275). In testing, fuzzy fonts have enabled proofreaders to achieve reading speeds at the computer screen that are comparable to those with paper (113). One group's performance increased from 60 percent to 98 percent of what it was with paper documents (38).

Jagged diagonal line

Antialiasing smooths edges

Dither to blend colors and tones

One way to extend the number of colors is to mix existing colors (or gray values) by juxtaposing them. This is exactly the technique used in photographic halftones and pointillist paintings. For instance, to create gray tones, black-and-white monitors simulate gray with patterns of dots. This technique, called *dithering*, trades screen resolution for a greater number of simulated gray levels. For instance, displaying a photograph with 17 gray levels effectively reduces resolution by 75 percent. A 100 dot-per-inch display is reduced to 25 dots per inch.

The relationship between screen resolution and gray levels is:

$$\text{gray levels} = \left(\frac{\text{max resolution}}{\text{effective resolution}}\right)^2 + 1$$

For colors, the principle is the same but the mathematics more complex.

Dithering trades resolution for levels of gray

Gray levels	Linear resolution (percent of maximum)
2	100%
5	50%
9	33%
17	25%
26	20%
37	16%
50	14%
65	12%
82	11%
101	10%

WHEN THE GRAPHIC WON'T FIT ...

Because online pictures are displayed at a lower resolution in a smaller area than paper documents, you must keep them as simple as possible. Reduce the number of parts in each illustration and avoid fine lines and tiny text. If necessary, divide a complex illustration into several separate, simpler pictures. Include an overview picture from which the user can zoom in on these component pictures for more details.

Eliminate unnecessary information

Purge the graphic of nonfunctional elements and objects best shown elsewhere, such as the following:

Point to items on screens

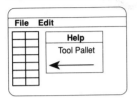

- **Objects shown elsewhere on the screen**. Point to things outside of the frame of the online document, provided the window appears in the same location relative to other objects on the screen.

Split screen between example and annotation

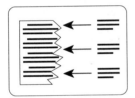

- **Unnecessary parts of examples.** Split the screen vertically and show the example on one half and the annotation for it on the other half.

- **Decorative elements.** Remove all embellishments such as frilly borders and textured backgrounds.

Reduce the size

If you can do so without reducing legibility, make the graphic smaller by shrinking it or by reducing the size of text or other elements. Use a smaller typeface for example screens or use a graphical editing program to shrink the example, provided this does not make it impossible to read.

Condense blocks of text intended for continuous reading but not for scanning targets. Higher density may actually increase the speed of reading of continuous text (164). Condensing text for continuous reading also frees space for text that is the target of scanning.

Divide large graphics

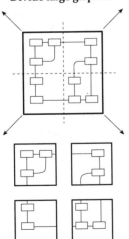

Use multiple pictures

You can divide a large graphic into a series of smaller graphics, such as the individual maps of an atlas. Use this technique with caution as viewers can easily get lost or discouraged before they find the graphic they need:

- Put the more important and more frequently used parts of the graphic early in the series (100).

- Do not split a diagram that must be viewed as a whole between separate displays (251). Use some other technique, such as zooming in.

- Overlap the coverage of the separate graphics, say by 10 percent.

Provide a scrolling view

If the graphic is continuous, put it in a window. Display part of the graphic at a time. Let the user scroll or slide the display to bring different zones of the graphic into view:

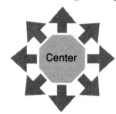

Controls for scrolling over a graphic

- If movements are primarily horizontal and vertical, provide scroll bars.

- If diagonal movements are common, provide a control to move the graphic vertically, horizontally, and the in-between diagonal directions.

- If small precise positioning movements are needed, let the user drag the graphic within the window.

Let users zoom in

Another way to handle oversized graphics is to give a zoomable view. Start with an overview with sparse detail. When the user selects a region of the graphic, this region expands to fill the complete display. As it does, more details become visible. The viewer can continue to zoom in for more details of a smaller area or zoom back out for a wider view with fewer details.

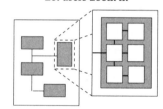

Let users zoom in

REDUCE DETAIL

The resolution of the screen limits fine details and may require redesigning graphics for a more streamlined image.

Fewer layers of detail

Online documents can display fewer layers or levels of detail. They have a shorter visual hierarchy than paper documents. Although a paper document can include as many as four or five levels of detail in a display, few online documents can display more than three levels of detail and even this requires using color and varying degrees of brightness.

Limit tiny details

Reduce reliance on fine details, points, lines, textures, and patterns. Limit the smallest size to one pixel and gradients to those possible in one-pixel increments.

Selectively display detail

Selectively display detail

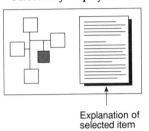

Explanation of
selected item

Limit the amount of detail shown at any one time. Let users selectively request and see details. Online illustrations can be self-annotating. The user just selects an object in the illustration, and an explanation appears in a reserved area on the screen or in a pop-up window.

Progressively disclose information

Start with a simple display and progressively—as the user requests—add more layers of detail (318). A simple form of progressive disclosure is called a *build*. You build up an image by continually adding to the display. You can add information to a display provided you do it in a way that is predictable and not distracting. For instance, you can build up the steps of a procedure by displaying them one at a time. Builds, sequentially adding information to the display, are less distracting than putting each step on a separate display and have the advantage that the user can see the steps together (342). Use builds to:

- Progressively reveal more detailed information
- Show a path on a map, a flow through a chart, or progress on a project tracking chart
- Depict the stages of a process or steps of a procedure

For example:

The display starts with a single box.

It adds an arrow to show the first process in a series.

A box shows the results of the first process.

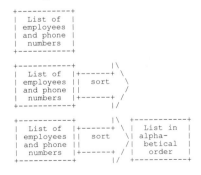

```
+-----------+       |\  +-----------+        |\
| List of   |+------+ \ | List in   |+------+  \
| employees || sort \| alpha-    ||  nroff   \
| and phone ||      /| betical   ||          /
| numbers   |+------+/ | order     |+------+  /
+-----------+       |/  +-----------+        |/
```

Another arrow represents a second
process.

```
+-----------+       |\  +-----------+        |\  +-----------+
| List of   |+------+ \ | List in   |+------+ \ |           |
| employees || sort \| alpha-    ||  nroff  \|  Phone    |
| and phone ||      /| betical   ||         /|  book     |
| numbers   |+------+/ | order     |+------+ / |           |
+-----------+       |/  +-----------+        |/  +-----------+
```

The results appear as the final box.

Selectively mask or filter information

Rather than build up complex graphics, we can start with a
dense but comprehensible display, and let users remove
details as if peeling away layers of acetate on which different
kinds of information are printed. For example, consider a
diagram showing a complex computer network serving a
corporation. The user could select one filter to see particular
kinds of network connections. The user could select another
filter to see particular kinds of computers or certain
departments.

Filters selectively remove details

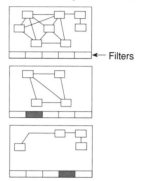

ELECTRONICALLY LINK TEXT AND GRAPHICS

Links are connections among blocks of text and graphics.
When a linked part of text is selected by pressing a key or
pointing to it with a mouse pointer, the related graphic or
block of text appears, either in a new window or area on the
screen or in place of the currently displayed information. Such
electronic links are the basis for hypertext and hypermedia.

Electronically link text and graphics

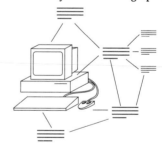

Link this ...	... to this
body text	supporting figure
graphic	related text
graphic	caption, legend, annotation, notes
part of graphic	annotation or description of the part
overview, picture of whole	detailed views of each of its parts
picture of an object or component	pictures of assemblies that include it

Consider all the ways users will want to read your document and provide the links they need.

MAKE TEXT LEGIBLE

Displayed text is generally less legible than printed text. Reading from the screen is 20 to 30 percent slower (170), slightly less accurate (347), and more variable in speed (33) than reading from paper. Improving the legibility of text requires attention to letter shapes, type size, display contrast, and layout.

Use well-formed character shapes

Most of the difference in reading speed between paper and online documents results from the low legibility of displayed characters compared to printed characters (113). By displaying text in well-formed characters, we can improve the legibility of displayed text relative to printed text. In addition to the recommendation in Chapter 15, pay special attention to the shape and size of characters for online documents.

"Serifs suffer from reproduction processes that cut off the thin serifs. Thus especially for on-line presentation, one wants to use slab serifs—the serif lines are 90 degrees to the verticals rather than serifs which curve on a diagonal which pixel densities on the screen make difficult to read." (335, p. 13-15)

Pick typefaces with:

- Simple functional letter shapes (275). Avoid stylized, decorative, and cursive typefaces.

- Square or slab endings. Fonts with smaller serifs may display irregularly because serifs that fall on pixel boundaries may not display at all.

- Distinct ascenders and descenders (100). These are the strokes that project above the body of the letter and below the base line.

- Standard, moderate letter proportions. Avoid condensed or stretched faces (145).

- Proportional spacing (133).

- Distinct strokes, at least one-twelfth the character height (145).

Consider high-legibility fonts, such as Stone and Lucida by Adobe, which are designed for low-resolution laser printers, fax machines, and computer screens.

Size type for reading conditions

The proper size for text depends on the reading distance. For paper documents, the viewing distance is not critical because it is easily adjusted by the user. The minimum recommended size for legibility and scanning are given in the following graph (145).

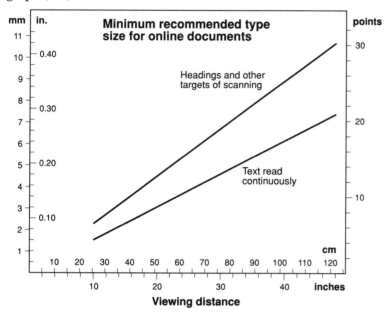

Remember, though, that these figures are for ideal readers under near-perfect conditions. Other factors can reduce legibility, and even with corrective glasses or contact lenses, most people have less than perfect vision (152).

MOTION

We live in a dynamic, changing environment, and we instinctively notice and attend to moving objects. Online documents can use the computer's power to display information in motion to focus attention and to communicate dynamic concepts. Online illustrations can incorporate animation and simulation to show exactly what happens when the device is used.

Use visual transitions to guide the eye and mind

Visual transitions are special visual effects to express the flow from one idea to another. Such visual transitions are especially important because the smaller display size means that the user views more separate displays than with paper pages and yet has fewer contextual or orienting cues. Visual transitions are commonly provided by tools for creating hypertexts and computer-based training lessons.

Use visual transitions to guide the user's eye to a specific area of the screen (132), to preserve coherence when shifting from one context to another (31), to alert the user to new objects and other changes in the display (14), and to reinforce the action being performed. Make such transitions distinct, smooth, and clear—especially when shifting context.

Visual transitions

Scroll down

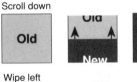

Wipe left

Zoom in

Dissolve

Fade to black

What you want to do or communicate.	Visual transition to use.
Move forward in a continuous series.	Scroll information from bottom to top of the display.
Move backward in a continuous series.	Scroll information from top to bottom of the display.
Move forward one display in a series.	Paint new information over old in a right-to-left wipe.
	Or scroll the new information onto the display from the right, pushing the old information off to the left.
Move backward one display in a series.	Paint new information over old in a left-to-right wipe; or scroll the new information onto the display from the left, pushing the old information off to the right.
Show more specific information on an item.	Zoom in on the item.
Show more general information.	Zoom out from the current item, collapsing it to an icon or label.
Suggest a smooth, gentle transition of ideas.	Dissolve or fade from one display into the next.
Move to a new, major topic in the series.	Fade to black between displays. That is, gradually darken the first before gradually lightening the second.

Segue between organizationally distant topics.	Fade out to a graphical view of the current topic, zoom out to show its immediate neighbors, slide over to a view of the new topic and its neighbors, zoom in on the new topic, and fade into the new topic (232).

You can combine visual transitions for special effects and to communicate compound actions.

Animate dynamic concepts

Animation is the illusion of motion. Animation makes exploded diagrams explode, procedures proceed, and working models work—all in front of the user's eyes (151). Animation can show abstract changes, such as the movement of data through a process (280).

Animation cannot fail to draw attention and stimulate interest (277). Simple moving line drawings are often more effective than complex shaded animations or fully detailed video segments (14).

So strong is the effect of motion in holding the eye that a cameraman "can simply center a moving image in his finder and regardless of poor composition, improper placement in the frame, unsatisfactory background or numerous other pictorial faults, hold the viewer's attention through sheer movement alone!" (199, p. 198)

Uses for animation

Use animation to communicate, not to decorate. Use it to convey change, movement, and progress. Use animation to:

 For more information on animation read:

- *Disney Animation* by Frank Thomas and Ollie Johnson (308)
- *Animation Techniques* by Roger Noake (227)

- Explain a complex mechanical device with many moving parts, such as a laser printer.

- Show increase, decrease, or change in some physical variable.

- Help the user recognize solid objects by peering slightly around and behind them (motion parallax).

- Simulate varying conditions. You might, for instance, teach a repair technician to recognize the circuits inside a piece of equipment under normal office lighting, under a spotlight, or by flashlight.

- Show processes and procedures. Because they unfold over time, processes and procedures are naturals for animation.

- Illustrate software dynamics, such as algorithms, data-communication protocols, and flows through program structures and loops. A whole field, called *program visualization*, has developed to animate and study dynamics of software.

- Analyze processes. Animation can reveal repeated patterns of action, bottlenecks, and relative speed of processes.

- Show rather than tell what a command does. Reveal what inputs it takes and what results it produces.

- Demonstrate how to operate a device.

How animation works

As inexpensive tools for animation have become available, many now find animation within their budget and schedule. Animation, however, is a difficult technique to master, requiring considerable study and experience. This section is not a primer on animation, but it does warn about the most common mistakes made by neophyte computer animators.

You can produce simple animations by repeatedly displaying the same picture with slight changes each time (280), as in this sequence for turning pages.

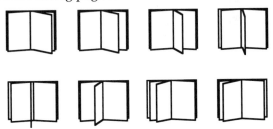

Draw and erase images smoothly and keep the distance between successive images small.

Design the pattern of motion

In designing animation, pay special attention to patterns of motion, especially repeated motions. A pattern of motion is sufficient to endow a graphical object with human characteristics, such as aggressiveness, persistence, nervousness, and fatigue (11).

Unvarying, symmetrical reciprocal motion can prove hypnotic or annoying. It communicates a mechanical, nonhuman feeling. Asymmetrical reciprocal motion creates a feeling of syncopation, rhythm, and swing (19). Zooming in pulls the viewer into the scene, inviting participation or interaction with the graphic (277).

Animated graphical objects are subject to the laws of physics. Graphical objects are perceived as having mass. In motion, they acquire momentum, preserving the direction and speed of any movement. Objects overcome resistance. Speed represents high power or low resistance. Acceleration is attributed to the power of the object; slowing down, to friction (11).

Depth is communicated by the change of size of graphical objects. When we walk down a hallway, it appears to expand

Objects do not burst into motion

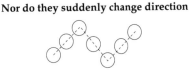

They accelerate and decelerate

Nor do they suddenly change direction

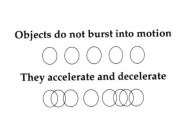

They round corners

and open ahead of us and contract and shrink behind us. This effect, called *parallelatic gradient*, is a valuable cue to pilots attempting to land on an aircraft carrier (129). The rate at which the size of the retinal image of an object changes tells us how fast it is approaching or receding (129).

Set the pace and tempo

To change the tempo of a scene, alter the length of the shots. Idle time seems to pass more slowly than time filled with activity (154). Use short shots for a quick tempo. D. W. Griffith perfected the technique of the cross-cut—jumping back and forth between two concurrent events—to increase the excitement of a chase scene. Relax the tempo with longer shots (129).

Don't overload the viewer by showing too much too fast. The display becomes distracting when we try to show too much spatially by crowding the display with objects or too much temporally by changing rapidly or too abruptly (14). Remember that users can pay attention to only one moving object at a time. If the animation includes simultaneous movements by separate objects, let the user cycle or repeat the scene.

"If response is sluggish, users will retreat to the fast, safe world of static text and static pictures." (14, p. 266)

Ensure continuity

For continuity in animation, repeat familiar objects, characteristics, and patterns from scene to scene (277):

- ☐ Use the same color and texture on different objects or in different scenes.

- ☐ Repeat shapes, especially simple geometric shapes that are recognizable even in complex scenes.

- ☐ Repeat distinctive patterns of motion. The pattern must be unique to the scene and clearly distinguished from other motion, or viewers will either not notice it or will be confused.

Prepare the viewer for changes

In animation, use a change of color, motion, or sound to prepare the viewer for a sudden or dramatic change of the visuals. Gradual changes can prepare the viewer for a new style of presentation or a new type of content (277).

To sneak something unnoticed into the display, move one or two other objects jerkily and quickly in a different part of the scene as you glide the new object smoothly and slowly into place. Stage magicians have used this trick for centuries.

Clarify the flow of time

Because few people can accurately gauge time durations and intervals without some clear frame of reference, film directors typically show the lapse of time by the change of clock hands, change of days on a calendar, change of season, or visible aging of characters. You can also show the passage of time by dissolving slowly from scene to scene or cutting away for a while to another scene (reaction shot) and then returning to the original scene.

Integrate with other media

If you are combining animation with sound effects, voice, or music, you must coordinate and precisely synchronize all these elements. Some uses for sound include:

- Voice-over narration to explain a simulation or example without cluttering the screen with text

- Change of musical tempo or tone to prepare the viewer for a sudden change

- Rhythm to reinforce a pattern of motion

- Realistic sounds to provide associated cues, such as the chirp of a disk drive head or the whir of a cooling fan

Simulate complex systems for hands-on experience

Computer simulations can outperform training on actual systems, especially when the actual system is expensive or dangerous or when the reaction time of the actual system is extremely fast or slow. A space shuttle simulator, for example, can show the results of an orbital maneuver immediately, jumping ahead several orbits without the expense or danger of an actual launch.

Where possible, give "hands-on" exercises on the actual system or at least on a high-fidelity simulation (99). Such training is more effective than any read-and-type exercises (204). By experimenting with the actual system and

---

Clearly show passage of time

"The tone, rhythm, and speed of the sound track should complement the weight and motion of the visual elements and underscore the emotional context of the scene. Research has shown that there is a direct correlation between sound and visual perception. Low-pitched sounds are associated with dark colors and large, rounded forms, while high-pitched sounds are perceived as smaller in size, sharper in contour, and brighter in color." (277, p. VC-19)

"If a picture is worth a thousand words, hands-on examples are worth a thousand pages." (212, p. 62)

"Simulation adds new dimensions to experiments and to their use in teaching because it makes visible many very small, very slow, or very rapid changes that cannot be observed in actuality." (195)

seeing the outcomes of their actions, learners form a more accurate mental model than by merely observing the system in operation or reading about it (156).

Simulating a system lets the user practice in a controlled, safe environment. An example is the QUIZDOC system, which lets the user run sample programs to learn programming concepts (18). You could include a simulation of the menus of a system, especially if selecting commands and entering data could be dangerous or confusing to novices.

Let the users stop, start, step through, and reverse the simulation.

Do-by-example exercises incorporate actual hands-on exercises into the document. In interactive tutorials, leave working area on the document for the user to try out commands and tools.

Use video to show real objects in motion

In its most advanced forms, online documentation grows to resemble television.

In the Movie Manual project, the Machine Architecture group at MIT included movies in a repair manual for the first time (31; 38). The user read the manual at a computer screen that displayed one page of the manual at a time. On the page might appear a still, color picture. When the user touched the picture, it turned into a short movie, complete with sound.

Interactive video has spawned entirely new forms of online documentation, such as *surrogate travel*, in which a computer lets users sample the sounds and sights they would experience on a stroll about the landscape (188).

Of course, producing interactive, dynamic multimedia documents such as these requires specialized equipment, an extensive team of expert professionals, and an ample budget. In producing such documents, follow a few simple guidelines:

- Use moving pictures for subjects that teach psychomotor skills or demonstrate three-dimensional devices in motion. Do not use them to discuss abstract concepts and philosophies.

- Show things moving, not just people talking.

Simulation of video control panel

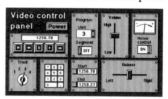

"Provide practice exercises in performing various tasks, but also allow the user to supply real information along the way so that the task is actually performed when the exercise is completed." (61, p. WE-161)

"If a picture is worth a thousand words, a dynamic picture of time-varying objects is worth a thousand static ones." (318, p. 893)

- Keep segments short. In television, few shots last longer than ten seconds (250). In rock-music videos, they may average less than a second.

Let the user control the action

Controls for online video and animation

Play the segment.

Freeze a particular frame.

Vary the speed from high speed to slow motion.

Run the movie forward and backward.

Loop the segment so it automatically starts over when it reaches the end.

Let the user control the rate at which information is displayed. In an interactive program, never arbitrarily erase information after a fixed time. Let the user signify when to erase or replace information in a display or when to move to the next display (342). In a passive demonstration program, display information as long as it takes to read it aloud (278).

Let the user control the animation. For instance, in CBT-32, a computer-based training program for informing managers and technical personnel about National Semiconductor's NS32532 processor, users may view animated sequences straight through, with or without accompanying narration. They may also freeze a frame, resume viewing, or step through the animation one frame at a time (93).

THE AFFECTIVE EFFECT OF GRAPHICS

11

Graphics work not only on the intellect but on the emotions of the reader as well. Though many technical communicators would deny it, successful computer documentation must tend to the emotional needs, resistances, and preferences of its readers. This chapter discusses how graphics can motivate, inspire, reassure, and tickle the reader.

 The tone, mood, or personality of a document is set long before the reader reads the first word. Format, more than any other factor, determines the reader's emotional response to a written work.

REMEMBER THE EMOTIONAL COMPONENT

Graphics designed objectively are perceived subjectively. The problem with objectively designed graphics is that the audience's emotions, memories, appetites, and misconceptions all actively affect how images are interpreted and even which images are selected. Our initial and subsequent reactions to a graphic or to an entire publication depend on subjective visual impressions (108; 254; 268).

"Our visual impressions are often more memorable than our understanding of the facts they describe." (259, p. 20)

Consider the whole viewer

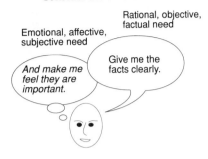

"Boredom is as much a threat in visual design as it is elsewhere in art and communication. The mind and eye demand stimulation and surprise." (76)

 Take care. The techniques appropriate for one purpose may be opposite those for another purpose. First, decide your primary purpose.

All graphics have both objective and subjective meanings (119). We must attend to both: We must present the facts and help the viewer understand what they mean.

Nigel Holmes, graphic designer for *Time* magazine, advocates a highly pictorial style in which the background for the graphic illustrates what the graphic is about. Such illustrations emphasize how the information affects people like the viewer. Often the shape of a plotted line or bar becomes part of the illustration. For instance, a bar chart showing financial losses by automobile companies is shaped as an automobile sliding over a cliff. Inside, the driver appears to be pulling back on the steering wheel as if to put more pressure on the brakes (141). Such graphics convey both fact and emotion.

MANAGING THE EMOTIONAL RESPONSE

You've spent many long hours to ensure that everything users need to know is in that manual. You're a good writer and the facts are all logically organized and clearly presented. But the users just don't read and follow the manual the way you hoped they would.

Merely recording the facts logically and clearly is often not enough. Remember, the user is not a computer to be programmed, but a human being. And communicating with human beings requires managing rather than ignoring the emotional response. Fortunately, we can design our graphics to manage this emotional response, and thus to ensure the graphics are interpreted correctly.

Motivate the reader to read and to act

Graphics can motivate users to read and study manuals and to follow the procedures they prescribe. To motivate users to follow complex procedures, show typical results, annotated to explain which steps contributed to the result. This provides a context and shows users what they are creating (256). It also motivates reading and study. Recipes that show completed dishes consistently draw more readers than those that merely list raw ingredients (230). A study by George Gallup of 70 advertising campaigns featuring before-and-after photographs failed to find any that did not increase sales (230).

To motivate readers to study critical graphics, include a range of questions or activities to awaken their curiosity and thereby encourage them to attend to the graphics. The questions must cover all the important concepts of the graphics. By focusing attention on certain concepts, questions increase learning of these concepts, but they may reduce learning of other concepts. Design the questions so they require interpreting the graphic, not just reading a value from it (341).

For positive reinforcement, reward the reader's glances with successive levels of detail. Layer the graphic in a clear visual hierarchy and reveal increasing layers of information to the probing eye. Zooming in from the big picture, the reader expects to find meaningful details (185).

Build the viewer's confidence

Complex technical and business information can seem frightening. To build the viewer's confidence that he can understand and use the graphic and the publication:

☐ **Keep the display simple**. Eliminate all unnecessary details and fine print.

☐ **Establish a clear visual hierarchy**. Emphasize primary information and make it stand out from secondary details.

☐ **Use graphical characteristics redundantly**. Don't depend on a single graphical characteristic alone. Team them up. For instance, you might make all primary objects large, red rectangles, rather than making them just large, just red, or just rectangular.

☐ **Use soft edges and rounded corners**. Just as sharp objects prick and stab us, sharp graphical objects produce a measure of anxiety in viewers. Grind off the hard-edge for a more humane graphic.

☐ **Choose soothing colors**. Avoid bright, warm colors. Prefer cool or neutral pastels. Reduce harsh contrast if doing so does not reduce legibility.

Keep the graphic simple and well-organized

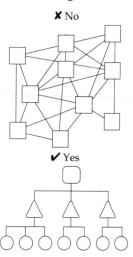

Win trust

To convince the viewer that what you say in the graphic is true, precise, and accurate, present the graphic openly and honestly.

Avoid misleading, decorative graphics

✗ No

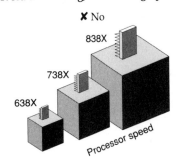

838X

738X

638X

Processor speed

✔ Yes

Processor speed

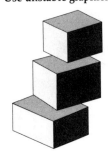

638X | 25 MHZ

738X | 33 MHZ

838X | 40 MHZ

Use unstable graphics

"A humorous approach to technical writing appeals to the reader's creativity and personal experience, and helps satisfy the reader on both technical and personal levels." (108, p. 90)

☐ **Use graphics to communicate, not to decorate**. Viewers are quick to recognize empty decoration and are likely to suspect that it is used to hide or distract from the meaning of the data. So remove purely decorative elements.

☐ **Make relationships explicit**. Don't hint, imply, or suggest—show.

☐ **Emphasize important but subtle differences**. If two things are similar but not the same, make the similarities and differences clear.

☐ **Avoid graphical distortions**. Don't use graphical tricks, such as three-dimensional bar graphs, that are easily misread. Remember this cardinal rule: The viewer's first impression must be true.

☐ **Allow verification of details**. Enable the viewer to check the facts. Post numbers in charts. Cite source materials.

☐ **Use hard-edged graphics**. Feature square-cornered shapes to imply an upright, orthodox view. Use fine lines and perhaps a grid background to suggest scientific precision.

Communicate urgency

When the purpose of the graphic is to propel the viewer into action, it must communicate a sense of urgency.

☐ **Use alerting colors**. Feature bright, saturated, warm colors. Use red to suggest danger and yellow to demand attention.

☐ **Keep the graphic simple**. Spartan. Stark.

☐ **Use "unstable" graphics**. Use graphical elements and characteristics that suggest urgency. Feature jagged edges and diagonal lines. Show objects in unstable positions or in mid-action.

Make the viewer laugh

Humor can be an effective tool in overcoming resistance and in focusing or holding attention. It can interest viewers in the message and help sell ideas and products. And it is especially effective in softening the blow of negative information (108). However, in technical documents, use humor to make a point, not to entertain (98). Unless humor contributes to your message, it distracts. It becomes noise.

Remember, however, that communicating humor requires some shared experience. For this reason, avoid humor in cross-cultural documents; certainly refrain from using puns in documents that will be translated. Consider Help for HyperCard 1.0 which uses two identical rabbits as a symbol for the Copy command. Might not other cultures see the rabbits as food or vermin?

Humor is a matter of personal taste. Will the Copy bunnies appear too cute? Cuteness may work 90 percent of the time, but you must decide whether the benefits of such humor outweigh the 10 percent failure rate.

Use humor with a light hand and subtle tone. Never make fun of the product and never, under any circumstances, make fun of the user. Avoid parody and satire, as they require a great amount of shared knowledge between creator and reader. Instead, strive for a whimsical tone more likely to produce a smile than a belly laugh.

Use humor for items of secondary importance (108). Use humor to reinforce, to support, to alert. Never use it as the primary carrier of critical factual information. With humor there is always the danger that the reader will not take seriously the point presented humorously. No one would suggest a message such as:

```
Hey dude, this process could wipe out all the neat stuff
on your hard disk. Then again it might not. Do you want
to risk it? Select F2 to say "No way" or F3 to say "Go
for it."
```

For effective humor, consider these graphical effects:

- **Antique photographs and prints** of analogous objects. For instance, the *Jot Times*, a publication about the APL computer language, included an old drawing of workers inside a circular section of steel pipe and referred to it as their first circular function (108).

- **Humorous examples.** While keeping examples and samples relevant to the user, you can still pick companies with amusing names ("Transylvania Midnight Airlines") or unusual products ("Puckerperfect pickles").

- **Cartoons of typical users.** Show simplified drawings of people the readers can identify with. Show them in relaxed positions where they seem to be enjoying themselves. Do not show them having tantrums or pulling their hair out—

"Humor is a great weapon in your visual arsenal. As long as it is not malicious, making people laugh with you will encourage a reader to remember your image and therefore the point of the chart." (141, p. 76)

"In other words, it is better to be too subtle and have the humor be missed than to try too hard for a laugh and have the whole message missed." (108, p. 90)

Optional equipment?

Concoct humorous examples

Transylvania Airlines Reservations

From

To

Blood type

unless you mean to imply that your product is hard to use and unreliable.

CARTOONS

A technical manual is not the comics page of the newspaper, and many writers of technical manuals hold that cartoons have no place in technical documents. But cartoons can do more than entertain and amuse. When used appropriately, cartoons can boost readership, focus attention on important information, and convey difficult messages diplomatically.

Uses for cartoons

Cartoons are useful in many technical documents, especially those for nontechnical audiences. You can use cartoons to:

- **Add a light tone** to an otherwise tedious document. As an example of cartoons used to good effect, look at Peter Aschwanden's cartoons in John Muir's *How to Keep Your Volkswagen Alive* (217).

- **Avoid personal characteristics**. A properly designed cartoon character should have no identifiable race or sex.

- **Show consequences of undesirable behavior** in a way inoffensive to the reader (158). It's a lot less expensive to crash a cartoon airplane (or computer) than a real one (126).

- **Attract attention to important messages**, such as safety warnings, tips and suggestions, maintenance reminders. (158; 312).

- **Present secondary or peripheral messages** that don't fit in the structure of your main message (312).

Cartoons are effective in communicating serious information to adults (279). They can communicate to multiple levels of technical experience, knowledge, and responsibility and can "humanize" or personalize a document (158).

One word of caution: because of their frequent use for humor cartoons may not be appropriate for highly formal documents (158).

"Cartoons are universally popular and possess an irresistible charm. They portray an imaginative and symbolic world that carries no direct threat or attack, but a world of vision and fancy that readers willingly enter because of the intellectual attraction of symbolic associations, their personal identity with the human condition being illuminated, and the sense of adventure, or escape, of belonging to a world apart for a space of time." (158, p. G-13)

Use cartoons to avoid personal characteristics

I'm the universal user

"Even the poorest comic book distributed by a company will be read by each employee and his family.... Cartoon strips can explain complicated industrial engineering concepts, industrial relations goals, the benefits of teamwork, and principles of supervision, to name a few." (98, pp. 86-87)

In using cartoons, remember that the purpose of the cartoon is to communicate information, not to evoke humor. If the cartoon communicates, it works; if it also amuses, then all the better.

Develop a cartoon character

Drawing cartoons is not difficult. They can be quite simple. And they can be irregular, asymmetrical, and out of proportion (158).

Though cartoons may be simple, viewers must automatically recognize ideas or objects symbolized. Identity can be conveyed by characteristic features of the object or even by identifying labels (158). Remember that cartoon characters are made up of permanent traits—representing the character's personality—and of temporary deviations—representing the character's emotions (111). Make the permanent characteristics recognizable and the temporary ones expressive.

Exaggerate features and movements of cartoon characters. Make sure the character can sit, recline, stand, walk, and run. Especially enlarge the head, hands, feet, and facial features (219). Cartoons that are just "talking heads" annoy or disappoint readers (98).

Create cartoon characters by animating objects from the reader's world of work: pencils, calculators, computer terminals, coffee cups, filing cabinets, copying machines, and even technical manuals (158). Make dangerous things look fierce and menacing; make helpful things look safe and likable (98).

Make the cartoon character one the audience can identify with. Avoid specific identifying characteristics such as sex, age, race, and position. Give the cartoon character a clear personality but make it flexible enough to cover all situations you will ever want to create. (126). Experiment with all the basic emotions the character must express and the environments in which it may appear (219).

Cartoon character

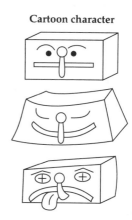

Animate real-world objects

The cartoon "... avoids the direct impact of written language in a negative communication, avoids attributing responsibility for a problem directly to a person, group, or department and avoids the appearance of the stinging hand of correction, an onerous business at best. The indirect message of the cartoon allows the reader to 'save face,' to preserve his professional ego, and so produces less inclination to respond negatively to the message." (158, p. G-13)

"

Another important use for cartoons is to provide a character for transfer of touchy subjects or undesirable personal characteristics away from sensitive individuals. Such a character can sidestep the tendency to accuse the trainee of ignorance or negative attitudes. You can show the effects of good or bad characteristics without appearing to preach or talk down to the trainee. The cartoon character can be dumb or foolish and get the message to the trainee without being degrading or threatening." (98, p. 86)

It's never done that before!

Use cartoons for negative messages

Probably the most effective use of cartoons is to warn the reader without offending the reader. Bluntly telling the reader not to do something foolish can backfire. Many readers would say, "Why, I would never do that! Do they really think I am that stupid?" Such a reaction alienates the reader and erects barriers against well intentioned and perhaps critical messages.

Writers for military and industrial users of dangerous and expensive equipment have found cartoons an effective way to deliver such messages without offending the reader. Gardner-Denver Company used a series of cartoons featuring the wasteful and careless Don Downtime and the ever-professional Rig Runright to show the wrong and right way to use and repair equipment in the oil field (312). The United States Air Force's *TAC ATTAC* uses a cartoon eagle called "Fleagle" to deliver safety warnings (126). Fleagle, who does not heed warnings and advice, continually crashes and gets shot down.

For cartoon story lines, collect humorous stories about using the product from users, customer-support staff, trainers, sales representatives, and service technicians (312).

PRETTY PICTURES

This book is not about making pretty pictures. But there are times when a pretty picture is warranted. Decorative graphics may well be necessary to motivate reading or to meet other emotional needs of the viewer. Base the relative priority of decoration on the purpose and audience of the graphic. For *USA Today* the priority is

Message + Redundancy + **DECORATION** + Noise

For the *Journal of the American Medical Association* it is

MESSAGE + Redundancy + Decoration + Noise

For your technical manual it is probably somewhere in between these extremes.

Reasons to use pretty pictures

Use pretty pictures for the same reasons you use all pictures in the publication, and for the same reason you use words to accomplish a purpose. The purposes of pretty pictures are as important to the success of a document as those met by purely functional graphics. Use pretty pictures to:

- Establish a visual theme or motif for continuity

- Set a tone or mood

- Catch the eye and arouse curiosity

- Seduce the reader

- Portray aesthetics of a product

- Meet expectations of the reader

- Provide visual relief and variety

- Break up solid blocks of text

What is beautiful?

For thousands of years artists, philosophers, scholars, and psychologists have studied and argued this notion called beauty. Yet, no universal principle of beauty tells us this is beautiful and that is not. We do not have an algorithm for creating beautiful images. Often we fall back on clichés such as, "I don't know art, but I know what I like," or "Beauty is in the eye of the beholder." In designing or selecting graphics for viewing by many pairs of eyes and various tastes, we can, however, follow a few simple guidelines to broaden the appeal:

☐ **Reduce the graphic to essential characteristics**. The standard of classical beauty is without expression and character (111).

☐ **Present an average.** Create a composite figure that averages the experiences of your viewers (54). To show a generic computer terminal, make its proportions and color an average of the terminals users see and use.

☐ **Make it functional.** Make the graphic as clear and effective as you can. Once you do, you may discover that it is also visually attractive.

"The most attractive people are not blessed with rare physical qualities others can only dream about. A knockout face possesses features that approximate the mathematical average of all faces in a particular population." (35, p. 298)

"Functional and aesthetic proportions, at their best, tend to be identical." (206, p. 78)

☐ **Test, test, test.** Seek the opinion of others, especially those who may have different standards of beauty. Show your rough sketches to those of a different culture, age, sex, job category, and political party. Revise, revise, revise.

How to use pretty pictures

With pretty pictures:

☐ Make the art visually attractive. Design it well and reproduce it impeccably.

☐ Relate the illustrations to the subject of the book or manual. Make the relationship clear and visual. Do not rely on a pun.

☐ Strive for consistency of style and approach in all illustrations. Don't mix photographs, watercolors, and cartoons in one manual.

Ideas for pretty pictures

The following are some suggestions for relevant and attractive visual images:

Enlarge an icon

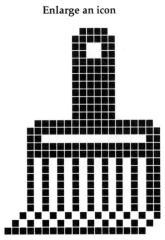

- Greatly enlarged icon or menu.

- Photographs of users applying the product to their problems.

- Stylized drawings or photographs of the product itself.

- Photographs of earlier technologies that performed the same tasks; archaic devices used to achieve the same result; tools from the field.

- Analogous objects. Chapters in the manual for Microsoft Windows 3.0 begin with photographs of windows of buildings.

- Cartoons of users of the product.

- Antique photographs and works of art.

- Page headers that carry out a graphical motif. For example, a manual for a MIDI music synthesizer featured the musical staff as a page header.

NEVER USE JUST PRETTY PICTURES

In a publication or a graphic, anything that does not contribute distracts. Every drop of ink, every pixel either furthers the message or obscures it in noise. Making graphics visually attractive can reinforce the message and convey it smoothly into the attention and memory of the viewer (340). Pictures that are beautiful, but not relevant, post no such benefit. Bud Sagendorf, cartoonist of Popeye, points out the weakness of relying on style alone: "A beautiful drawing seldom sells a weak idea, but many times a strong idea will sell a poor drawing" (219, p. 120).

"There is a criticism of overdesigned or overillustrated and embellished graphics, and it is well founded criticism if the charts in question are published in specialist or technical journals. Where an audience knows its business, do not dress up the facts." (141, p. 90)

GLOBAL GRAPHICS

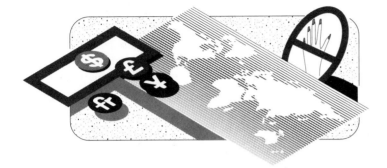

Today when a manufacturer ships a product, its destination may be one of a dozen countries. For this reason, documents which accompany products must communicate across barriers of language and culture. Over the globe about 5000 languages and dialects are spoken, of which about 100 are used in business and technical pursuits (79). Even within a single language, there are many variants. The French spoken in Paris differs somewhat from that of Montreal and greatly from that of the southern parishes of Louisiana. Differences in meaning, style, and emphasis separate the English used in the United Kingdom, Canada, the United States, and Australia.

Even products marketed within a single country must overcome language barriers. Many countries have multiple official and unofficial languages. India's 1-rupee note contains the words "one rupee" in the 15 official languages using 11 scripts (220). In industrialized countries more and more work is done by "legal aliens" or "guest workers" from distant lands and different cultures. By the year 2000, it is estimated that the majority of Canadians will speak neither English nor French as their first language. And in many areas of the United States now, Spanish, Chinese, French, Japanese, Vietnamese, Korean, and other languages are the first or only language of residents.

"If a picture can save you a thousand words, then that same picture can save you another ten thousand words if it is in a document that will be translated into ten other languages." (321, p. 330)

RELY ON GRAPHICS

Despite the hard work of some linguists, Esperanto, Ido, Volapuk, Interlingua, Suma, Ro, and other attempts at a universal language have not achieved widespread use. (79). Nor are graphics always universally understood. Yet, with careful design they can bridge barriers of language and culture. In interlingual and intercultural documents, use graphics to:

- **Reduce translation**. The more you say graphically, the less you must translate. The less you translate, the lower the cost of translation and the less the risk of mistranslation.

- **Ease learning**. A visual image is less ambiguous and easier to remember than a verbal image expressed in an unfamiliar language.

- **Make text easier to understand**. Viewers recognize and understand the main idea of a graphic immediately. The understanding imparted by the graphic helps readers translate the text.

- **Give documents an international look**. Rather than an impenetrable gray wall of text, readers see a series of recognizable images, such as the signs in international airports and at sporting events.

- **Reduce the size and number of editions of documents**. If only labels and brief annotations must be translated, multiple translations can fit in a single document.

International graphics

Multilingual labels

Power switch
Interruptor fuerza
Interrupteur moteur
der Wechselschalter

CONSIDER READING SKILLS AND HABITS

The way and extent to which graphics can use language depends on the language skills of the reader.

If the reader...	Then design the graphic to...
Reads English as a first language	Use English freely.
Reads English as a second language	Use simple words. Prefer concrete nouns and verbs. Avoid words with multiple meanings.
	Avoid abbreviations since many languages abbreviate differently from English. Some do not abbreviate at all (130).
Does not read English	Do not use English for any critical distinction. Either repeat words in the reader's language or test the graphic to ensure it works without language.
Will read the document in translation	Use concrete words and simple sentence structures to promote more accurate translation.
	Avoid abbreviations (130).
	Leave room in case more text is required in the target language.

The viewer's accustomed reading direction affects the direction in which they scan a graphic and the order in which they read a sequence of graphics. An advertisement for laundry detergent in the Middle East showed dirty clothes on the left, a box of the detergent in the middle, and clean clothes on the right (130). It failed because Arabic is read right to left.

Determining reading direction is not always easy. I have seen a Taiwanese newspaper with text reading left to right, right to left, and top to bottom in columns read from left to right and in columns read from right to left—all on the same page.

Consider reading direction

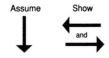

If viewers have different reading directions, make graphics read from top to bottom and use arrows to show sequence and to direct the eye about the graphic.

CONSIDER ARTISTIC CONVENTIONS AND EXPECTATIONS

Visual or verbal communication depends on a common foundation of shared conventions. Many primitive cultures can't recognize photographs or understand vanishing-point perspective. Studies of African peoples unfamiliar with pictorial materials found that both children and adults required training to recognize familiar objects shown in photographs and line drawings, and they perceived depth only with difficulty and only when overlap was present (74). Australian aborigines, however, objected to overlap used to show depth and perspective in pictures of birds because the overlap hid a wing or foot (111). Likewise many people in Western cultures don't "understand" modern art.

Most societies that use computers do understand the standard graphical forms common in computer documentation. Problems arise, though, in the use of symbols and the way objects are depicted. The only insurance against cultural miscommunication is testing with expected viewers.

GENERALIZE GRAPHICS FOR AN INTERNATIONAL AUDIENCE

For international symbols design objects "sufficiently abstract that the audience does not have a preconception of their meaning." (119, p. 141)

Pick graphics your international readers can identify. A strategy of including specific details to make objects more recognizable may backfire for international documents when readers are unfamiliar with the details shown. For such readers we may have to deliberately make images more general and abstract.

☐ Disguise or diminish national differences, such as the shape of power plugs (321) and the on-off position of power switches (249).

☐ Choose a viewpoint that hides audience-specific details.

☐ Use a simplified drawing or visual symbol rather than a realistic drawing or photograph (321).

☐ Avoid provincialism in graphics. Landscapes, office decor, clothing styles, climate, and even bodily features vary widely around the globe. Baseball may be familiar in the United States and Japan but not in Romania or Nepal.

International details best disguised

 Australian

 North American

 Swiss

 United Kingdom

 Universal European

ACCOMMODATE DIFFERENT LEARNING AND RHETORICAL STRATEGIES

The preferred style for documents varies around the world. Americans want it short and sweet. Step by step. To the point. Germans prefer more details and background information and will tolerate larger amounts of information than others. The French favor a more formal and authoritative educational stance. Japanese learners would appreciate instructions that are presented accurately yet with polite deference to the reader. Arabs demand grandiloquent and florid prose, passionate with style. In China, the master or teacher lays out philosophical principles—it is the responsibility of the student to infer the details.

How can graphics and documents meet such diverse requirements and expectations? I suggest a three-part policy:

Avoid personal characteristics

✘ No   ✔ Yes

Moderation   Take a middle position between two extremes. For instance, to balance formality and informality, you might round the edges of shapes but maintain precise, mechanical lines. Moderation minimizes the confusion and offense any graphic may offer.

Set formality to suit audience

Formal   Moderate   Informal

Suggest, but do not compel, a reading order

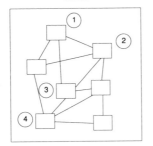

Neutrality	Graphics are inherently more neutral in tone and emotion than text. We can maintain this neutrality by avoiding techniques that give the graphic a definite personality; for instance, we need to avoid being either stuffy or chummy.
Multipurpose	Design graphics that can be read in different ways for different purposes. For instance, give users a map with numbered items along a suggested route. Those who want a step-by-step procedure can follow the route; those who prefer to learn on their own can explore.

CONSIDER CULTURAL VALUES AND SYMBOLS

Miscommunication can also result when underlying cultural values differ. The art, science, and literature of each culture and civilization embody and reflect its values. Ancient Egyptian art stressed order and predictability. Ancient Greek art emphasized balance and rationality. Oriental art espouses harmony of opposites. Similar cultural values affect how people interpret modern technical documents.

Symbology

The symbols we may use to encode meaning or to decorate a graphic can have vastly different associations in different cultures. We must ensure that the different associations do not contradict our intended meaning.

Colors

 For more on color, read Chapter 13.

Since the symbolic meaning of color varies from culture to culture, ignorance about color associations can cause us to miscommunicate. Designers for the United States Indian Service, for instance, inadvertently biased voting in a Navajo election by using color codes for candidates. To the Navajo, colors are ranked, with blue being good and red bad. Colors were replaced by photographs of the candidates (122).

Cultural associations for color come from a culture's religion, literature, and graphic arts (68; 79; 309; 333):

Culture	Red	Yellow	Green	Blue
Europe and Western Hemisphere	Danger	Caution, Cowardice	Safe Sour	Masculinity Sweet Calm Authority
Japanese	Anger, Danger	Grace, nobility Childhood gaiety	Future Youth, energy	Villainy
Chinese	Joy, festive occasions	Honor Royalty		
Arabic		Happiness Prosperity	Fertility, strength	Virtue, faith, truth

Gestures

Almost all configurations of the human hand are obscene or rude gestures somewhere in the world. For instance, the circle-sign made by forming a ring with the thumb and forefinger means money in Japan, OK in England and the United States, zero or worthless in the south of France, and an obscene insult in Sardinia. It is found in Mediterranean works of art over two thousand years old. Likewise, the thumbs-up symbol, which means OK in the United States, is an obscene gesture in many Mediterranean countries.

Communication can go awry when we fail to account for the differences in the meanings of hand gestures. When General Motors introduced the Monza in Greece, they took out ads that showed a young woman dressed in blue and white, the Greek national colors, standing with her palm to the audience in the gesture of a traffic cop signaling traffic to stop. In Greece that palm-out gesture is considered obscene (22). This gesture, which ironically is called the *moutza*, dates back to Byzantine times when free men would humiliate new captives by scooping up horse droppings and with this gesture rub them into the faces of the captives (215).

What do these mean?

Are you sure?

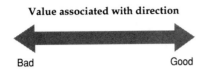

Value associated with direction

Bad   Good

Position and orientation

In paintings and theater of Christian cultures, good things are on the right and evil on the left. The word *right* is both a direction and a synonym for correct and proper. Other positive words like *adroit* and *dexterous* derive from the word for *right* in other languages, just as the words *sinister* and *gauche* come from the words for *left*. Tools and appliances are often designed for right-handed operators. This bias is shared by Arabic culture where the left hand is used only for "unclean" tasks; in the Chinese tradition, however, honor dwells on the left hand and the right is self-destructive and violent (68).

Modesty and taboos

Sights common in one culture may be deeply offensive or troublesome to another. In some cultures, showing the human figure is forbidden; and in others, certain parts of the body must not be shown. Standards of modesty vary widely:

- Nudes are readily accepted in advertisements in Western Europe, but not in the United States (230).

- In some Islamic countries only women's hands and eyes may be shown.

- The underside of the foot must not be shown in the Orient (141). Japanese viewers object to bare feet, even out of doors.

Sexual stereotypes and gender roles

Cultures differ in the roles women play and the jobs they can perform. In Europe, Australia, Canada, and the United States, we expect to find women at all levels and in all departments of business working alongside their male colleagues. Though a relatively recent development, this trend is so pervasive that a graphic showing an all-male group of computer users would be thought of as odd or dated.

This equality is not universal. In many parts of the Orient, Africa, and the Middle East, the jobs and roles of men and women differ greatly. Even within a single nation or culture, we find extremes. In some Islamic countries, women play little or no role outside the home. In Pakistan, however, a woman has served as Prime Minister. In still other Islamic countries, women can fill technical professional jobs, but cannot work in direct contact with men in the same roles (119).

How then, can you produce graphics that workers in different cultures can identify with? Some suggested strategies are:

☐ Avoid pictures of people. Unless the subject is a person, you may get by with just pictures of equipment and computer screens.

☐ Show hands only when they are performing procedures and stylize the hands so they are not clearly male or female.

☐ Use unisex figures. Draw people as simplified line drawings, cartoons, and stick figures without any identification as to gender.

☐ Prepare separate graphics for regional editions of documents. Remember, you may have to translate some graphics.

Create generic hands

✘ No   ✔ Yes

Clearly female hand   Unisex hand

Checklist for cultural and national differences

The following table recaps many of the cultural and national differences you may encounter and what you can do to make your graphics more international:

Difference	What to do
Racial characteristics	Use simple, abstract figures, devoid of recognizable bone structure or hair style.
	Use unshaded line drawings of people. Omit any indication of skin color.
Relations between sexes	Use simple unisex cartoons or stick-figure drawings of people, hands, and faces.
Clothing	Simplify drawings of clothing to omit seams, folds, buttons, and belts.
Modesty	Do not show bare arms, shoulders, legs, or feet.
Gestures	Avoid hand gestures. If you show a hand, show the right hand holding or pressing something.
Color associations	Define and explain color symbology. Use colors in a technical context only.

Familiarity with graphical formats	Limit yourself to common, well-established formats.
Sense of humor	Avoid humor, especially puns.

LEAVE SPACE FOR TRANSLATION

As a rule, text expands when translated from English to other languages. This means you must leave extra room for text that will be translated (130).

Leave extra space for translation

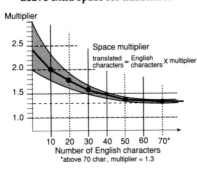

Number of characters in English	Number of characters after translation
5	15
10	20
20	35
30	50
40	60
50	70
60	80
70	90
over 70	1.3 x English

To ensure adequate space:

- Arrange all labels, callouts, and other text in the graphics so that the translated text will fit and the illustration will not have to be redrawn..

- Never place text overlapping other graphical objects (321).

- Use large type in English documents and then reduce the type size when translating to other languages (44).

WORDLESS INSTRUCTIONS

"For the customer, word-free setup instructions can prevent unintentionally hilarious translations of setup instructions, or obscure passages that yield to no amount of deductive reasoning." (101, p. 17)

Since pictures are easily understood and require no translation, wordless instructions would seem the ideal way to cater to an international market. For instance, wordless instructions on decals attached inside the covers of office equipment have been effective in showing how to load paper, change ribbons and cartridges, and clear a paper jam (321).

However, producing effective wordless instructions is far from easy. The South African Chamber of Mines designed a three-panel wordless message intended to tell illiterate miners to remove rocks from rail tracks. It showed, left to right, a worker encountering a rock, picking it up, and carrying it away in a cart. The sign failed as many workers began piling rocks on the tracks. They had read the sign right to left (79).

Developing nonverbal instructions requires teamwork, testing, and a visual approach (43):

Example of wordless instructions

- ☐ Use wordless instructions for step-by-step procedures involving simple physical actions, not for conceptual tasks that require branching and looping. Wordless instructions can show how to unpack and set up hardware; they cannot teach programming or show how to operate a complex application.

- ☐ Start with a storyboard with word descriptions of steps in the one column and photographs of the steps in the other column (101). Test and revise until the basic instructions work well.

- ☐ Or, start with a videotape of a typical user performing the procedure. Capture individual frames for use in your storyboard.

- ☐ Make the reading sequence obvious. Clearly indicate whether pictures are read by row or by column and whether sequences go from left to right or right to left. Remember that the viewer's native language may suggest a reading direction other than the one you intended.

- ☐ Box the pictures of a sequence and group them into modules of related steps (322).

- ☐ Eliminate unnecessary details that might distract viewers (349).

- ☐ Test the document extensively, and revise until you get it right (43).

COLOR

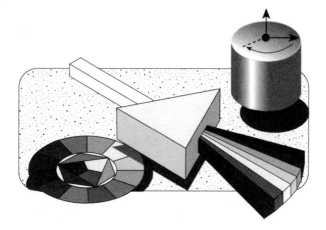

Most animals are color-blind. Only human beings, a few other primates, day-active birds, reptiles, fishes, mollusks, and bees see color. Frogs, salamanders, dogs, cats, horses, cows, and sheep are all color-blind (94). Our evolutionary heritage or Creator did not endow us with color vision without good reason. Color helps us deal with a complex, ever-changing environment rapidly and surely.

In technical documents, make color functional first, last, and always. Where possible, make colors pleasant and appealing—but never at the expense of clear communication. Color is so important to effective communication today—and so difficult to use well—that I have chosen to discuss it here in a separate chapter.

Difficulties in using color can be cured by:

- Understanding what color is and how it works

- Taking into account background color as well as foreground color

- Using color schemes appropriate for the purpose at hand

"Color produces immediate reaction and is the exclamation point of graphic symbols, so it must be reckoned with." (79, p. 21)

Understanding these three issues will guide you in deciding how many colors you need, picking effective colors, and using them meaningfully.

WHAT IS COLOR?

For more on the theory of color, see:

- *Theory and Use of Color* by Luigina De Grandis (72)

- *Using Computer Color Effectively* by Lisa Thorell and Wanda Smith (309)

Throughout this book I have tried to avoid long theoretical discussions, feeling it was my job to digest and refine concepts for use by busy practitioners. I have included references for those interested in the theory or in checking my recommendations. For color, I cannot avoid some conceptual knowledge. I will forego anatomical discussion of rods, cones, ganglia, and synapses—interesting though they may be—in favor of a concise, workable conceptual model.

What we speak of as color is really three related perceptual dimensions or components:

How many colors?

16,777,216	Number of colors possible with 24-bit color computer display
7,500,000	Measurable colors (154)
1,000,000	Colors trained colorists can distinguish under **ideal** conditions (315)
50	Color codes viewers can recognize with **extensive** training (169)
7	Colors viewer can easily distinguish when shown in same field of view (121)
4	Color codes recognized when shown alone without training (121; 309)
1	Best for fastest search (target in unique color) (83)
0	Best for legibility (black and white) (323)

Hue	What we most often speak of as color. Hues are designated by names such as red, yellow, green, and blue. Hue is a property of the wavelengths of light. (See color Figure 1.)
Lightness or value	Amount of white or black in the color. Some hues are inherently lighter or darker than others and some hues exist in a range of lightness values. (See color Figure 2.)
Saturation	Purity of a hue. Red is more saturated than pink. Navy blue is more saturated than sky blue. Each color can be thought of as a mixture of a pure hue (fully saturated) and an achromatic color (black, white, or gray). The portion of pure hue is the degree of saturation. Saturation is related to the number of wavelengths mixed to produce the color. (See color Figure 3.)

Value or lightness is usually considered separately from color. Most people would not think of black, white, and grays as color. These *achromatic* colors lack hue and saturation.

Ways of specifying color

In 1905, artist Alfred Munsell produced the first systematic way to specify color. The Munsell color system is based on standard color swatches arranged in a twisted spherical shape. Hue is represented by 40 slices radiating from a central axis. Each slice from the axis outward represents one distinct hue. Lightness increases in 10 steps vertically and saturation in up to 16 steps radially. Because hue, lightness, and saturation are interrelated, not all combinations exist and the resulting color space is more spherical than cylindrical. The Munsell system, although widely used in North America, is not prevalent elsewhere. Modern computer color displays can produce many more colors than are designated in the Munsell system (218). Despite these limitations, the Munsell shape provides a convenient, yet scientific, model of color.

Munsell shape

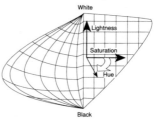

In the HLS (hue, lightness, saturation) system developed by Tektronix specifically for computer displays, color is specified in a cylindrical space. Hue is specified as an angle around the circumference, starting at 0 degrees for blue and proceeding through magenta (60 degrees), red (120 degrees), yellow (180 degrees), green (240 degrees), and cyan (300 degrees). Lightness is specified along the axis vertically, and saturation as a radial distance from the axis. Lightness and saturation are specified in percentages ranging from 0 percent to 100 percent (218). Though convenient for specifying color for computer displays, these scales do not closely match human perception. The human eye is not equally sensitive to changes in all three variables nor is it equally sensitive to a variable throughout its range. A 10 percent difference in one variable may be unnoticed while a 10 percent change in another variable completely reverses the viewer's interpretation of a scene.

HLS cylinder

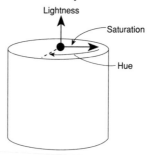

The RGB system specifies display colors as levels or percentages of the three primary display colors red, green, and blue. As such, this system describes color as a cubical space with black, blue, magenta, red, cyan, green, yellow, and white at the corners (218). Like the HLS system, the RGB system does not correspond to the sensitivity of the human perceptual system.

RGB cube

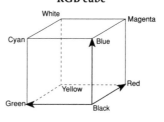

CIE chromaticity diagram

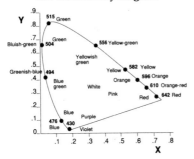

The CIE 1931 Chromaticity Diagram positions colors on a flat surface according to perceived differences in hue. On such a diagram, colors appear as a lopsided triangle. Around the top of the triangle are the pure colors of the spectrum. Along the bottom and inside the triangle are colors that can be produced by mixing these primary colors. Distinct pairs of colors are far apart; similar colors are close together. Colors are identified by an X and Y coordinate on this surface. Such a chart is useful in picking distinct sets of colors because the distinctiveness is proportional to the distance on this diagram and can be calculated from the X and Y coordinates (218).

This chart is also valuable because it accurately predicts the results of mixing colors. Two colors when mixed can produce any of the colors on the straight line connecting these two colors on the diagram. Similarly, when mixing three colors, the resulting colors all lie inside the triangle produced by connecting the three colors on the diagram.

Pure colors can be specified as the wavelength in nanometers (nm) of the dominant hue. Throughout this chapter the terms for pure colors are used as follows:

Color definitions

Color name	Dominant wavelengths (nm)
Red	642
Orange-red	610
Orange	596
Yellow	582
Yellow-green	556
Green	515
Bluish-green	504
Greenish-blue	494
Blue	476
Violet	430
Cyan	515 + 476
Magenta	642 + 476

Color circles

Newton, Goethe, Munsell, and others have devised color circles depicting relationships among colors. You can think of a color wheel as a slice through the Munsell color solid along the diagonal plane of maximum saturation. These color wheels differ in the positions and even the order of colors (72). A more tractable, though less scientific, color wheel may be that of Joseph Itten (color Figure 4). It is arranged by aesthetic rather than perceptual criteria (148). Though positions do not represent perceptual relationships precisely, they are close enough for picking contrasting and complementary colors.

Color scales

Human perception imposes a natural order on colors but not in the way most people think. Colors arranged by wavelength reveal hues in the order seen in a rainbow or the spectrum produced by a prism: red, orange, yellow, green, blue, indigo, violet. Though people can be taught this scale, it must be taught and is not recognized spontaneously (24). Human perception does, however, naturally rank colors along two related perceptual scales.

"Thus it seems that the important visual scale is not the Newtonian spectrum. For all its beauty the spectrum is simply the accidental consequence of arranging stimuli in order of wavelength. The significant scale for images runs from warm colors through neutral colors to cool colors." (175, p. 293)

One natural scale is lightness. Given sample colors, people can reliably arrange them from lightest to darkest. What we refer to as the lightness of a color is just a manifestation of the graphical characteristic of value. (See color Figure 2.)

The other ranking is based on the subjective "temperature" of the color. Warm colors are red, orange, and yellow. They are associated with fire and sunlight. Cool colors are blues and greens. They are associated with water and shade (343). (See color Figure 5.)

The scales of lightness and temperature are related because the so-called warm colors tend to be brighter than the cool ones. We react to light and dark, not just hue (11).

For reliable color scales, then, we must forego the spectrum and arrange colors light to dark and warm to cool.

WHY USE COLOR?

When displays are studied leisurely, graphics and color appear to offer little advantage. However, when viewers or readers are impatient or must act quickly, properly designed color graphics work better (165; 258).

For more information on the use of color to improve performance of computer users, see *Color and the Computer*, edited by John Durrett (83)

- **Color aids decision making**. Color helps viewers make quicker and more accurate decisions about complex and detailed information (83; 92). By organizing and classifying information, color lets people to handle more information, process it more efficiently, and apply simpler and more efficient decision-making strategies (258).

- **Color focuses attention.** Color grabs, directs, and holds attention, ensuring that more viewers attend to critical information (24; 79; 92).

- **Color increases learning.** Colored pictures are recalled more accurately than black and white ones (62). We remember material we pay attention to; therefore, when color is used to direct attention, it increases the speed and accuracy with which we absorb that material (24; 83; 92).

- **Color reveals organization and pattern.** Color helps viewers isolate and separate different items in a display and thus organize complex information (40; 88).

- **Color adds dimensions.** Color adds more dimensions with which to represent information (92). Practitioners of scientific visualization, which uses computer displays to make complex scientific and engineering phenomena understandable, have extended the number of dimensions of data that viewers can comprehend from four to seven by using color (274).

- **Viewers prefer color.** Survey after survey has demonstrated that computer users prefer a color display; some even regard color as a necessity (92; 316). Operators who feel more secure with color-coded displays find that color helps them locate objects on the screen and notice details. Users also consider color displays less monotonous and feel they reduce discomfort and eye strain (62; 309).

- **Color makes images more realistic.** With color we can more faithfully reproduce actual appearances, especially where color is a meaningful part of the scene (91; 92). Realistic color makes images more recognizable and reduces search time (62). On computer screens, color can reduce jagged edges to enhance realism and improve legibility (269; 274).

- **Color speeds search.** For tasks which involve searching for information in a complex display, color coding works better than shape, brightness, and other coding techniques (16; 309). (See color Figure 6.) Color coding can reduce search time up to 80 percent (60; 152).

"Indeed, one's attention is often captured by color before the form or composition is completely distinct." (79, p. 231)

"Given the appropriate environmental conditions, color enhances an organism's ability to identify visible objects, determine their physical properties, (e.g., ripe compared to immature fruit), and can play an important role in visual communication. For example, sexual displays and body markings are typically based on color cues in organisms with color vision." (94, p. 235)

"With the ability to quickly render full-color scenes on the computer, we can simulate three-dimensionality and provide richer, more effective, and easier-to-understand metaphorical interfaces." (274, 274)

- **Color sells.** Advertisers have long known the value of color in improving readership and sales. Adding spot color to a black-and-white advertisement typically increases costs 20 percent but draws over 60 percent more readers and sales (332). Four-color advertisements cost about 50 percent more than black-and-white ones but are twice as memorable (230).

- **Color stirs the heart ... and other vital organs.** Color affects blood pressure, circulation, breathing rate, endocrine functions, skin conductance, perceived temperature, eye blinks, brain wave patterns, and muscular strength (72; 104; 148; 309). The effect increases on this color scale: blue, green, yellow, orange, and red (11).

PROBLEMS CAUSED BY IMPROPER USE OF COLOR

All the listed advantages of color are peppered with the words *can*, *may*, *sometimes*, and *potentially*. Just as proper use of color enhances communication, haphazard or mistaken use of color confuses and bewilders. Though common, most of the problems with color are easily corrected or avoided.

- **Prior associations interfere.** The perception of color is highly subjective and personal (218). Private associations may interfere with the intended message. Consider the emotional associations of colors. We turn purple with rage, go green with jealousy, blanche with fear, blush with embarrassment, develop a yellow streak of cowardice, get into a brown study, and sink into a bad case of the blues (333).

- **Color distracts.** Excessive or irrelevant use of color can distract viewers and hinder performance by drawing attention away from information the viewer seeks (62; 309; 323). (See color Figure 7.) The more colors in a display, the longer it takes to react to a single color and the greater the confusion between colors (187). The distraction of irrelevant colors thwarts desired viewing patterns, such as the line-by-line progression of reading a paragraph of text (60).

> "Displaying more than four colors at once often seems 'too much.'" (100)

- **Color tires the eyes.** Long exposure to broad areas of color can prove fatiguing. Red causes the greatest fatigue, blue the least (72).

- **Color reduces legibility.** Without lightness contrast, no color combination is easy to read. (See color Figure 8.) Color-on-color displays make text, small objects, and thin lines hard to see (309).

- **Color is limited to central vision.** Since color perception is acute only in central (foveal) vision, color coding is effective only within 10 to 15 degrees of the center of vision (288). Widely spaced colors are difficult to compare.

- **Color produces fuzzy edges.** Objects formed of a combination of primary colors may appear fuzzy because of misregistration, especially near the edges and corners of a computer screen (337).

- **Designers lack experience with color.** Lacking experience with color, designers tend to use color in excessive, contradictory, and nonfunctional ways. These failings resemble those observed when desktop publishing systems first gave writers control of many typefaces and styles. As with type, the poor use of color will fade as designers gain experience, as good models appear, and as the novelty wears off.

- **Color is not standardized.** We lack a single, simple standard to define colors independent of circumstances. The color with a wavelength of 600 nanometers is alternately described as chrome, orange, golden poppy, spectrum orange, oriental red, Saturn red, cadmium red orange, bittersweet orange, and red orange (11). And because different processes are used to print color on paper and display it on the screen, no simple, obvious calculation can exactly match printed to displayed colors. However, precisely calibrated computer displays now promise a way of previewing a limited range of printed colors with fidelity accurate enough for most publications (320).

- **Color perception is relative.** The color we see at any point in a scene depends greatly on colors elsewhere in the scene. The perception of color depends not on the presence of three or more wavelengths of light but on the proportion of short and long wavelengths relative to the average of the scene (175). The subtle colors of magazine photographs are often distorted by the garish tones of advertisements on facing pages.

- **Color is unpredictable.** Color is fickle. The exact color we perceive depends on many variables: the texture of the surface; the lightness of the surface; any film or dust on the

surface; the size, orientation, and shape of the surface; the
relative position of the object and the observer; the direction
and distance of the illumination; the type of illumination;
other colors in the observer's field of vision; atmospheric
haze or smog; and individual perceptual differences (72).
Ambient color depends on time of day and weather
conditions. Daylight in shade is generally bluish. In the
shade of trees, it is greenish. On cloudy days daylight is
sometimes purplish. Throughout the day, daylight changes
from reddish at dawn, to white during the middle of the
day, to yellow and eventually gold in the afternoon, to red
fading to pink at sunset, and to deeper and deeper blues at
night (91).

Color illusions

Color perception, on initial study, seems quirky and
downright unreliable. Closer study reveals that what appear to
be mistakes or illusions are just ways that our eyes compensate
for the various lighting conditions under which we see color.

As designers, we need to understand these laws that govern
the way color is perceived. We can then use this understanding
not only to avoid viewer misperception but to sharpen and
focus perception.

Effect	Description
Luminance shift	For most colors, hue seems to change as luminance increases or decreases, but for the colors blue (470 nm), green (505 nm), and yellow (572 nm) hue remains constant throughout the range of luminance. These colors are exactly the ones identified as purest blue, green, and yellow (218). **Use these colors where constancy is important.**
Variable sensitivity	The ability to discriminate between two hues varies along the spectrum. We are most sensitive to differences around 420 nm (violet), 480 nm (blue), and 580 nm (yellow) and least sensitive to differences for hues between 440–450 nm and 500-540 nm (218). **Space color codes accordingly.**
Additive desaturation	Colors made up by adding primary colors contain a wider band of wavelengths and hence appear less saturated than do primary colors (218). **Use desaturated colors for viewers blind to primary colors.**

McCullough effect	Staring at one predominant color for a long period of time shifts color perception toward the complementary color (color Figure 9). This aftereffect may last seconds or even days (305). **Avoid big areas of pure color.**
Color adaptation	Exposure lowers sensitivity to the dominant color and makes it appear less saturated (309). **Use unique colors for search targets.**
Purkinje effect	In bright light, red appears brighter than blue, but in dim light, blue appears lighter (but colorless) than red, which appears nearly black (72). **Avoid using red in dim light.**
Simultaneous contrast	Each color alters our perception of other colors (color Figure 10). A pure color shifts adjacent colors toward its complement (148). **Use complementary colors to enhance contrast.**
Chromo-stereopsis	The optics of the human eye is not color corrected. The lens of the eye brings different colors into focus at different distances behind the lens. Blue objects come into focus nearer the lens than red objects. As a result, red objects appear closer than blue ones (color Figure 11). This effect creates an illusion of depth (291). **Use this effect to enhance depth perception. Use blue as a background.**
Chromatic aberration	The eye sees a dot of white as a white point fringed with color. This distortion is especially severe at the blue end of the spectrum (324). **Avoid pure blue for small objects or text.**
Size-color effect	Warm colors (red, orange, yellow) appear larger than cool colors (green, blue, violet) (306). **Assign color codes accordingly.**

HOW TO USE COLOR FUNCTIONALLY

For more guidelines on using color in publications, see *Color for the Electronic Age* by Jan V. White (333).

To harness the potential of color while avoiding problems, we must consciously use color to communicate.

To use color well, you must be clear about your purpose for using color since this purpose should determine the techniques you choose.

Often your purposes will overlap and you must decide which are primary and which are secondary; techniques that further one purpose may thwart another. Pick one primary purpose and ensure that the techniques for secondary purposes do not conflict with those for the primary.

To control attention

We can use color to focus the viewer's attention on specific objects and areas in the graphic.

To call attention to a small item

To call attention to a small object, give it a distinct, conspicuous color. Choose a color that contrasts with the background and other objects. Pick a distinctive hue with background contrast of at least 7:1 (305; 309; 314). Use only one color as the highlight color (157). If only one color is used to highlight, it need not be a bright color. Anything in color will stand out (333).

For marks to carry any perceptible color they must be at least 1.5 mm (0.06 in. or 0.22 degrees visual angle) in diameter. (See color Figure 12.) The larger the marks, the more colors viewers can distinguish (24). If the object cannot be enlarged, consider color coding the background around the object (color Figure 13).

For photographs and printed documents, red is distinctive, yet not overpowering (141; 333). Red is used as an accent color in *Scientific American* and in the U.S. Army's New Look publications (209). For light-on-dark computer screens, a yellowish-green at a wavelength of 560 to 570 nm is distinctive (218).

To strengthen the saturation of a small colored item, surround it with its complementary color, whose afterimage is the same as the surrounded color (97; 343). (See color Figure 14.)

Emphasize an area

To emphasize a small area, use a distinct color with moderate (5:1 to 3:1) lightness contrast with its background (309). For large areas use lower-contrast pale or dark colors, especially if they represent secondary information, ongoing themes, or motifs (309; 333). (See color Figure 15.)

Proper selection of high-contrast colors helps viewers spot patterns, trends, and otherwise invisible features. The technique called *pseudocolor* assigns prominent colors to areas

"Give color meaning: don't miscue the audience by using different colors for the same elements, or by assigning different meanings to one color." (157, p. VC-4)

Ensure adequate contrast

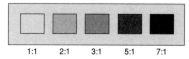

Size colored marks

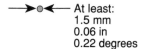

At least:
1.5 mm
0.06 in
0.22 degrees

For a second color in print, "Red simply does the best job on all counts: versatility of tonal variation, graphic clarity, most straightforward signaling of a point to be emphasized, and greatest contrast with black." (141, p. 37)

of particular lightness in a gray-scale image, such as to highlight hot-spots in infrared photographs or cracks in X-ray photographs. *False color* images remap the colors of the visible spectrum, typically to make ultraviolet and infrared light visible. LANDSAT images typically use false color to highlight areas of pollution or agricultural development.

Deemphasize an object

To deemphasize or hide an object, display it in a color close to the background color (color Figure 16). Give it a lightness contrast of no more than 3:1 with the background (309). Select a hue within 90 degrees of the background color on a color-harmony wheel (343). (See color Figure 4.) Surrounding a color with such a similar color weakens its saturation and contrast.

Show associations

Color effectively shows which objects are the same or similar and which are different.

Group spatially separate items

Color can show which of several separate objects are related. To show that objects are of the same class, category, or type, show them in the same color (color Figure 17). Display similar or related objects in distinguishable but similar colors (337). The eye groups first identical and then complementary colors (11).

Distinguish or discriminate items

Use different colors for different ideas (337). Viewers may inadvertently associate ideas merely because they were presented in the same colors (92).

To make colors easy to discriminate, select distinct, bright, saturated colors (288). To further enhance contrast, use complementary colors (97). Display the colors over a large enough area (11) close to the center of view (288). For more accurate comparisons of the hue and lightness of adjacent colors, separate the areas with a thin line in a neutral color. Doing so cancels the illusion of Mach bands that exaggerates the contrast at boundaries between similar colors (309). (See color Figure 18.)

For discrimination tasks, there is no limit to the number of colors you can use, provided adjacent colors contrast sufficiently (309). Trained colorists can distinguish between one million colors—compared two at a time, adjacent to one another, under ideal conditions (314). Most viewers can identify subtle differences in juxtaposed colors but are not so sure when remembering colors or comparing separated areas of color (11). If the viewer must attach a meaning to the colors, as well as discriminate between colors displayed together, use no more than six or seven colors (121; 157; 169; 288).

Speed search for objects

To help viewers find information in a display, assign colors to different categories of information. This technique, called *color coding*, can improve search performance up to 80 percent (60). Color coding reduces search time when and to the degree that:

- The display is unformatted (169; 288).

- Information is presented at high density (56; 258).

- Legibility is reduced (169).

- Information is searched (152).

- Target information is in a color that is rare or unique to the display (56; 152). At least 30 percent of the items in the color should be true targets (16).

- The display contains only a few colors (56).

- Color codes relate to the task at hand (169; 288).

- The viewer knows in advance the color of the target (152).

There is a fundamental tradeoff in color coding between the number of codes and the number of items in each coded category. Search time is least with one item in one color and increases as codes or items per color increase (83). If the viewer must recognize a color shown alone, limit colors to three or four. If the viewer must distinguish between colors displayed together, allow up to six or seven colors (121; 157; 169; 288).

Represent value with color codes

Color can represent information directly when colors are assigned systematically.

Categorize items

To categorize objects, assign a different color for each category. Use up to six or seven colors and categories (121; 157; 169; 288).

Strive for a natural, concrete, and objective assignment of color codes that relates to the categories they represent. For instance, a graph of fruit consumption might use red for apples, orange for oranges, yellow for lemons, green for limes, and purple for grapes. Or a map might use dark blue for water, light blue for wetlands, tan for desert, dark green for forest, and light green for grassland (309). Use dark, saturated colors for heavy objects and light, bright colors for lighter objects (72). Use complementary colors for mutually exclusive categories (309).

Ranked items

If the categories are ranked or naturally ordered, assign colors in order of lightness or value, not by hue or wavelength. A color spectrum of pure hues contains two scales of value on either side of yellow. The warm scale is red, orange, and yellow. The cool scale is violet, indigo, blue, green, and yellow. For ordered concepts, never mix the two scales. Value, even within colors, is a stronger ordering force than hue (24).

Cool and warm color scales

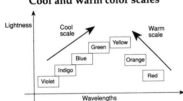

Range of values

You can also use color to express quantities of values along a range. A continuous range of colors can represent a range of values between two extremes. For instance, you can represent temperatures with a scale from deep blue to bright red. If the range includes positive and negative values, use two distinct colors, one warm and one cool, for ends of the scale and a neutral one for the zero point. (Also see color Figures 19 and 20.)

Attract and hold viewers

Though you do not want to let decoration dominate functional use of color, you can rely on aesthetic qualities of color to lure, please, and sustain readers.

Color perception is so highly subjective that precise rules for color harmony and aesthetics are impossible. Still, we can use guidelines to avoid color combinations that many people find ugly or offensive. We can also consistently use colors to unify rather than disrupt publications.

Balance colors

Balance colors over any display the viewer sees for more than a few minutes. Staring at one predominant color for a long period of time shifts color perception toward the complementary color. This aftereffect, called the *McCullough* effect, may last seconds or even days (309). (See color Figure 9.)

A mixture of colors is generally balanced and harmonious if the colors mix to produce white, gray, or black (148). To pick harmonious and balanced colors:

• Select proven color combinations. Find an established, successful color combination and use it. Look at successful publications in your field.

• Use colors from opposite sides of a traditional color-harmony circle (309). (See color Figure 4.)

• Consult guides that catalog samples of thousands of combinations (301). Pick a few different combinations that you like and then let typical readers have the final say.

Avoid garish colors

Avoid colors people dislike. If your document is intended for adults, avoid overuse of primary colors when more subtle and pleasing colors are available. Western viewers tend to prefer colors in this order: blue, red, green, purple, orange, and yellow (191).

For colors widely used throughout a publication, consider colors that have remained popular throughout different cultures and eras. If your publication will be in service for more than a year, avoid the trendy, vogue colors that are the favorites of fashion designers and interior decorators. An evening gown is not a diagram and a kitchen is not an icon. What is chic today may be stale tomorrow. In general, avoid extremes of value or saturation. Consider colors neither too bright nor too dark and neither pure nor pastel. Then test, test, test your choices with potential viewers.

Avoid conflicting colors

Pick optically compatible colors. Avoid putting spectrally distant pure colors, such as red and blue, side by side (color Figure 21).

Likewise, do not overuse pairs of opponent colors: red and green or blue and yellow (color Figure 22). Opponent colors are ones that in human perception are mutually exclusive or antagonistic. You cannot see a bluish yellow or a reddish green. Such opponent colors leave afterimages and suggest shadows (100).

Use color consistently

"A single color used throughout a publication provides continuity, unity, and character. Consistency gives the product identity. In a broader context, it helps to build a corporate identity." (333, p. 38)

For unity and coherence, use the same color scheme and color codes (319). For a coherent set of colors, start by picking one dominant color. Then select a set of compatible, secondary colors:

- Use different tints of the same hue (color Figure 3) (92).

- Darken or lighten the basic hue (color Figure 2) (343).

- Select colors from symmetrical positions around a color circle (color Figure 4), such as red, blue, and green (148).

For harmony, combine images that share a common hue. Don't juxtapose full-color images containing too many different hues. When mixing spot- and full-color images, use a spot color that repeats one of the prominent colors of the full-color image (333).

Use low contrast, desaturated or darker shades for colors that are repeated frequently or used over wide areas, as with ongoing themes and design motifs (309).

Show appearances exactly

Considering wide variations in lighting and the vagaries in human perception, it would seem quite impossible to show the exact appearance of any colored object. Yet we readily recognize colored objects, even in ill-lit, poorly exposed photographs.

1. Spectral color series

2. Scale of lightness

3. Scale of saturation

4. Itten color wheel

5. Scale of temperature

6. Color speeds search

Find the square   Find the yellow
shape

7. Color distracts

Notice how using
several bright colors
makes it hard to pay
attention to this word
and not this word or this
one or this one.

8. Color reduces legibility

Color on color   Black on white

9. The McCullough effect

Stare at this   Then stare at
for 1 min.   this area

10. Simultaneous contrast

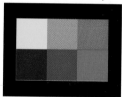

Complimentary   Similar colors
colors

11. Chromostereopsis

Do some colors seem nearer?

12. Enlarge marks that
carry color

13. Color code backgrounds

✘ No   ✔ Yes

14. Complimentary colors strengthen saturation

Complimentary   Contrasting

15. Emphasizing an area

16. Deemphasizing objects

17. Color shows associations

18. Distinguishing adjacent colors

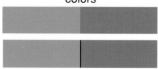

19. Warm scale

20. Cool scale

21. Adjacent spectrally distant colors

✘ No   ✔ Yes

22. Adjacent spectrally distant colors

23. Avoid low-contrast combinations

✘ No   ✔ Yes

24. Improve contrast

✘ No   ✔ Yes

25. Blue as background and foreground

26. Combine color with other graphical characteristics

✘ No   ✔ Yes

In depicting objects, we must distinguish between *local color* (how we typically think a thing appears) and *atmospheric color* (how it looks at the moment). Local color is uniform and flat. Atmospheric color varies, especially in value, across the surface of the object (69). What we remember and what we recognize is an object's local color. What we see in a picture is atmospheric color, but what we infer is the object's local color. If the picture lets us determine local color accurately, we will recognize the object.

The local color of the computer on which I am writing this book is a cream white. In the morning, by a north-facing window, its atmospheric color varies, but has a predominantly bluish cast. As I move toward a west-facing window later in the day, its atmospheric color shifts toward a pink tint. Yet if you ask me what color it is, I'll respond cream white, because unless I consciously pay attention to atmospheric color, it is local color I remember.

 Without looking, try to imagine the exact color of your computer. Now look at your computer and see how close you were.

The color rendition of most manmade objects in color photographs is seldom questioned because viewers do not have strong opinions of correct color. Pictures of people and foods, however, must be rendered with great color fidelity to be acceptable (91). For computers and other electronic equipment, a close color match is usually sufficient.

For realistic rendition of physical objects:

☐ Maintain relative warm and cool colors in the scene. It is not necessary to reproduce wavelengths exactly (175).

☐ For brighter and more saturated colors, print on glossy paper. The glossy surface reduces diffuse reflection that decreases contrast. The glossy coating also traps printing dyes on the surface of the paper rather than letting them be absorbed by the fibers of the paper (309).

☐ Don't detract from full-color images by adding colored borders, bright arrows, or other gewgaw (333).

If you cannot keep all of these rules in mind, stick to black and white, or pick one of these combinations:

Background	Use	Avoid
White	Black	Yellow
	Blue	Cyan
	Red	
Black	White	Blue
	Yellow	Red
	Green	Magenta

Ensure adequate contrast

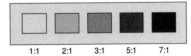

1:1   2:1   3:1   5:1   7:1

"Remember, even color comic books have the words of the text printed in black." (295, p. 268)

Ease reading

It is easy to choose a color combination that increases legibility of text, thin lines, and fine details: Use black and white. Or white and black, if you prefer. No color combination has the contrast and hence legibility of black and white. Reading colored text is often slower and more error-prone than reading black and white text.

If you must use chromatic colors for text and small details, follow these guidelines, especially the first:

☐ Ensure lightness contrast between foreground and background of at least 7:1 (309). Avoid low-contrast combinations such as yellow on white or navy blue on black (24). For a light background, use a pure color from either end of the spectrum, such as blue or red. For a dark background, pick a desaturated color from the middle of the spectrum, such as green or yellow (305). (See color Figure 23.)

☐ For better contrast, darken light pure colors (yellow and green) when they appear on a light background. Likewise, lighten dark pure colors (red and blue) when they appear on a dark background. (See color Figure 24.)

☐ Print in a primary color. Most printing, photographic, and computer display processes generate colors by combining dots of three or four primary colors. Objects formed of a combination of primary colors may appear fuzzy because of misregistration.

☐ If you use a pure blue, use it as a background. Many people cannot clearly focus on blue objects. If you must use blue as a foreground color, mix green with the blue. The green component will make the object come into focus more easily without shifting its apparent color, but the mixture will not have as sharp an edge as pure red or pure green alone (288). (See color Figure 25.)

☐ Avoid putting spectrally distant pure colors, such as red and blue, side by side. If you must use these colors together, reduce their saturation (305). (See color Figure 21.)

☐ To strengthen the saturation of a color, surround it with its complementary color, whose afterimage is the same as the surrounded color (343). (See color Figure 14.)

☐ For brighter, more saturated colors, print on glossy paper. The glossy surface reduces diffuse reflection that decreases contrast (309).

COLOR CODING

Dozens of human factors studies covering a wide range of test subjects, display conditions, and experimental methods have demonstrated that color coding out performs shape, brightness, and other coding techniques (16; 309):

- At Prudential Insurance Company, colored displays lowered training time and reduced errors of claims processors. Operators strongly preferred the colored displays.

- Air traffic controllers at Gatwick Airport located planes 16 percent faster with color displays.

- With business graphics, 70 percent of viewers of multihued graphics made optimal decisions, compared to only 33 percent with graphics in black and white.

To decide which colors to use for coding you must consider several interrelated issues, including the number of codes required, the background color, the size of the objects coded, and how color is produced in the display.

Case study of assigning color codes:

1. Colors are needed to highlight items on computer screens that display menus in white text on a black background. We need to flag these items: error messages, cautions and alerts, information entered by the user, and notes and advice presented to the user. Thus, we will need four codes.

2. We pick red, yellow, green, and blue.

3. Red is widely used for safety warnings and yellow for cautions. Green and blue have more positive or calming associations.

4. We decide to use red for error messages as they are the most serious warnings. We then assign yellow for cautions and alerts which are not so serious. That leaves blue and green. Because user-entered text must be highly legible, we'll put it in green which stands out from the dark background. Blue we assign for supplementary but not essential information.

"The more colors that are used, the less the impact of each, and no color has the contrast value of black on white." (323)

Assign codes in a meaningful manner

To assign color codes for a particular graphic or publication, balance resources and needs:

1. List the categories you need to distinguish. This will tell you how many codes you need.

2. Pick candidate colors.

3. Assign generic meanings consistent with the viewer's associations, government standards, and corporate usage.

4. List specific meanings in particular contexts—based on the tasks the viewer is to perform and the distinctions critical to those tasks.

The simple answer: red, yellow, green, and blue

For tasks that involve learning color codes, you are probably safe if you pick red, blue, green, and yellow. These colors are seldom confused with other colors (309). Such bright, high-contrast, saturated colors are processed more rapidly in the brain (309). Tests across age groups, cultures, and even primate species found these colors easier to learn and remember than others. As human languages add words for colors, these are the first colors named after light and dark. The order in which these *focal* colors are assigned names is light, dark, red, green, yellow, blue, brown, purple, pink, orange, and gray (11).

Use as few colors as possible

Although we can print or display millions of colors and the eye can distinguish thousands of colors, the mind can remember only a few color codes. The number of colors usable for color coding generally range from three to seven (288). The more colors in a display, the longer it takes to react to a single color and the greater the confusion between colors (187).

Recommended combinations

For more demanding tasks, you may have to pick more codes and must consider background color as well as other factors. The following table lists discriminable color combinations (169; 174; 258; 309).

Pick distinguishable colors

For this number of colors:	On a white background use:	On a black background use:
1	Red Green	Yellow Cyan Green
2	Red, blue Red, green Magenta, green	Magenta, cyan Magenta, green
3	Red, blue, green	Red, blue, green Red, blue, violet Magenta, cyan, yellow
4	Red, blue, green, yellow	Red, blue, green, yellow Magenta, cyan, yellow, green
5	Red, orange, green, blue, violet	Red, orange, yellow, green, blue
10	Red, orange-red, orange, yellow, yellow-green, green, bluish-green, greenish-blue, blue, violet	Red, orange-red, orange, yellow, yellow-green, green, bluish-green, greenish-blue, blue, violet

 For example, if you need two colors that can be distinguished on a black background, you'd pick magenta and cyan or magenta and green. If the same two colors had to remain distinctive on a white background, you'd select magenta and green because this combination occurs in the column for white and the column for black.

Define and display codes clearly

When using color codes, ensure that the color codes appear the same throughout the graphic and anywhere else they appear.

Use a neutral background color for color-coded information (309). In a test comparing red, blue, green, yellow, violet, and gray backgrounds, the gray background was the only one with consistently low error rates for red, blue, green, yellow, and violet color codes (252).

 Black and white are also neutral colors.

Size colored marks

 At least:
1.5 mm
0.06 in
0.22 degrees

Avoid tight textures of color

✘ No   ✔ OK

5 cycles/cm   2.5 cycles/cm

Make colored marks large enough to carry color. To see color in an object, it must be at least 1.5 mm (0.06 in. or 0.22 degrees visual angle) (24; 309). The larger the marks, the more colors viewers can distinguish (24). If the object is too small to carry color, such as a dot or fine line, color code its background instead (color Figure 13) (309). Don't use color for tight patterns, greater than four cycles per cm (ten cycles per inch or three cycles per degree of visual angle) (309). If color coding text, color code entire words, not individual characters. For faster discrimination, but slower reading, code the background of the word (309).

Provide color legends if the meaning of colors is not universally understood or if using more than five colors (309). Designate color by showing a swatch of the color, not by mentioning its name. Make the color symbols in the legend the same as those in the graphic. Remember, the appearance of color depends on the size of the graphical object. A small area of color will appear darker; a larger area, lighter and brighter. Thus, text printed in a color will appear darker than a color swatch of the same color (157).

RELY ON LEARNED COLOR ASSOCIATIONS

When you select colors, consider the meanings viewers have already adopted for these colors. If you can, pick colors in ways consistent with these meanings. If you must use color in ways contrary to these associations, alert your readers to your unconventional use of color and teach your meanings.

Remember that no color is limited to a single meaning. Despite advice that red be used only for warning, it is one of the most popular colors when people devise their own color codes (274). This should come as no surprise for red is used for many different purposes without causing great confusion. At the same time, red is the color of stop signs and stop lights, the *Down* button on elevators, a popular color for sports cars and fire trucks, the skin of a ripe apple, an accent color for graphics in *Scientific American*, and the emblem of socialism.

The meaning of a color depends on its symbolic context, too. The color symology for religious art, for instance, may not translate to expectations for technical graphics.

Natural associations

Use natural color codes; that is, color associations learned from nature. Such associations are readily understood worldwide:

Color	Associated with	Meaning
Red	Blood	Danger
	Fire	Heat
Yellow	Sun	Warmth
Blue	Water	Cool
Green	Young leaves	Life, youth
Brown	Dead vegetation	Age, death
Paler colors	Atmospheric haze	Distance

Military cockpit displays use natural and mimetic color codings, such as showing the sky in blue, to speed search and interpretation (258). One scheme for showing the age of computer files represented them as icons that progressively yellowed and turned brown (274). Remember that warm colors suggest action; cool colors, inactivity or reserve (100).

"Throughout the entire world, water, seas, and rivers are never red, fire heat, and dryness are not generally accompanied by a blue sensation, vegetation is most often green." (24, p. 90)

Business conventions

Every domain has its own color conventions. Graphics should respect these conventions to avoid confusing viewers. For example, in Western societies, the following color conventions are widespread:

Field	Red means	Other color associations
Finance	Loss	Black = gain
Politics	Radicalism	
Temperature	Warm	Blue = cool
Mapping	Primary roads	Blue = water, green = vegetation
Traffic signs	Stop	Yellow = caution, green = go
Safety	Danger	Yellow = caution, green = safety

ANSI Standards for color in signs (10)

Red	Danger
	Stop
Orange	Dangerous parts of equipment
Yellow	Caution
Blue	Nonsafety messages
Green	Safety
Black on yellow	Radiation
Black on white	Traffic markings

 For more information on handling cultural differences for graphics, see Chapter 11.

Institutional standards

Many standards contribute to our sense of color usage. For example, I have never seen a blue river. I have seen brown, green, reddish, and yellowish rivers. Yet blue is the recognized symbol for water, and on a map I recognize a meandering line of blue to represent a river. In traffic lights and signs worldwide, red means stop or no, yellow means caution, green means go, and blue means yes (79).

Be aware of cultural differences

The symbolic interpretation of color varies from culture to culture. However, many problematic color associations do not pertain in cultures sophisticated and cosmopolitan enough to use computers. Confusion occurs mostly in primitive cultures or in religious or social contexts.

COMPENSATE FOR COLOR-BLINDNESS

Total color-blindness (monochromatism or cone blindness) is extremely rare, afflicting only 0.003 percent of men and 0.002 percent of women. More common, however, are difficulties perceiving fine details in blue and in distinguishing red and green. Most people are blue-blind (tritanopic) in central vision (145), and about 8 percent of men and 0.4 percent of women cannot reliably distinguish red and green.

To overcome problems caused by color-blindness:

☐ **Use color as a redundant signal**. Make monochrome reproductions of the graphic decipherable by combining other graphical characteristics, such as shape, pattern, or value with chromatic color (24). (See color Figure 25.)

☐ **Avoid problem colors.** Don't use red versus green for any critical distinction. Use pure blue only as a background. By avoiding problem colors you remove problems of color discrimination for 99.995 percent of men and over 99.997 percent of women (288).

☐ **Use colors with different lightness values.** Even persons with total color-blindness can still discriminate between light and dark (288). (See color Figure 2.)

☐ **Select colors everyone can distinguish.** Use a bright yellow, medium green, and dark red. Use color combinations most persons can distinguish: red and blue, red and cyan, blue and yellow.

☐ **Limit the number of colors viewers must distinguish.**

☐ **Put colors to be compared close together, especially if similar in lightness.** Place color legends close to the colors they decode (309).

☐ **Screen viewers.** Applicants for some jobs—military pilots, for instance—are screened for color perception.

TEST, TEST, TEST

Test your color choices under actual viewing conditions. Color theory is often overruled by practical considerations. Colors seen by the viewer depend on environmental lighting as well as on printed colors of the display. Is the document read in a room lit by incandescent lights, fluorescent lights, or natural lights? Some computers are used out of doors in bright sunlight and others under blackout conditions. Background illumination and glare often make displayed colors appear less saturated or "washed out," and a strong predominant color can shift color perceptions.

First make the graphic work in black and white. Only then add color to improve its performance.

Yet for most simple coding and recognition tasks, the human perceptual system more than adequately compensates for varying conditions. To be sure it does, and to fine tune color assignments, test with representative viewers under actual viewing conditions.

ENRICHING GRAPHICS

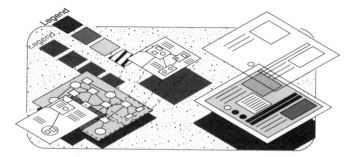

Effective graphics are more than a single picture. They may incorporate multiple pictures and rich textual annotations. This chapter explains how to augment the basic graphical image with secondary images and with textual labels and notes to produce complete, self-sufficient graphics.

CREATE COMPOSITE GRAPHICS

Composite graphics combine multiple graphical forms to provide alternative views of information. Use composite graphics:

- To show the same information in two ways

- To provide secondary details and reference information

- To enable different groups of readers to use the same graphic

- To layer information so that details are progressively revealed in a way that does not swamp the reader with information

Inserts

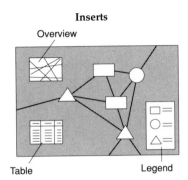

Inserts
Overview
Table   Legend

Inserts are areas of additional information included within a graphic to supplement its basic elements. Typical uses for inserts in computer documentation include:

- Explanatory text
- Table of related data
- Key or legend of symbols
- Enlargement of a region of dense detail
- Overview or wide-scale map

Box the insert only if the insert might otherwise be confused with the main graphic.

Combinations and overlays

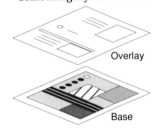

Combining layers of detail
Overlay
Base

To compare dissimilar items or to show two aspects of the same data, you can combine two or more types of graphics into one. The two types must be compatible, and one must remain the primary form.

You can think of the primary form as the base over which you superimpose additional layers of information. For example, over a photograph of an open equipment cabinet you might superimpose a line drawing of proposed modifications. The overlay would call attention to the circuits, cables, and connectors to be added.

Be careful mixing radically different forms, such as drawings and charts (as does *USA Today*). Viewers may confuse objects in the base with objects in the overlay and not know where one ends and the other begins (64).

 Some online documentation systems let users display or hide several different layers of detail.

Small multiples

"Small multiples resemble the frames of a movie: a series of graphics, showing the same combination of variables, indexed by changes in another variable." (315, p. 170)

Small multiples or *data multiples* can be compared to the frames in a movie. Several design elements—scales and grids, for instance—are repeated for related items of information. The unchanging parts provide a stable basis for the parts that change from frame to frame. Use small multiples to:

- Show changes with respect to another variable beyond the ones shown in the individual graphics

- Distinguish constant from variable parts, such as between standard and optional equipment

- Demonstrate that many variations are possible

Small multiples show variations

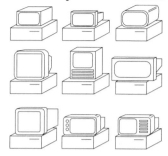

Overview and closeup

A common problem in many highly detailed graphics is how to show the details without losing context. One technique is to combine detailed closeups with an overview graphic. To combine an overview and closeup:

☐ Show one graphic but progressively increase detail in the area of interest. Increased detail draws the eye and focuses attention.

☐ Superimpose a blow-up of a small area onto a view of the entire area. Connect the blow-up to the related area of the main graphic with lines or arrows.

☐ Add a second graphic showing a closeup of an area in the first graphic. On the first graphic, show the areas enlarged on the second graphic. This technique lets one overview serve as an index for several detailed views.

Show the overview and closeup view from the same viewpoint.

Closeups reveal details

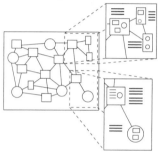

USE WORDS IN PICTURES

Unless graphics are attended to in sequence with the text, they must be completely self-explanatory (346). For this reason we must design the graphic and accompanying text as one visual unit (340). Few pictures can stand alone without words. Many require and most benefit from well-chosen labels, annotations, and notes. Include text in graphics to:

- Quickly identify the graphic (24)

- Tell people what strategy to use to read the graphic (339)

- Tell what all the objects in the graphic have in common

- Identify different types of objects and tell how they are organized (24)

"Few pictures are self-explanatory. Don't forget that a picture is an equal partner of words, not a replacement for them." (66)

Words in pictures

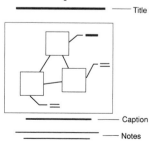

- Explain how the graphic relates to other graphics, such as whether it is a continuation of another graphic (337)

Don't, however, state conclusions in text that are more easily observed from the graphic ("Signal AB goes from Pin 12 to Jumper J4-1") (201).

CAPTION AND TITLE

The caption identifies the graphic and relates it to body text. It may contain anything that applies to the whole graphic (192). The caption should not, however, include:

- Detailed information found in the text (196)
- Unnecessary background information
- Information obvious in the graphic (192)
- Information contained in labels or headings of the graphic (117)

Captions may be omitted altogether if the graphic is simple, if it appears exactly where mentioned in the text, and if it is introduced by preceding text (335).

The caption may include any of these elements:

- Number
- Title
- Description

In some graphics, the number and title appear at the top of the graphic and the description appears at the bottom where it is almost an explanatory note.

"Picture captions are the most undervalued and therefore misused page component in most publications. That is because they are usually written under the deadline gun and are not much more than afterthoughts. They tend to be seen as those less-than-important words needed to explain or identify a graphic item, which in turn is seldom deemed as important as the text. To most writers and editors, captions, legends, or cutlines are a nuisance." (335, p. 124)

Parts of caption

Figure 14. **Contrast control**   Adjusts relative lightness of foreground and background

Number graphics referred to elsewhere

Unless a graphic appears right where it is mentioned in text, number it and refer to it by number in the text. Number graphics in the order they appear and are cited.

Conventionally, tables are numbered separately from figures. Figures usually include line drawings, photographs, charts, and diagrams. You can, however, number both tables and figures in a single series, calling them all figures or exhibits. In any event, do not create separate numbering series for different types of figures (335).

Number in a single sequence

✘ No	✔ Yes
Table 7-1	Figure 7-1
Photo 7-1	Figure 7-2
Chart 7-1	Figure 7-3
Diagram 7-1	Figure 7-4

Follow the same numbering scheme for graphics as for pages. If pages are numbered sequentially throughout, number graphics continuously from first to last. If pages are numbered by chapter or section, number graphics likewise; for example, Figure 5-7 for the seventh figure of Chapter 5. If appendixes contain graphics, number these graphics using the same scheme as for the rest of the work. For example, if graphics are numbered sequentially throughout the text and the last graphic in the text is Figure 42, then make the first graphic in the appendix Figure 43. If graphics are numbered by chapter or section, make the first graphic in Appendix B Figure B-1.

Separate a graphic's number from title with a period and a space or with a dash (118). Use arabic numerals, which are easier to read than Roman numerals (51; 311).

Title to identify graphics

The title of the graphic announces what the graphic shows. Give the graphic a unique title that clearly distinguishes it from other graphics in the same work. If all titles are similar, readers soon stop reading them (45). Feature the distinction; do not bury it deep in the title. Avoid a series of titles that all begin with the same words. Such long titles obscure the most important and useful part of the title.

The title should introduce the graphic well enough that the viewer does not have to go back to the body text (348). Word titles succinctly, answering *What? When? Where? Why?* Keep titles less than two lines (192; 276). Use "thematic titles" to sum up the key idea of a graphic and serve as an advance organizer to alert the reader to what information is most important (323).

To make titles easy to read, use standard grammar and terminology:

☐ Make terminology in the title consistent with that in the body of the text (118).

☐ In general, compose the title as a noun or noun phrase. Avoid relative clauses; use participles instead.

☐ Write titles, not telegrams. Do not omit articles and relative pronouns, unless space is tight.

 If tables and figures are numbered in a single sequence, you may omit the word *figure*. To make the number stand out, you may need to enlarge it or set it in bold type.

Figure 7.1. Opening a file
becomes
7.1 Opening a file

Pages numbered in sequence	Pages numbered by section	Figures in appendix
Figure 1	Figure 1-1	Figure A-1
Figure 2	Figure 1-2	Figure A-2
Figure 3	Figure 1-3	Figure A-3
Figure 4	Figure 2-1	Figure B-1
	Figure 2-2	Figure B-2

Use Arabic numerals

✗ No	✔ Yes
Figure VII	Figure 7

Focus on differences that matter to the viewer

✗ No	✔ Yes
Model 6339A display brightness control	Adjusting brightness
Model 6339A display contrast control	Adjusting contrast
Model 6339A display color mode switch	Displaying color

Nonthematic title	Thematic title
SMOOTH Command applied to line segments	Smoothing rounds corners and softens shapes

Phrase titles as participles

✗ No	✔ Yes
The report which results	The resulting report

Use standard grammar

✗ No	✔ Yes
Program reformats data you entered	The program reformats your data

Avoid nominalizations

✘ No   ✔ Yes

The program's drawing of a chart

The program draws a chart

☐ Avoid nominalizations; that is, turning verbs into nouns (323).

Include the description to guide the viewer

In addition to a title, the caption may include a longer description. This is a perfect location for an important message. Readers will attend to captions up to 45 words or three lines long (335). Use the description for:

- **How to read the graphic** (315). Explain the graphical form so that even a graphical illiterate can understand it (340). ("Alternative choices. Pick one.")

- **What to attend to in the graphic.** What is especially important, new, or significant (335). ("New menus, shown in red, let you edit individual frames.")

- **Why the graphic is important** (335). Implications for readers. Why they should bother viewing the graphic (340). ("Five ways to safeguard your data.")

- **Conclusions the reader should draw** (340). This sets the schema and enables top-down processing to fill in the particular reasons for the general conclusion (155). ("Use HyperZIP for databases and spreadsheets, but not for freeform word processing files.")

Write captions using concrete words in descriptive sentences that guide the reader into the illustration (191). Make sure the caption adds useful information. If all captions are similar, readers soon stop reading them (45).

Put caption with its figure

✘ No   ✔ Yes

Display the caption with the graphic

Place the caption so that it is clearly associated with its graphic and not confused with the body text. Caption figures separately, not in blocks of captions (335). The proper placement depends on whether the title is included with the description or displayed separately.

Place the caption

Traditionally, the caption goes below the graphic. This makes good sense, because otherwise people would skip it to get to the illustration. Three exceptions are tables which are read top to bottom, figures that bleed off the bottom of the page (118; 335), and captions that are only a title. To tie the caption to the figure, align the caption to one of the edges of the figure or center it symmetrically along an edge. If the caption is to the left of the figure, right justify it (335).

Leave twice as much space between the caption and following text as between the caption and the illustration (335).

Place the caption so it reads in the same direction as the figure (335). Set the caption in type 70 to 100 percent the size of body type. Make single-line captions as long as necessary. Break captions over 60 characters (335).

If the title is separate

If the title is separate from the rest of the caption, design it so it is noticed before the graphic is read. Place the title at the top of the graphic, just outside the border of the graphic (276). Set titles in the largest type used in the graphic (276). Center one- or two-line titles horizontally over the graphic (118). Centering the title helps to visually associate it with the graphic and distinguish it from the text. Left justify titles over three lines.

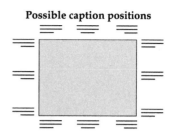
Possible caption positions

Keep captions near figure
Body text
Graphic
Caption
Body text

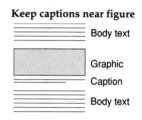
Put title above graphic
Title
Description

LABELS AND ANNOTATIONS

Labels provide information about parts of the graphic. They draw attention to important components, answer questions the viewer may have, and remove ambiguity in the graphic. Labels are typically words or phrases that identify specific parts. They can also be sentences that describe and explain parts. These longer, more extensive labels are called annotations. Throughout this section, the term *label* refers to both short labels and more extensive annotations.

Why label?

Labels may be the most important text in your document. Information in callouts to an illustration is better remembered than information in body text (230). Although labels will not redeem a misleading or ambiguous graphic, they do limit misunderstanding (11; 315). Often the key to seeing an image as a three-dimensional shape is a label that identifies the object (223).

Use labels and annotations to:

- Add important observations and comments
- Explain exceptional values and special cases
- Call attention to important trends
- Make categories of graphical objects clear
- Explain how to view a new graphical format

Connect objects and labels

Label objects in the most direct way possible (276). Do not make the reader shuttle between text and graphics to figure out the meaning (64; 335). In comparing different ways of labeling graphics, consider speed, accuracy, and dependability. A separate legend may be accurate, but it is slow and many may not bother to consult it. Some options, arranged from most direct to least direct, for connecting labels and objects are:

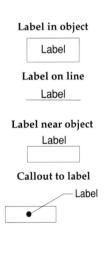

Label in object

Label

Label on line

Label

Label near object

Label

Callout to label

Label

Symbol beside object

▲ ▲ = Label

- ☐ **Put label on object.** If space permits, place labels inside or on the boxes or objects they name (8; 64; 180). To save space, place labels along, rather than beside, lines.

- ☐ **Place label near object.** If the label cannot go on the object, place it next to the object (180). Put labels above, not below, a line. Words have fewer descenders than ascenders (314), and the eye tends to travel above a line rather than below (19).

- ☐ **Connect object and label by callout line.** If the label cannot go on or beside the object, connect it to the object by a callout line thinner than lines in the object.

- ☐ **Put symbol near object and define the symbol.** If space does not permit word labels, place a graphical symbol near or on the object and define the symbol in a key or legend.

☐ **Share graphical characteristics.** To connect an object or area with its label, you can give both common graphical characteristics. For example, to connect annotations with areas of a menu or report, use a different background color for each area and its annotation. Or place a small swath of the color near the start of the annotation. For color-coded blocks of text, put a label in the margin. Put it in reverse type on a saturated color block (white type on red). Mark the related text by printing it on a background of a desaturated version of the same color (black on pink).

Label keyed to graphical characteristic

☐ **Label analogous graphics.** As an alternative to conventional labels, supplement the main graphic with a second one from the same viewpoint that includes labeled areas corresponding to objects in the primary graphic (223).

Label analogous graphic

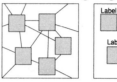

Phrase labels carefully

Use language in expected, predictable ways in labels. In addition, use complete words and avoid unnecessary abbreviations and contractions (100). Avoid the tendency to omit small words, such as articles and prepositions, which are necessary to understand the label. Make terminology in labels consistent with that in the text body (118).

Use standard language

✗ No   ✔ Yes

2nd Int Ctrlr Bd   Secondary interrupt on the controller board

Use familiar symbols for labels

If you are using symbols, rather than words, for labels, pick symbols that are visually distinct from the graphic and from one another, that are familiar to the reader, and that are simple in form (34; 100). Display and use symbols consistently throughout the graphic and the document. In selecting symbols, avoid:

- Upper- and lowercase versions of the same letter (223)
- Symbols found in the graphic itself (335)
- Numeric and alphabetic codes of more than a few characters (34)
- Mixtures of letters and numbers (100)
- Greek letters that look like roman letters (223)
- The characters I, 1, o, O, and 0 in alphanumeric codes that mix letters and numbers (337)

If an item is duplicated, repeat the symbol, perhaps with an addition, such as: A, A′, A′′, and so forth (223).

Labels clockwise

Labels in rows

Finding parts		Finding names	
Audio mix	3	1	Disk drive
Back control	6	2	Camera input
Camera input	2	3	Audio mix
Disk drive	1	4	Edit knob
Edit knob	4	5	Forward control
Forward control	5	6	Back control

Make annotation stand out from background

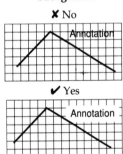

Index labels

Large graphics must be self-indexing. Arrange and label objects in an order and pattern that lets the viewer quickly find an individual item (223). Refer to items in the illustration in systematic order: top to bottom, left to right, clockwise, or counterclockwise (335).

If using numbers or letters as labels, arrange them sequentially about the object. Start in the upper left and proceed either clockwise around the figure or horizontally in two rows, one above and one below the object (118).

The way you index the parts of a graphic depends on whether the viewer knows the name and is looking for the part or knows the part and is seeking the name. For finding parts, the list should be alphabetical by part name with the name preceding the number. For finding names, it should be alphabetical or numerical by key, with the symbol preceding the name (223).

Make labels and annotations visually distinct

Design labels and annotations so they stand out from the background but remain subordinate to the subject matter. To distinguish labels and annotations, give them distinctive graphical characteristics—more conspicuous than those of the background but less prominent than those of the subject.

☐ If the background is a texture, pattern, or grid, blank it out underneath the label. Otherwise the text will be hard to read.

☐ If the subject is unboxed, box the annotation. However, don't add to the plethora of lines by unnecessarily boxing annotations.

☐ If the subject is boxed (a pop-up menu perhaps), do not box the annotation. In this case, boxing the text wastes space and fails to distinguish it from the subject.

☐ If the subject is largely text, make the text of the label smaller, lighter, or styled differently.

☐ If the subject matter has a rectangular geometric shape, draw it with a drop shadow to identify it as an object and to elevate it above labels and annotation (223).

☐ Display labels in a distinctive color, perhaps darker or less saturated than the subject.

☐ For an informal tone, use a speech balloon for comments to the reader.

Speaking to reader

Arrange labels about the subject

Arrange labels to avoid clutter and to ease reading. Do not label more items than are discussed on the same page or a facing page (26). Don't let dimensions or other secondary details clutter the drawing. Subdue them or possibly pull them off to the side (8).

Do not stack up the words or characters of a label (100). Inverted or vertical text thwarts our habitual left-to-right eye movement and hence is harder to read (260).

Keep labels close to the thing labeled, even if connected by leader lines. However, arrange labels so there is ample room in case labels expand when translated to another language.

Separate labels from object

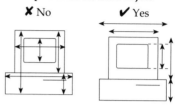

Avoid stacked text

✘ No   ✔ Yes
S   t   Horizontal
t   e   text
a   x
c   t
k
e
d

Use callout lines to connect label and object

If you cannot put labels on or next to objects, use short, simple lines to connect labels to objects.

Clearly connect label and object

Make clear what the callout line points to. End the line with a symbol that clearly identifies the object, objects, or area labeled (118):

Callout line

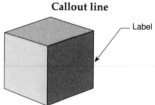

To point to ...	End the callout line with ...	Example
Edge of object	Arrowhead	
Interior of object	Dot	
Range of items	Bracket or dimension line	
Group of items	Lasso loop around items	

Make sure the callout line leads unambiguously to the label. A short, but distinct, shoulder line is common (118).

Callout lines direct the eye to labels

Make object lines stand out from callout lines

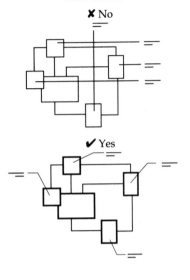

Make callout lines distinctive

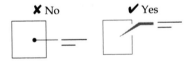

Annotate text items

```
item
----
 |
 |
 +-- This is the
     annotation
     on that
     item
```

Route lines carefully

Take care that callout lines do not turn the graphic into a confusing spider web.

Keep callout lines short and avoid running them parallel to nearby subject lines (118).

Route callout lines over unoccupied or unimportant areas of the picture. Do not take them across edges of objects, flow lines, labels, busy areas of the illustration, or other callout lines (256).

Draw nearby callout lines parallel (118). Placing all callout lines at the same diagonal angle helps separate them from the horizontals and verticals of the object.

Make callout lines distinctive

Clearly distinguish callout lines from subject lines. Some techniques to try:

☐ Make callout lines 30 percent less prominent than subject lines.

☐ Taper callouts from wide at the label to thin at the object identified. This gradient gives them a definite sense of direction without the implied motion of arrows. However, it may draw too much attention to the callout line.

☐ If most subject lines are horizontal or vertical, make callout lines diagonal.

☐ Surround callout lines with blank space to separate them from overlaid objects, lines, and areas.

Annotate computer programs

One of the most effective ways to use labels is to embed instructions and commentary right into programming examples. Almost all programming languages allow the writer to include nonexecutable statements or comments in the body of the program. The writer can thus use typewriter characters to connect notes to elements of the program to explain what they accomplish. For example:

```
WRITE (1, TEXT) RECORD.ZXT
-----  |  ----  ----------
  |    |   |        |
  |    |   |        |
  |    |   |        +-- file to send
  |    |   |
  |    |  .+-- format of the file
  |    |
  |    +-- channel
  |
  +-- command to transmit files
```

Such annotations do not require the programmer to consult a
separate document to understand what each statement in the
example program does.

DECODE SYMBOLOGY OF THE GRAPHIC

Explain the symbology and conventions of the graphic fully.
Itemize the objects and the symbologies used to represent
each. Label axes in charts. Provide legends defining colors and
textures. Provide a key of all shapes and visual symbols (24).

Legends and keys

A legend defines the symbologies used in the graphic. It is a
list of the graphical objects or characteristics and their
meanings. The legend may contain swatches of color, value,
texture, and pattern or samples of lines, shapes, and other
graphical codes. Each swatch or sample is accompanied by its
definition. Make the swatches the same size and on the same
background as in the graphic.

Example of a legend

Orientation cues

Tell the viewer how the scene in the graphic relates to what is
experienced in the real world. Such orienting cues include:

- **Orienting arrow**. For maps that do not put north toward
  the top, include a northward pointing arrow to show
  direction.

Orienting arrow

Orienting map

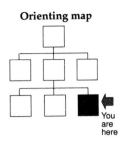

You
are
here

- **You-are-here overview**. Detailed graphics often need to show how their details fit into some larger context.

- **Mapping projections**. Global maps specify the projection scheme used to render the spherical surface of the earth onto a flat surface. Projections, such as Mercator or polyconic differ in which areas are exaggerated and which are diminished.

- **Perspective projection**. Perspective drawings may use different ways of rendering three-dimensional objects on a two-dimensional surface. Techniques such as isometric, dimetric, 1-point, and 2-point, differ in the distortions introduced into the scene and the measurements that may be made from the drawing.

Scales

We consciously and unconsciously gauge the size of objects relative to our own size. In 5 BC, Polyclitos related all sizes to the typical length of the middle finger; and in the 1940s, Le Corbusier based his *modulator* on human body proportions (179). In design, man truly is the measure of all things. When we see a graphic of a real object, we immediately want to know how large it is compared to our bodies and the objects in our daily experience.

To estimate distances on the graphic, the viewer must have a clear sense of the scale of the graphic. The scale is simply the relationship between distances on the graphic and distances in the real world. This relationship can be communicated in the following ways:

Type scale	Example	Notes
Number ratio	1:200 200X	This example indicates that distances in the real world are 200 times those on the graphic. The advantage of such a ratio is that it is independent of units. One inch on the graphic represents 200 inches in the real world; one centimeter represents 200 centimeters. A mathematical ratio also simplifies calculation. To relate a graphic distance to a real-world distance, we simply multiply by the ratio.
		The American Society for Testing and Materials recommends these standard enlargements: 5X, 10X, 25X, 50X, 75X 100X, 150X, 200X, 250X, 500X, 750X, 1000X, 1500X, 2000X (138).

| Units ratio | 1 in. = 1 ft | This example indicates that each foot in the real world is represented by one inch on the graphic. Units ratio scales let the viewer apply convenient units for measurement. Few would measure graphic distances in kilometers or land distances in centimeters. The format is |

graphic distance:object distance
or
graphic distance = object distance

Graphical scale		A graphical scale gives the real-world length of a reference line or shows a ruler calibrated in real world units. The graphical scale has two clear advantages. First, it requires no other measuring device to read graphic distances. Second, a graphical scale remains accurate if the graphic is enlarged or reduced.
Known shape	Person, hand, or finger tip	Include a familiar object in the scene. Don't, however, let the scale-giving object dominate the scene (138).
Grid	Longitude and latitude lines in a map	Show the object on a background of equally spaced parallel lines.
Distance numbers	Dimensions in blueprint	Label important dimensions of the object and distances between objects.

In numerical and units ratios, take into account any enlargement or reduction that will be done as part of the publications process (138).

NOTES

Place detailed, seldom needed information in a visible but out-of-the-way location, such as in a note to the graphic (81).

Use notes for secondary information

Use notes for secondary reference information that is not necessary to understand the graphic but that some viewers may find useful.

Use notes sparingly. They interrupt and possibly distract viewers. Don't use notes for information that takes little more space than the note reference. The value of the information in the note must exceed the effort expended to find and read it (192). Viewers who consult the note must remember where to go back to (346).

Place notes beneath the graphic

Graphical notes are not page footnotes

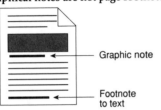

Graphic note

Footnote to text

Place notes flush with the left margin of the graphic, immediately below the caption, if any. If the graphic is boxed, enclose the notes inside the box—again, at the bottom of the graphic.

On multipage graphics, put graphic notes for each page at the bottom of that page, or put all notes at the end of the graphic. If you put the notes at the end of a multipage graphic, put a note on the bottom of each page that contains note references. Let it say "See notes at end of graphic."

Do not mix text footnotes and graphic notes; number them separately. To avoid confusion, don't put graphic notes on the bottom left of the page (81; 118). Display graphic notes only with the graphic; display text footnotes at the end of the page, section, or book.

Set graphic notes in smaller or less emphatic type than the title and caption of the graphic.

Kinds of notes

Placing notes for graphics

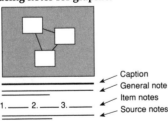

Caption
General note
Item notes
Source notes

Graphics can have three kinds of notes: general notes, item notes, and source notes. They are usually included in that order (161).

General notes	Provide information about the whole graphic, such as the scope of the information presented, limitations of accuracy, and possible exceptions.
Item notes	Describe particular parts of the graphic, such as a cell or heading in a table, a symbol in a diagram, or a component in a drawing.
Source notes	Identify the originator or authority for the information presented in the graphic.

Source notes

Source notes go at the foot of the graphic (or the first page of multipage graphic) after any other notes.

Introduce source notes with SOURCE: or SOURCES: in emphatic type (conventionally SMALL CAPS). Acknowledge the source of information if it is not original or widely known. Use the same form as for footnotes in text.

Give credit to illustrators and artists who author an image (138). If your illustration is copied or derived from another work, you generally will require permission of the copyright owner to use it. Unless the copyright owner requires a different form, follow these examples for wording credit lines (137):

Criteria	Example
The illustration is an original for which the author holds copyright. Consider crediting the originator.	Illustration by Dave Oliver.
The originator of the unpublished, uncopyrighted work is letting you use it without fee.	Courtesy of Hillsdale Museum of Science.
Statistical values from another publication are presented in an original graphic.	Data from Figure 7-2, p. 122, Aston 1970. Copyright 1970 by Joseph Aston.
The source illustration has been redrawn with changes to both data and the graphic.	Redrawn and adapted, by permission, from Figure 7-2, p. 122, Aston 1970. Copyright 1970 by Joseph Aston.
The source illustration is redrawn. Although some stylistic changes may have been made, the data are the same.	Redrawn, by permission, from Figure 7-2, p. 122, Aston 1970. Copyright 1970 by Joseph Aston.
The source illustration was photoreproduced and then the graphic and data were modified.	Adapted, by permission, from Figure 7-2, p. 122, Aston 1970. Copyright 1970 by Joseph Aston.
The source illustration is reproduced photographically with no changes except to scale or color.	Reprinted, by permission, from Figure 7-2, p. 122, Aston 1970. Copyright 1970 by Joseph Aston.

General notes

General notes include abbreviations, qualifications, limitations, and other information pertinent to the graphic as a whole or to large parts of it (348). Information appropriate for general notes includes:

- Abbreviations or symbols used throughout the graphic

  NOTE: ■ = maximum, □ = minimum, ▲ = increasing, ▼ = decreasing

- How accurate or reliable is the information

  NOTE: Equipment calibration limits accuracy to two decimal places.

- How data have been calculated, manipulated, rounded off, or approximated.

  NOTE: Data from the three studies were converted to common units of measurement and merged. No attempt was made to adjust for inconsistencies in reporting procedures.

- Other related information. Cross-references.

  NOTE: For a cost estimate for this project, see Figure 14.

Place general notes before any other notes, at the foot of the first page of the graphic. Introduce general notes with **NOTE:** or **NOTES:** set in emphatic type.

Item notes

Item notes provide additional information about a few items in the display. Item notes are not the same as labels keyed to objects by shared symbols. An item note provides additional information about a particular object in a scene or about a specific column, row, or cell in a table. They are referenced by symbols in, on, or beside the referenced object.

Mark item notes with symbols that stand out from the other objects in the graphic. Separate note references that occur together with spaces, not commas. If a note occurs in a blank table cell, put the note reference in parentheses.

"It is wrong to assume that an asterisk can correct the discrepancy in the visual presentation by meekly stating the fact underneath it. Charting is a visual presentation; too many footnotes defeat the purpose." (141, p. 176)

Symbols for notes

Type data	Use	Avoid
Numeric	Letters	Numbers
Text	Numbers	Letters
Formula	Special	Numbers, letters
Statistics	Letters	* and **

Put item notes at the bottom of the graphic on the page on which they occur. If the same notes occur on multiple pages, gather all item notes at the end of the graphic.

Place item notes in the order readers will most likely find them in the graphic. For tables, this is in paragraph reading order, starting in the upper left. For free-form graphics, arrange notes clockwise from upper left.

Extend notes across the full width of the graphic. You may, however, put several short notes on a single line.

[1] First note   [2] Second note   [3] Third note

PAGE AS PICTURE

Graphics seldom stand alone. Even the best graphics fail unless they are properly integrated with body text into effective pages. To design effective graphics and integrate them into pages and other composite displays you must mix text and graphics in ways that legibly and clearly reveal information.

In this chapter we consider placing graphics onto pages and the graphical aspects of the resulting pages. These are important topics because most pages today are designed for words only and accept graphics grudgingly and awkwardly. The result is often less effective than either the text or graphics alone.

DESIGN PAGES FOR GRAPHICS

Pictures are more powerful than text. When a page contains graphics, they are noticed first, studied longer, and returned to more often than text. Labels, annotations, and captions to graphics are read more often than body text or headings. Yet most page designs used in computer documentation and other technical documents treat graphics as secondary and even as an unwelcome violation of the pure design of the page.

"Readers look first at the illustration, then at the headline, then at the copy." (230, p. 88)

"Images take precedence over written material, and large images tend to attract the eye before small ones." (272, p. 29.)

265

"Yet it is precisely the pictorial graphic items (with their verbal explanations) that are looked at first when the new page is revealed. They are glanced at and studied before the text and often even before the title is read." (335, p. 124)

"Every time a new page is looked at, the first element to be notice and studied is the visual, nontextual one—the diagram." (333, p. 47)

Writers, skilled and experienced in using words, may not realize that their readers will not have the same fascination with the written word. Graphic designers, concerned only with making a pretty page, will distort graphics to fit them to a preconceived page design. Fortunately, enlightened writers and graphic designers now realize that their job is not to put words on paper or to make pretty pictures, but to communicate. They are taking steps to put pictures and text together into effective pages.

DESIGN PAGES AS GRAPHICS

People view and process a page in much the way they do any graphic image. Upon first glance, figures tables, headings, and blocks of text are just unexplored graphical objects of the larger picture that is the page. Understanding how viewers process pages can help us design pages that effectively combine text and graphics toward a single goal.

Pages are viewed and processed in a sequence of four overlapping activities (157; 198):

Design headings as labels for associated blocks of text.

Phase	Visual cues
Chunking. Unconsciously the reader divides the page into three kinds of graphical objects: paragraphs, headings, and graphics.	Blank space surrounding objects, different levels of indentation, boxing of groups of objects, alignment and juxtaposition of objects.
Ranking. These chunks are then ordered or queued.	Position on page or relative to other objects, contrast with background, brightness of color, size.
Sorting. The ordered chunks are classified into distinct categories.	Color, size, shape, indentation, and any other shared graphical characteristics.
Abstracting. The function of various chunks and groups is inferred.	Patterns of graphical characteristics repeated on the page or throughout the document.

For this process to succeed, we must design entire pages with the same care and principles as we do individual graphics. Designing effective visual cues into the text benefits all readers (146).

List what will appear on a page

The first step in designing pages is to list the elements that can appear on the page. This list will include things like paragraphs of body text, various levels of headings, page headers and footers, lists, tables, and other graphics. Decide which of these items must be visually distinct from others. For instance, you may choose to distinguish paragraphs that present conceptual information from ones that describe an example. You will probably want to distinguish lists of alternatives from lists of requirements. You will certainly want warnings, cautions, and notes distinct from regular body text.

Rank elements by importance

Divide the ranked list into four or five distinct levels of importance: that is, the order in which you want them to be noticed. Viewers can readily recognize only about five levels of emphasis. These levels are the basis for the visual hierarchy of the page. For example, a typical page might have these levels of elements in its visual hierarchy:

 For online documents that appear on alphanumeric screens, you may have to reduce the number of levels to only three or four.

Level	Items
1	First-order heading Safety warning
2	Second-order heading Caution
3	Body text Tables Graphics
4	Bullet-list items Figure captions Notes to body text
5	Page headers and footers Notes to text and graphics

Assign graphical characteristics

To separate the different levels of importance and to distinguish items within each level, select appropriate graphical characteristics for each page element.

"Develop size, weight, caps/lowercase, spacing and indentation formats relative to body text. Use the minimal number of visual characteristics necessary to differentiate between headings, as each difference implies an additional structural significance." (198, p. VC-34)

"Successful design sets up elements to visually reflect the organization of the document's contents. The visual characteristics of headings and white space around them should indicate the level of generality of that heading and its function in the overall structure of the document." (198, p. VC-34)

Start with body text. Design its characteristics for maximum legibility. Then using body text as a baseline, assign graphical characteristics to add emphasis for higher levels and reduce it for lower levels. Each level should be between 30 percent and 60 percent more conspicuous or prominent than the one below it.

For textual elements, like paragraphs, headings, lists, and tables, you can use size, boldness, indentation, and spacing before and after the element to vary the level of emphasis.

Adjust characteristics so that different elements at the same level of emphasis are visually distinct. The form of the element may provide this distinction. For instance, few would confuse a diagram for a paragraph of text. Likewise, checklists, numbered lists, and bulleted lists are all distinguished by the symbol next to each block of text.

The resulting set of specifications is called a *style sheet* or *property sheet*.

Put elements on the page

Make pages predictable. The more text and graphics are mixed on the page, the greater the value of an orderly, predictable layout. Decide where constant and recurring elements should appear on the page and always put them in these locations. To enhance coherence of the page, align visuals and blocks of text (25; 272).

To make pages predictable, create a page template that designates specific areas and zones for different page elements. A page template puts illustrations and text blocks in predictable locations, removing confusion about what is text and what is illustration (a problem with word-heavy illustrations) and allowing a richer display.

Conscientiously follow your page template, but allow variations for special cases. Slight violations of a page template, say 10 percent of the time, are OK.

Example of a page template

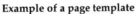
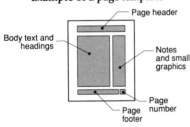

Page header

Body text and headings

Notes and small graphics

Page number

Page footer

Test the design

To test the page design, create a sample page and give it the "squint" test. Close and then gradually open your eyes. Note the order in which you notice objects. Your design works if:

- One object is clearly the most prominent.
- More important objects are noticed before less important objects.
- Objects noticed at about the same time are of the same level of importance.

To test the aesthetics of a composition, turn it upside down. It should still look good (272).

PLACE GRAPHICS BY RELATIONSHIP TO TEXT

Should you place a graphic above, below, beside, or apart from related text? The answer depends on how you are using graphics, the size of the graphic, and the relationship between the graphic and body text.

Put graphics near related text

Avoid graphical apartheid. Place the illustration near related text (8; 118). If pictures are not placed near the corresponding text, the reader may never look at them (323), so don't make readers flip pages to find the graphics (314). Eighty percent of the users of NASA technical reports said they read illustrations with text and preferred them integrated with text unless there were more than four pages of illustrations per page of text (243).

"… placing graphics close to the reference is more important than balancing text and graphics on the page for esthetic effect." (323)

Repeat graphics as necessary

Repeat rather than cross-reference graphics (209), especially if the graphic is more than five pages from a repeated reference (118). Descartes repeated the same illustration 11 times in his *Principia* rather than send readers scurrying from page to page (314).

Likewise, if you can't put all annotations with one figure, repeat the subject in two illustrations, each with different annotations. Clearly explain what type of information each figure provides.

"Although many technical editors and publications managers will resist the suggestion, I urge you to repeat an exhibit rather than committing that most serious error: referring to an exhibit that cannot be seen." (330, p. 101)

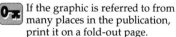 If the graphic is referred to from many places in the publication, print it on a fold-out page.

Put supporting graphics after related text

Place graphics and text according to their relationship. Readers are more likely to refer to a graphic if it occurs right after it is mentioned in the body text. To keep from confusing and sidetracking readers, never place a supporting graphic before the spread in which it is mentioned (161).

If the graphic summarizes or recalls information in the text, place the graphic after the text. Doing so provides a context for the graphic, reduces possible misinterpretations, and encourages the reader to review the text and thus remember more (45).

Consider how graphics are read

The relative placement of text and graphics depends on the sequence in which text and graphics are read and the specific relationship between them.

Text and graphics read ...	Situations	Place text and graphics	Illustration
Alternately	Graphic summarizes, recaps, or supports text.	Place graphic immediately after the related text (45).	
	Graphic introduces text.	Place graphic before the related text (45).	
	Graphic bridges blocks of text.	Place graphic between blocks of text (45).	
In parallel	Graphic explains concepts.	Place graphic to left of related text.	
	Graphic defines term.	Place graphic to right of term.	

Separately	Graphics are not necessary to understand text.	Place graphics together at the end of the chapter, section, or document.	
	Graphics are primarily reference.		
	Graphics and text require different printing processes or paper, such as a color insert.		
	Many graphics span multiple columns.		

REFER TO GRAPHICS IN TEXT

If graphics are referred to from the text and cannot appear directly where they are referenced, number each graphic and refer to it by number in the text. Graphics cited in text are easier to find and readers refer to them more often than unmentioned graphics (255). Number graphics in the order they appear and are cited.

Cite graphics directly, at the end of a sentence (117):

Set the DIP switches for duplex communication, as shown in Figure 6.

If you must refer to figures within a sentence, write it as a parenthetical phrase (118):

... the interrupt controller (see Figure 4) is located on the mother board (see Figure 5).

If the parenthetical reference occurs within a sentence, capitalize and punctuate it as a phrase. If it occurs between sentences, treat it as a sentence:

Model 3629 contains five circuits. (See Figure 7–3.) Later models add advanced circuits.

When online documents appear in a small window or on a small screen, the user may be unable to see graphics and related text at the same time.

Do not refer to a graphic by its relative position, as with "the above graphic" or "the following graphic" (138). The process of typesetting and laying out the page may require the graphic to be positioned other than where you planned.

Try to refer to graphics only at the end of a paragraph. If you send the reader to a graphic in the middle of a paragraph, the reader may not read the rest of the paragraph or may find it difficult to resume reading at the right spot. Since the mental state of the reader is sufficiently different after viewing the graphic, a paragraph break is usually warranted.

Avoid unnecessary cross-references. Repeat short, simple graphics if necessary. In the general notes, explain that the graphic is a repeat.

NOTE: This table is the same as Table 6-2.

For proper learning and interpretation, direct attention to the graphic at the most appropriate moment. Doing so provides a context for the graphic and reduces possible misinterpretations (45).

DESIGN PAGES FOR SEARCHING AND READING

When searching, readers use headings as signposts for locating needed blocks of information.

Few people approach technical manuals and other forms of computer documentation as if they were novels. Almost nobody reads computer documentation word-by-word from cover to cover. Instead, readers skim, they scan, they skip fore and aft. Page designs should assist rather than hinder these searching strategies.

Make blank space work for you

"Surprisingly, for most books, the main body of the text only occupies 50 percent to 60 percent of the page. Thus the ratio of text area to page area is about 1:2. A visual illusion creates the impression of greater coverage of text. People shown pages with 50 percent text coverage estimated that about 75 percent of the pages were actually text." (269, p. 168)

Blank space is often one of the most important components of a page. It is not just what is left over after text and graphics are dropped on the page. Blank space serves two valuable functions: as margins to separate the page's contents from the environment and as indentation and vertical space to separate elements on the page and show relationships among them.

Leave adequate margins

So-called *passive* blank space separates the page from its environment. It consists of the margins around the edge of the page. Provide adequate margins to:

☐ Let readers hold the page without covering text or graphics. Allow at least 15 mm (1/2 in.) for the side margin.

☐ Visually isolate the page's contents from other things in the reader's field of view.

☐ Let mechanical grippers pull pages through the printing press. Usually 10 mm (3/8 in.) is sufficient.

☐ Accommodate binding. Three-hole binding requires about 25 mm (1 in.). Perfect binding takes about 20 mm (3/4 in.).

Very little passive space is necessary (or even available) for online documents.

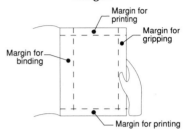

Margins

Use space to communicate

The functional use of blank space to separate blocks of information and to show their interrelationships is called *active* blank space.

Balance the use of blank space. With too little blank space, the page appears crowded and cluttered. Search takes longer and skimming is difficult. Too much blank space, on the other hand, wastes space and maroons text and graphics in an ocean of white (272). In general, cover only about 50 percent of the paper page with text and graphics (311).

☐ Leave at least the equivalent of two blank text lines above and below graphics.

☐ Leave space in examples and procedures for readers to write in the values they should enter, codes they should remember, and other information unique to their situation.

☐ If the page is scanned more than read, increase the amount of active blank space. If the page is read from beginning to end, reduce blank space to pack more information onto the page and reduce page flipping.

☐ Leave extra blank space if the document will be translated.

Make graphics easy to find

Because graphics are used for quickly finding an individual fact or reading a single data value, it is essential that the scanning reader be able to recognize graphics on the page. While integrated with the flow of text, graphics must be visually distinct. Normally the extra margins and rectangular layout of graphics are sufficient clues for the reader. If not, visually announce graphics:

Highlight the background

Place line before and after

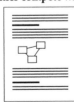

☐ Print the graphic on a light-colored background. The background should be no more than 10 percent black. Avoid using a dot pattern to create a gray background, especially if the graphic contains marks with thin lines or numbers with decimal points.

☐ Place heavy lines before and after the graphic. This draws attention to the graphic and tends to separate it from the text.

Box the graphic

Highlight column headings

☐ Box the graphic. Readers refer to boxed graphics more quickly and more often than unboxed ones (255). Box similar illustrations when juxtaposed lest the viewer see them as one illustration (219). Do not use unnecessary boxes or lines to segregate text from graphics. Because the subject cannot extend all the way to the border, borders waste space (223).

☐ If a document is primarily tables, highlight the column headings, for instance, with a background color. This helps separate individual tables and guide the eye to the head of the table.

Balance headings and graphics

Graphics compete with text

Graphics are unbearable hams, and the page is their stage. Given half a chance, they'll steal the show from stalwart text and sturdy headings. You cannot readily mix headings and graphics in a single column. The visual magnetism of the illustrations will overpower all but absurdly large headings. To integrate pictures on pages without overpowering the headings you can:

☐ Gray or halftone the illustration.

☐ Draw illustrations with very fine lines.

☐ Make illustrations smaller. Most can be quite small without any loss of effectiveness (315).

☐ Put headings in a separate column from text and graphics, especially when headings label or comment on the text and graphics rather than mark a boundary in the discussion (327).

☐ Put graphics in a separate column. This allows continuous reading without interruption.

☐ Keep text in one contiguous area in the display. Book publishers traditionally sink pictures to the bottom of the page or float them to the top of the next page. This procedure may, however, separate the graphic from the related text.

Halftone the graphic

Headings in separate column

Graphics in separate column

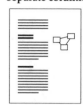

Text in contiguous areas

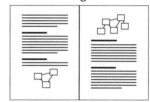

Allow continuous reading

Graphics placed amid text can disrupt reading of that text by those who are not interested in the graphics or who do not need the graphics (177). Awkward placement or styling of graphics can thwart habitual reading strategies and established perceptual skills. To avoid these problems, integrate graphics with text in ways that promote efficient scanning and reading:

Situation	Solution	Notes
Many wide graphics	Gather all graphics together at the end of the text.	Do this only if the graphics are not necessary to understanding the text.
Full-column graphics	Float graphics to top or bottom of the next available column or page.	This technique is widely used in book publishing.
Half-column graphics	Run text around the graphic.	When using runarounds, ensure the resulting text column is wide enough for uniform word spacing. This can be especially difficult when paragraph breaks and headings fall into this space (335).

Text runs around graphics

Graphics in margin

How do you read this?

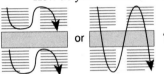

or ?

Narrow graphics	Place graphics in the margins next to related text.	
Very small graphics	Integrate graphic in-line with text.	Such illustrations include small visual symbols (➡), key-symbols (<RETURN>), and simple drawings.

Avoid the ambiguity that results when a graphic interrupts multiple columns of text. If more than half the figures span more than one column, use a single-column layout of text (52).

One column or more?

Should you arrange body text in one, two, or more columns on the page? Aesthetics aside, there are practical reasons to choose one over the other.

Single column

Simpler to produce. Even the simplest word-processing packages can lay down a single column of text.

Expected and preferred by many readers of technical documents (243).

Better handles wider graphics (52).

Multiple column

More flexibility in placing figures (311).

Shorter line length improves legibility of text (311).

Special cases: up, down, left, right?

Because of the concentration of visual functions in the right hemisphere of the brain, you may obtain a slight advantage in the speed with which visuals are processed by placing graphics to the left of text. Visuals on the left are processed first by the more visually oriented right hemisphere of the brain and text on the right by the more literate left hemisphere (103). Placing graphics to the left of text also aids processing by using the left visual field to review the graphic each time the reader scans a line of text (123). This advantage is most pronounced with Western men and less with women or those raised in Japanese or Chinese cultures.

In glossaries, however, put the text to the left of the graphic so that attention naturally flows from the term to the graphic that explains it.

If practical, place illustrations in the display in positions compatible with their viewpoints. For instance, an overhead view of the back-right corner of a cabinet should be at the bottom, right corner of the page. A view of the upper-left corner of a room should be in the upper-left of the page (223).

Position consistent with viewpoint

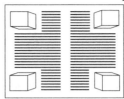

FIT GRAPHICS TO THE PAGE

Design graphics to fit the page where they appear. Do not, however, distort graphics to force them into page layouts and templates designed for text only. Design the page layout and graphics to work together.

Size graphics meaningfully

Consistently scale illustrations rather than fit them to fixed column widths. The extra space draws undue attention to the illustration (8). Scale graphics so they can be read from the same distance and orientation as the rest of the document. The reader should not have to turn the page, hold the book closer, or zoom-in the window to view the graphic (276).

For a dynamic layout, vary the size of graphics on a page (168). When combining graphics on a page, make one graphic dominant, since a single dominant graphic provides a nucleus for smaller graphics. Make the dominant graphic at least twice the size of other graphics and make the secondary graphics distinct in size, shape, and tone. This style is called the hen-and-chicks principle (168).

As a rule, shrink graphics that communicate factual details or reference information and enlarge graphics used to motivate, inspire, or please the reader. Most of the computer manuals I have seen would lose little and gain much if all their graphics were half their current size. Reducing oversized graphics puts more information in the reader's field of view, makes patterns and trends easier to spot, and frees up space for other purposes.

"Beware the one- and two-column straitjacket. Unthinkingly many editors size illustrations to fill either one column or the page width." (8, p. W-153)

One graphic dominates

"Many data graphics can be reduced in area to half their currently published size with virtually no loss in legibility and information." (315, p. 169)

"Select one-third of the photos you were going to publish, and print them three times the intended size." (245)

Orient graphics with text

✗ No   ✔ Yes

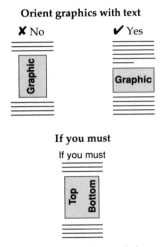

If you must

If you must

Replace with overview and closeup

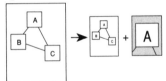

Subdivide large graphics

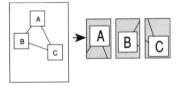

Binding divides graphic

Avoid sideways graphics

Align graphics with reading text (131). Avoid rotated graphics, especially in documents to be displayed on computer or microfiche screens, which cannot be turned as easily as a paper page (244).

Turn the graphic sideways only if the illustration cannot be simplified, reduced, or reproportioned (8), or the page cannot be enlarged or reshaped to accommodate the graphic (302). Orient sideways graphics so the bottom of the graphic is toward the right of the page (118).

Reduce or divide oversized graphics

First, try to shrink the graphic. Reduce the overall scene but call out and discuss a full-scale insert of the area of interest (26).

If you cannot shrink the graphic, subdivide it. Large diagrams can be subdivided laterally into abutting views at the same level of detail or hierarchically into telescoping views expanding out lower levels of detail (196).

If you cannot subdivide the graphic, continue it on subsequent pages. If the graphic is numbered, repeat the graphic number. Follow it with a phrase that tells where the current page fits in the sequence of pages:

> Figure 4-2 (Page 3 of 6)

Do not repeat the full title if the graphic is numbered. If the graphic is not numbered, repeat the title (or a short form of it) followed by the same phrase, thus:

> Compressing digitized images (Page 3 of 6)

or just

> Compressing (Page 3 of 6)

Divide with care

Watch out lest binding unduly divide a two-page illustration. Black comb or wire bindings often intrude on white-backgrounds and overpower split line drawings. White bindings can do the same for photographs and drawings with a dark background. Also be careful if the artwork contains lines or textures similar in width, orientation, and color to the binding.

If the illustration continues across a two-page spread, limit the number of objects split. Try to split only simple geometric elements whose regularity simplifies matching the two halves. For instance, split the two ends of a cable, but not an intricate circuit board.

If you cannot split the graphic cleanly along a straight line, overlap the coverage of the two halves by 5 percent to 10 percent and tell the viewer of the overlap.

Limit objects split

✘ No ✔ Yes

CONSERVE SPACE

One of the objections to using graphics is that including them will increase the number of pages. However, we can usually redesign the document to use space more efficiently, thus accommodating the graphics without reducing effectiveness (350):

☐ Increase page size.

☐ Use narrower margins (not necessarily longer lines).

☐ Set type in multiple columns of shorter lines.

☐ Use smaller type, especially for headings.

☐ Decrease line spacing.

☐ Use run-in headings, which can be smaller and which do not add extra blank space.

☐ Reduce the size of graphics.

MAKE TEXT LEGIBLE

Text—whether a label in a graphic, a caption to the graphic, or an accompanying paragraph—must be legible, not just recognizable. Improving the legibility of text requires attention to letter shapes, typesize, display contrast, and the layout of text.

Size type

Size type for legibility, emphasis, and aesthetics. Proper size depends on so many factors that it is impossible to prescribe exact sizes, but the following provides a starting point for design:

Element	Type size (points)		
	Min	Mid	Max
Chapter titles	18	24	36
1st order headings	14	18	24
2nd order headings	10	12	18
Body text	8	10	12
Figure captions	6	8	10
Figure labels, notes	6	7	10
Page headers and footers	6	8	10
Annotations in graphics	5	6	8

Plan the size and reductions of graphics so that in the final publication all text in illustrations is consistently scaled (8).

Pick simple, standard typefaces

For legibility, simple, familiar typefaces work best. Pick typefaces with:

- Simple functional letter shapes (275). Avoid stylized, decorative, and cursive typefaces.
- Distinct ascenders and descenders (100). These are the strokes that project above the body of the letter and below the base line.
- Standard, moderate letter proportions. Avoid condensed or stretched faces (145).
- Proportional spacing and variable-width characters (133).

Some graphic designers chafe at this advice, yet good aesthetic design is possible within these rules. In a survey, ten graphic designers were asked if they were limited to five families of type, which five they would pick. The votes were (299):

New Times Roman	6
Helvetica	5
Garamond	5
Caslon	4
Goudy Oldstyle	4
Bodoni	3.5

Only two felt such a limitation would adversely affect their work and two said it would improve their work.

Use no more than two or three typefaces on one page. Using more confuses and distracts the reader and slows reading. Combine two classic typefaces with a clear difference in weight. Do not combine two similar faces or two intricate faces (157). If the graphic, especially a list or table that is primarily text, is integral with the body text, set it in the same type size and style (335).

Style paragraphs for legibility

If text is read continuously, rather than at a glance, design it to maintain adequate legibility:

- ☐ Use high contrast between text and background (286). Color contrast alone is not sufficient; light-dark contrast is required (49; 292).

- ☐ Use upper- and lowercase letters, not ALL CAPS. Doing so ensures that text is read more quickly (310) and more accurately (283).

- ☐ Increase line spacing and blank space. Make line spacing at least one-thirtieth of the line length (34). Such spacing gives the eye a definite downward angle for the return swing after reading a line of text and ensures that the eye reliably finds the start of the next line.

- ☐ Keep lines short. Limit lines to 40 to 60 characters (100) or about the length of the 26 uppercase and 26 lowercase letters as displayed (135).

- ☐ Left justify rather than fully justify the text. (132). Full justification reduces reading rates about 10 percent (313).

- ☐ Limit the variety of type in text and graphics (323). Generally limit type sizes, styles, and colors to three sizes, three styles, and three colors per page and five sizes, three styles, and four colors per document.

PAINT IDEAS WITH PICTURES AND TEXT

What is the proper mix of text and graphics? A working technical document, I maintain, is more like a comic book than a novel, especially for today's reluctant readers.

"IDEA PAINTING, as its name implies, is simply a methodical arrangement of text and graphics, closely integrated for maximum impact." (65, p. E-32)

Pictures alone are understood quickly, but not accurately. Words alone are understood accurately, but not quickly. The best combination of speed and accuracy of understanding often results from using pictures first and words second (32). A visible format allows selective learning and enables efficient skimming by letting readers identify and skip unimportant information (270).

Perhaps the proper model for technical communication, then, is not the novel but the comic book. In Europe, South America, and Japan, the graphic novel—an expanded form of the child's comic book—is a popular and respected genre. In Japan such works account for one-third of all publications sold (281). In an era of declining literacy, Epic Comics sells 72 million copies a year (294). Similar rich mixtures of text and graphics are succeeding at communicating technical information too:

- Students in a high school history class scored consistently higher when taught from material in comic book form than from traditional textbooks (262).

Place text as annotation

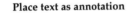
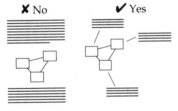

- Using annotated pictures has proven effective in communicating procedures to military personnel (32). The U.S. Army's New Look format for publications relies on graphics with a minimum of words (209). The U.S. military's Functionally Oriented Maintenance Manuals (FOMMs), likewise, are primarily graphic with only minimal supporting text (183).

- The *super comic book* or *text picture* style, which presents as much information as possible in graphics, has been used by Pratt and Whitney, John Deere, IBM, and others to simplify instructions and lower translation costs (44).

- WHIF (When and If) drawings arrange the instructions or descriptions around the image of the equipment and use arrows to lead the reader from the starting point to each piece of text in sequence. Names of critical parts are boxed and connected with lines to the part in the drawing. Such WHIF drawings have been used by GM in diagnostic and repair procedures (98).

When and If diagram

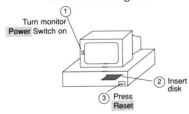

Design coordinated modules of graphics and text to work together:

1. The graphic draws attention.

2. The caption conveys the verbal message.

3. The graphic reinforces the message.

4. The body text elaborates the message.

Or put all the information needed directly on the graphic. Eliminate body text altogether and place textual information into labels, annotations, titles, captions, and notes within the graphic. The reader gets one story and never has to look elsewhere.

THE CHALLENGE OF THE FUTURE

As the complexity of computer systems increases and the quantity of information necessary to operate them grows, so does the challenge to the communicator who must select, sort, and express this information to increasingly overloaded readers. Turning mountains of data and oceans of facts into knowledge and skill will require new techniques and new technologies. Communicators of the future must master emerging technologies, such as hypermedia, holography, artificial intelligence, and virtual reality. They must combine pictures with words and numbers and sounds. Their methods and tools will be new, yet their goal will be that of our primitive ancestors whose articulated grunts first conveyed understanding from one human mind to another.

References and Bibliography

1   Adams, Ansel. *Artificial-Light Photography*. Hastings-on-Hudson, NY: Morgan & Morgan, 1969.

2   Adams, Ansel. *Camera and Lens: The Creative Approach*. Hastings-on-Hudson, NY: Morgan & Morgan, 1970.

3   Adams, Ansel. *Natural-Light Photography*. Hastings-on-Hudson, NY: Morgan & Morgan, 1969.

4   Adams, Ansel. *The Negative*. Hastings-on-Hudson, NY: Morgan & Morgan, 1969.

5   Adams, Ansel. *The Print*. Hastings-on-Hudson, NY: Morgan & Morgan, 1968.

6   Adams, K. A., I. M. Halasz, and R. J. Adams. *Handbook for Developing Computer User Manuals*. Lexington, MA: Heath, 1986.

7   Alexander, Christopher. *A Pattern Language: Towns, Buildings, Construction*. Oxford: Oxford University Press, 1977.

8   Amsden, Dorothy. "Get in the Habit of Editing Illustrations." In *Proceedings of the 27th International Technical Communication Conference*. Arlington, VA: Society for Technical Communication, 1980, pp. W 147-154.

9   Anderson, Harold E. "System/38 Syntax Diagrams: A Better Idea." In *Proceedings of the 31st International Technical Communication Conference*. Arlington, VA: Society for Technical Communication, 1984, pp. WE 56-59.

10 ANSI. *Safety Color Code for Marking Physical Hazards* (ANSI Z53.1). New York: American National Standards Institute, 1979.

11 Arnheim, Rudolf. *Art and Visual Perception: A Psychology of the Creative Eye*. Berkeley, CA: University of California Press, 1974.

12 Attneave, Fred. "Multistability in Perception." In *Image, Object, and Illusion*. San Francisco: W. H. Freeman and Company, 1974, pp. 91-99.

13 Baddeley, Alan. *The Psychology of Memory*. New York: Basic Books, 1976.

14 Baecker, Ronald and Ian Small. "Animation at the Interface." In *The Art of Human-Computer Interface Design*. Reading, MA: Addison-Wesley, 1990, pp. 251-267.

15 Bailey, M. C. and W. Pferd. "Graphics-Based Instruction for Interactive-Graphics-System Training." *IEEE Transactions on Professional Communication*, 25 (2), 1982, pp. 67-73.

16 Banks, W. W. and M. T. Clark. *Some Human Engineering Color Considerations Using CRT Displays: A Review of the Literature* (AD-B-81-001). Idaho Falls, ID: EC&G, 1981.

17 Barnard, Phil and Tony Marcel. "Representation and Understanding in the Use of Symbols and Pictograms." In *Information Design: The Design and Evaluation of Signs and Printed Material*. New York: John Wiley & Sons, 1984, pp. 37-75.

18 Barr, Robert I. "An Online Manual for a Programming Language: A Case Study in Computer Interface Design." In *Proceedings of 35th International Technical Communication Conference*. Arlington, VA: Society for Technical Communication, 1988, pp. RET 84-86.

19 Barratt, Krome. *Logic and Design in Art, Science, and Mathematics*. New York: Design Press, 1980.

20 Benson, P. J. "Writing Visually: Design Considerations in Technical Publications." *Technical Communication*, 32 (2), 1985, pp. 35-39.

21 Berger, John. *Ways of Seeing*. England: Norwich, 1977.

22 Berlitz, Charles. *Native Tongues*. New York: Grosset & Dunlap, 1982.

23 Berry, Elizabeth. "How to Get Users to Follow Procedures." *IEEE Transactions on Professional Communication*, 25 (1), 1982, pp. 22-25.

24 Bertin, Jacques. *Semiology of Graphics*. Green Bay, WI: University of Wisconsin, 1983.

25 Bethke, Deanna D. "Simple Graphic Techniques for the Technical Writer." In *Proceedings of the 25th International Technical Communication Conference*. Arlington, VA: Society for Technical Communication, 1978, pp. 32-35.

26 Bethke, Deanna D. "Simple Graphic Techniques for the Technical Writer II." In *Proceedings of the 26th International Technical Communication Conference*. Arlington, VA: Society for Technical Communication, 1979, pp. V 11-16.

27 Bewley, William L., Teresa L. Roberts, David Schroit, et al. "Human Factors Testing in the Design of Xerox's 8010 'Star' Office Workstation." In *Proceedings of CHI'83 Human Factors in Computing Systems*. New York: Association for Computing Machinery, 1983, pp. 72-77.

28 Biederman, I. and G. Ju. "Surface Versus Edge-Based Determinants of Visual Recognition." *Cognitive Psychology,* 20 (1), 1988, pp. 38-63.

29 Blaiwes, Arthur S. "Formats for Presenting Procedural Instructions." *Journal of Applied Psychology,* 59, 1974, pp. 683-686.

30 Bliss, Charles K. "Semantography: One Writing for One World." In *Symbol Sourcebook: An Authoritative Guide to International Graphic Symbols.* New York: Van Nostrand Reinhold, 1984, pp. 22-23.

31 Bolt, Richard A. *The Human Interface: Where People and Computers Meet.* Belmont, CA: Lifetime Learning Publications, 1984.

32 Booher, Harold R. "Relative Comprehensibility of Pictorial Information and Printed Words in Proceduralized Instructions." *Human Factors,* 17 (3), 1975, pp. 266-277.

33 Bork, Alfred. "A Preliminary Taxonomy of Ways of Displaying Text on Screens." *Information Design Journal,* 3 (3), 1983, pp. 206–214.

34 Bouma, H. "Visual Reading Processes and The Quality of Text Displays." In *Ergonomic Aspects of Visual Display Terminals.* London: Taylor & Francis, 1980, pp. 101-114.

35 Bower, Bruce. "Average Attractions: Psychologists Break Down the Essence of Physical Beauty." *Science News.* May 12, 1990, pp. 298-299.

36 Bower, Gordon. "Mental Imagery and Associative Learning." In *Cognition in Learning and Memory.* New York: John Wiley, 1972, pp. 27-47.

37 Brady, Richard, J. Peter Kincaid, Paul Scott, et al. "Illustrated Formats to Teach Procedures." *IEEE Transactions on Professional Communication,* 25 (2), 1982, pp. 61-65.

38 Brand, Stewart. *The Media Lab: Inventing the Future at MIT.* New York: Viking, 1987.

39 Braz, Lisa M. "Visual Syntax Diagrams for Programming Language Statements." In *Proceedings of SIGDOC '90.* New York: Association for Computing Machinery, 1990, pp. 23-27.

40 Breen, Paul T., P. E. Miller-Jacobs, and Harold H. Miller-Jacobs. "Color Displays Applied to Command, Control, and Communication Systems." In *Color and the Computer.* Boston: Academic Press, 1987, pp. 171-187.

41 Briggs, J. and F. D. Peat. *Turbulent Mirror: An Illustrated Guide to Chaos Theory and the Science of Wholeness.* New York: Harper, 1989.

42 Briles, Susan M. and Henning P. Jacobshagen. "Improving Communications Between Artists and Writers." *Technical Communication,* 28 (4), 1979, pp. 12-14.

43 Bring, Robert C. and S. Gayle Wyman. "Developing Nonverbal Operating Instructions." In *Proceedings of the 32nd International Technical Communication Conference.* Arlington, VA: Society for Technical Communication, 1985, pp. VC 19-22.

44 Brockmann, R. John. *Writing Better Computer User Documentation: From Paper to Hypertext.* New York: John Wiley, 1990.

45 Brody, Philip J. "Affecting Instructional Textbooks Through Pictures." In *The Technology of Text: Principles for Structuring, Designing, and Displaying Text.* Englewood, NJ: Educational Technology Publications, 1982, pp. 301-316.

46 Broer, Jan W. "Integrating Text and Figures." In *Proceedings of the 25th International Technical Communication Conference.* Arlington, VA: Society for Technical Communication, 1978, pp. 36-40.

47 Brooke, J. and K. Duncan. "An Experimental Study of Flowcharts as an Aid to Identification of Procedural Faults." *Ergonomics,* 23 (4), 1980, pp. 387-399.

48 Bruner, Jerome. *On Knowing: Essays for the Left Hand.* Cambridge, MA: Harvard University, 1961.

49 Buck, J. R. "Visual Displays." In *Human Factors: Understanding People-System Relationships.* New York: John Wiley, 1983, pp. 99-136.

50 Buehler, Mary Fran. "Report Construction: Tables." *IEEE Transactions on Professional Communication,* PC-20 (1), 1977, pp. 29-32.

51 Buehler, Mary Fran. "Table Design—When the Writer/Editor Communicates Graphically." In *Proceedings of 27th International Technical Communication Conference.* Arlington, VA: Society for Technical Communication, 1980, pp. G 69-73.

52 Burnhill, P., J. Hartley, and Margrette Young. "Tables in Text." *Applied Ergonomics,* 7 (1), 1976, pp. 13-18.

53 Burns, Michael J. and Dianne L. Warren. "Formatting Space-Related Displays to Optimize Expert and Nonexpert User Performance." In *CHI'86 Proceedings.* New York: Association for Computing Machinery, 1986, pp. 274-280.

54 Burt, C. *A Psychological Study of Typography.* Cambridge, England: Cambridge University Press, 1959.

55 Cahill, M. "Designing Features of Graphic Symbols Varying in Interpretability." *Perceptual and Motor Skill*, 42, 1976, pp. 647-653.

56 Cahill, M. C. and R. C. Carter. "Color Code Size for Searching Displays of Different Density." *Human Factors*, 18 (3), 1976, pp. 273-280.

57 Campbell, Jeremy. *The Grammatical Man: Information, Entropy, Language, and Life.* New York: Simon & Schuster, 1982.

58 Carliner, Saul. "Lists: The Ultimate Organizer for Engineering Writing." *IEEE Transactions on Professional Communication*, PC 30 (4), 1987, p. 218.

59 Carroll, J. M. "Word Frequency and Age of Acquisition as Determiners of Picture Naming Latency." *Quarterly Journal of Experimental Psychology*, 25, 1973, pp. 85-95.

60 Carter, R. C. "Search Time with a Color Display: Analysis of Distribution Functions." *Human Factors*, 24, 1982, pp. 302-312.

61 Charland, Dennis A. "Online Documentation: Promises and Problems." In *Proceedings of 31st International Technical Communication Conference.* Arlington, VA: Society for Technical Communication, 1984, pp. WE 158-161.

62 Christ, R. E. "Review and Analysis of Color-Coding Research for Visual Displays." *Human Factors*, 17 (6), 1975, pp. 542-570.

63 Cleveland, W. S. and R. McGill. "Graphical Perception and Graphical Methods for Analyzing Scientific Data." *Science*, 229 (4716), 1985, pp. 828-833.

64 Cochran, Jeffery K., Sheri A. Albrecht, and Yvonne A. Green. "Guidelines for Evaluating Graphical Designs: A Framework Based on Human Perception Skills." *Technical Communication*, 36 (1), 1989, pp. 25-32.

65 Cohen, Gerald. "The Missing Half." In *Proceedings of the 29th International Technical Communication Conference.* Arlington, VA: Society for Technical Communication, 1982, pp. E 32-33.

66 Cohen, Gerald and Donald Cunningham. *Creating Technical Manuals: A Step-by-Step Approach to Writing User-Friendly Instructions.* New York: McGraw-Hill, 1984.

67 Cohen, Nancy E. "Online Documentation: Not the Only Solution." In *Proceedings of 34th International Technical Communication Conference.* Arlington, VA: Society for Technical Communication, 1987, pp. ATA 64-66.

68 Cooper, J. C. *An Illustrated Encyclopedia of Traditional Symbols.* London: Thames and Hudson, 1978.

69 Cornford, Christopher. "The Language of Painting." In *Understanding Art.* New York: Random House, 1981, pp. 94-135.

70 Cronbach, L. and R. Snow. *Aptitudes and Instructional Methods.* New York: Irvingon, 1976.

71 Dalton, Stephen. *Split Second: The World of High-Speed Photography.* Salem, NH: Salem House, 1983.

72 De Grandis, Luigina. *Theory and Use of Color.* New York: Abrams, 1986.

73 Debes, John L. and Clarence M. Williams. "The Power of Visuals." *Instructor*, 84, 1974, pp. 31-38.

74 Deregowski, Jan B. "Pictorial Perception and Culture." In *Image, Object, and Illusion.* San Francisco: W. H. Freeman and Company, 1974, pp. 79-85.

75 Dickey, G. L. and M. H. Schneider. "Multichannel Communication of an Industrial Task." *International Journal of Production Research*, 9, 1971, pp. 487-499.

76 Dondis, D. *A Primer of Visual Literacy.* Cambridge, MA: MIT Press, 1973.

77 Doss, Madge Conyers. "Keeping a Graphics Scrapbook." In *Proceedings of the 30th International Technical Communication Conference.* Arlington, VA: Society for Technical Communication, 1983, pp. G&P 7-9.

78 Douglis, Phil N. *Communicating with Pictures.* Chicago: Lawrence Ragan Communications, 1976.

79 Dreyfuss, Henry. *Symbol Sourcebook: An Authoritative Guide to International Graphic Symbols.* New York: Van Nostrand Reinhold, 1984.

80 Duffy, T., T. Curran, and D. Sass. "Document Design for Technical Job Tasks." *Human Factors*, 25 (2), 1983, pp. 143-160.

81 Dukes, Eva. "Table Construction: Do's and Don'ts." *IEEE Transactions on Professional Communication*, 32 (1), 1989, pp. 36-40.

82 Dunker, John. "Making and Selecting Photographs for Publication." In *Proceedings of the 36th International Technical Communication Conference.* Arlington, VA: Society for Technical Communication, 1989, pp. VC 42-44.

83 Durrett, H. John and D. Theron Stimmel. "Color and Instructional Use of the Computer." In *Color and the Computer.* Boston: Academic Press, 1987, pp. 241-253.

84 Dwyer, Francis M. *A Guide for Improving Visualized Instruction.* State College, PA: Learning Services, 1972.

85 Edwards, Betty. *Drawing on the Right Side of the Brain: A Course in Enhancing Creativity and Artistic Confidence.* Los Angeles: J. P. Tarcher, 1979.

86   Ehrenberg, A. S. C. "Rudiments of Numeracy." *Journal of the Royal Statistical Society,* 140, 1977, pp. 277-297.

87   Einstein, Albert. "Letter to Jacques Hadamard." In *The Creative Process.* New York: New American Library, 1952, pp. 43-44.

88   Engel, F. L. "Information Selection from Visual Display Units." In *Ergonomic Aspects of Visual Display Terminals.* London: Taylor & Francis, 1980, pp. 121-125.

89   Enrick, Norbert L. *Handbook of Effective Graphic and Tabular Communication.* Huntington, NY: Robert E. Kreiger, 1980.

90   Fantz, Robert L. "The Origin of Form Perception." In *Perception: Mechanisms and Models.* San Francisco: W. H. Freeman and Company, 1972, pp. 334-340.

91   Feininger, Andreas. *Total Picture Control.* New York: Chilton Books, 1970.

92   Filley, Richard D. "Opening the Door to Communication Through Graphics." *IEEE Transactions on Professional Communication,* PC-25 (2), 1982, pp. 91-94.

93   Finkelstein, J. "A Computer-Based Training Program for Describing an Advanced 32-Bit Microprocessor." In *Proceedings of 35th International Technical Communication Conference.* Arlington, VA: Society for Technical Communication, 1988, pp. ATA 20-23.

94   Fischler, Martin and Oscar Firschein. *Intelligence: the Eye, the Brain, and the Computer.* Reading, MA: Addison-Wesley, 1987.

95   Ford, Donald F. "Packaging Problem Prose." In *Proceedings of 31st International Technical Communication Conference.* Arlington, VA: Society for Technical Communication, 1984, pp. WE 52-55.

96   Frascara, Jorge. "Design Principles for Instructional Materials." In *Information Design: The Design and Evaluation of Signs and Printed Material.* New York: John Wiley & Sons, 1984, pp. 469-478.

97   Frutiger, Adrian. *Signs and Symbols: Their Design and Meaning.* New York: Van Nostrand Reinhold, 1989.

98   Frye, Robert H. "Artistic Technical Training." *IEEE Transactions on Professional Communication,* PC-24 (2), 1981, pp. 86-89.

99   Gaines, B. R. "The Technology of Interaction Dialogue Programming Rules." *International Journal of Man-Machine Studies,* 14, 1981, pp. 133-150.

100   Galitz, Wilbert O. *Handbook of Screen Format Design.* Wellesley, MA: QED Information Sciences, 1989.

101   Gange, Charles and Amy Lipton. "Word-Free Setup Instructions: Stepping into the World of Complex Products." *Technical Communication,* 31 (3), 1984, pp. 17-19.

102   Gates, Charlene. "Winning Contracts Graphically." In *Proceedings of the 30th International Technical Communication Conference.* Arlington, VA: Society for Technical Communication, 1983, pp. G&P 24-26.

103   Gatlin, Patricia L. "Visuals and Prose in Manuals: The Effective Combination." In *Proceedings of the 35th International Technical Communication Conference.* Arlington, VA: Society for Technical Communication, 1988, pp. RET 113-115.

104   Gerard, Robert. "Differential Effects of Colored Lights on Psychophysiological Functions." *American Psychology,* 13 (340), 1960, pp. 127-138.

105   Gesell, Arnold. "Infant Vision." *Scientific American,* 182 (2), 1950, pp. 20-22.

106   Gettys, Deborah. "IF You Write Documentation, THEN Try a Decision Table." *IEEE Transactions on Professional Communication,* PC 29 (4), 1986, pp. 61-64.

107   Gibson, James J. *The Perception of the Visual World.* Boston: Houghton Mifflin, 1950.

108   Gleason, James P. "Humor Can Improve Your Technical Presentations." *IEEE Transactions on Professional Communication,* PC-25 (2), 1982, pp. 86-90.

109   Glenn, John. "Can Flow Charts Be Overdone?" *Technical Communication,* 34 (3), 1987, p. 172.

110   Glinert, P. and L. Tanimoto. "Pict: An Interactive Graphical Programming Environment." *IEEE Computer,* 17 (11), 1984, pp. 47-59.

111   Gombrich, E. H. *Art and Illusion: A Study in the Psychology of Pictorial Representation.* Princeton: Princeton University Press, 1969.

112   Goodman, N. *Languages of Art: An Approach to a Theory of Symbols.* New York: Bobbs-Merrill, 1968.

113   Gould, J. "Why is Reading Slower from CRT Displays than From Paper?" In *Proceedings of the 30th Annual Meeting of the Human Factors Society.* Santa Monica, CA: Human Factors Society, 1986, pp. 834-835.

114   Gould, Steven J. *Wonderful Life: The Burgess Shale and the Nature of History.* New York: Norton, 1989.

115   Green, R. Dennis. "The Graphics Oriented (GO) Proposal Primer: Harnessing the Power of Data in Graphics." In *Proceedings of the 32nd International Technical Communication Conference.* Arlington, VA: Society for Technical Communication, 1985, pp. VC 30-33.

116   Gribbons, William M. "Visual Literacy in Corporate Communication: Some Implications for Information

Design." *IEEE Transactions on Professional Communication,* 34 (1), 1991, pp. 42-50.

117 Griffith, George W. "Formal Table Talk." In *Proceedings of the 27th International Technical Communication Conference.* Arlington, VA: Society for Technical Communication, 1980, pp. W 155-157.

118 Grimstead, Deborah. "Quality Graphics: Writers Draw the Line." In *Proceedings of the 34th International Technical Communication Conference.* Arlington, VA: Society for Technical Communication, 1987, pp. VC 66-69.

119 Grove, Laurel K. "Signs of the Times: Graphics for International Audiences." In *Proceedings of the International Professional Communication Conference.* New York: Institute for Electrical and Electronics Engineers, 1989, pp. 137-141.

120 Haber, Ralph N. "How We Remember What We See." *Scientific American,* 202 (5), 1970, pp. 105-115.

121 Haeusing, M. "Color Coding of Information on Electronic Displays." In *Proceedings of the Sixth Congress of the International Ergonomics Association.* International Ergonomics Association, 1976, pp. 210-217.

122 Hall, Edward T. *The Silent Language.* Garden City, NJ: Anchor Press, 1959.

123 Hand, James D. "Brain Functions During Learning: Implications for Text Design." In *The Technology of Text: Principles for Structuring, Designing, and Displaying Text.* Englewood, NJ: Educational Technology Publications, 1982, pp. 91-120.

124 Haney, Richard W. "The Effect of Instructional Format on Functional Testing Performance." *Human Factors,* 11 (2), 1969, pp. 181-188.

125 Hanks, Kurt and Larry Belliston. *Draw! A Visual Approach to Thinking, Learning, and Communicating.* Los Altos, CA: William Kaufmann, 1977.

126 Hardison, Stan. "The Fun of Drawing Funny." In *Proceedings of the 24th International Technical Communication Conference.* Arlington, VA: Society for Technical Communication, 1977, pp. 131-132.

127 Harmon, Leon D. "The Recognition of Faces." In *Image, Object, and Illusion.* San Francisco: W. H. Freeman and Company, 1974, pp. 100-112.

128 Harris, Ron. "Costs to Society: Dropout Not the Only One Who Pays." *Los Angeles Times,* 29 May 1989, Section I, p. 33.

129 Hart, Russ A. "The Psychological Basis of Iconic Messages: A Means of Developing a Visual Language and Effective Communication with TV and Film." In *Proceedings of the 25th International Technical Communication Conference.* Arlington, VA: Society for Technical Communication, 1978, pp. 171-176.

130 Hartshorn, Roy W. "Writing for International Markets." In *Proceedings of the 37th Technical Writers Institute.* Troy, NY: Rensselaer Polytechnic Institute, 1989, pp. 129-135.

131 Haverill, Lawrence R. and Thomas L. Kraft. *Technical Report Standards: How to Prepare and Write Technical Reports.* Rockville, MD: Banner Books, 1977.

132 Heines, Jesse M. *Screen Design Strategies for Computer-Assisted Instruction.* Bedford, MA: Digital Press, 1984.

133 Helander, Martin G., Patricia A. Billingsley, and Jayne M. Schurick. "An Evaluation of Human Factors Research on Visual Display Terminals in the Workplace." In *Human Factors Review.* Santa Monica, CA: Human Factors Society, 1984, pp. 55-129.

134 Hemenway, K. "Psychological Issues in the Use of Icons in Command Menus." In *Proceedings on Human Factors in Computer Systems.* New York: Association for Computing Machinery, 1982, pp. 20-25.

135 Henderson, Allan and Annette Bradford. "Online Information: A Practical Approach." In *Proceedings of 31st International Technical Communication Conference.* Arlington, VA: Society for Technical Communication, 1984, pp. WE 154-157.

136 Henno, J. "User-Friendly Syntax: Design and Presentation." *International Journal of Man-Machine Studies,* 28 (5), 1987, pp. 551-572.

137 Hester, Mary C., Jacquelyn L. Monday, and John I. Snead. "Documenting Illustrations." *Technical Communication,* 36 (2), 1989, pp. 102-113.

138 Hill, Mary and Wendell Cochran. *Into Print: A Practical Guide to Writing, Illustrating, and Publishing.* Los Altos, CA: William Kaufmann, Inc., 1977.

139 Hodgkinson, Richard and John Hughes. "Developing Wordless Instructions: A Case Study." *IEEE Transactions on Professional Communication,* PC-25 (2), 1982, pp. 74-79.

140 Holdaway, Jill. "Developing Manuals in the Age of Visual Communication." In *Proceedings of the 37th International Technical Communication Conference.* Arlington, VA: Society for Technical Communication, 1990, pp. VC 7-9.

141 Holmes, Nigel. *Designer's Guide to Creating Charts and Diagrams.* New York: Watson-Guptill, 1984.

142 Horton, William. "Toward the Four-Dimensional Page." In *Proceedings of 30th International Technical Communication Conference.* Arlington, VA: Society for Technical Communication, 1983, pp. RET 83-86.

143 Hudelson, Donna J. "Avoiding Sexism in Illustrations and in Their Interaction with Text." In

Proceedings of the 27th International Technical Communication Conference. Arlington, VA: Society for Technical Communication, 1980, pp. W 189-192.

144 Huff, Darrel. *How to Lie with Statistics.* New York: W. W. Norton & Company, 1954.

145 Human Factors Society. *American National Standard for Human Factors Engineering of Visual Display Terminal Workstations* (ANSI/HFS 100-1988). Human Factors Society, 1988.

146 Idestein, P. "Underlining Versus Repetitive Reading." *Journal of Educational Research,* 65 (7), 1972, pp. 321-323.

147 International Association of Business Communicators. *Without Bias: A Guidebook for Nondiscriminatory Communication.* San Francisco: IABC, 1977.

148 Itten, Joseph. *The Elements of Color.* New York: Van Nostrand Reinhold, 1970.

149 Jarvenpaa, Sirkka L. and Gary W. Dickson. "Graphics and Managerial Decision Making: Research Based Guidelines." *Communications of the ACM,* 31 (6), 1988, pp. 764-774.

150 Jaxtheimer, Bodo W. *How to Paint and Draw.* New York: Weathervane Books, 1962.

151 Jong, Steven. "The Challenge of Hypertext." In *Proceedings of 35th International Technical Communication Conference.* Arlington, VA: Society for Technical Communication, 1988, pp. ATA 30-32.

152 Kantowitz, Barry H. and Robert D. Sorkin. "Vision." In *Human Factors: Understanding People-System Relationships.* New York: John Wiley, 1983, pp. 99-136.

153 Kat, A. and J. L. Knight. "Speed of Reading in a Single Column Versus Double Column Type." *Science News,* 118 (9), 1980, p. 296.

154 Kaufman, Lloyd. *Perception: The World Transformed.* New York: Oxford University Press, 1979.

155 Kent, Thomas. "Rhetoric and Visual Design: Translating Principles of Cognitive Psychology into Design Guidelines." In *Proceedings of the 37th International Technical Communication Conference.* Arlington, VA: Society for Technical Communication, 1990, pp. ET 128-130.

156 Kessel, C. J. and C. D. Wickens. "The Transfer of Failure-Detection Skills Between Monitoring and Controlling Dynamic Systems." *Human Factors,* 24 1982, pp. 46-60.

157 Keyes, Elizabeth. "Visual Literacy for Effective Business Communication." In *Proceedings of the 37th International Technical Communication Conference.* Arlington, VA: Society for Technical Communication, 1990, pp. VC 2-4.

158 Kittendorf, Dorothy Krueger. "The Cartoon as Technical Communication." In *Proceedings of the 28th International Technical Communication Conference.* Arlington, VA: Society for Technical Communication, 1981, pp. G 11-13.

159 Klimowsky, Brian Frederick. "Setting Up a Photographer to Do a Good Job." In *Proceedings of the 26th International Technical Communication Conference.* Arlington, VA: Society for Technical Communication, 1979, pp. V 52-56.

160 Knapp, Beverly G., Franklin Moses, and Leon H. Gellman. "Information Hiding in Complex Displays." In *Directions in Human/Computer Interaction.* Norwood, NJ: Ablex Publishing, 1982, pp. 95–215.

161 Knecht, Thomas W. "The Editing of Tables." In *Proceedings of the 13th Practical Conference on Communication.* Oak Ridge, TN: East Tennessee Chapter, Society for Technical Communication, 1989, pp. 117-122.

162 Kodak. *Basic Scientific Photography.* Rochester, NY: Eastman Kodak Company, 1977.

163 Kodak. *Close-Up Photography and Photomacrography.* Rochester, NY: Eastman Kodak Company, 1977.

164 Kolers, P. A., R. L. Duchinicky, and D. C. Ferguson. "Eye Movement Measurement of Readability of CRT Displays." *Human Factors,* 23, 1981, pp. 517-527.

165 Kopala, C. J. "The Use of Color Coded Symbols in a Highly Dense Situation Display." In *Proceedings of the Human Factors Society—23rd Annual Meeting.* Santa Monica, CA: Human Factors Society, 1981, pp. 736-740.

166 Kosslyn, Stephen Michael. *Ghosts in the Mind's Machine: Creating and Using Images in the Brain.* New York: W. W. Norton & Company, 1983.

167 Kostelnick, Charles. "Designing for Readability: An Index for Evaluating the Visual Language of Technical Documents." In *Proceedings of the 35th International Technical Communication Conference.* Arlington, VA: Society for Technical Communication, 1988, pp. VC 44-47.

168 Krause, Carolyn. "Photo Finish: Making and Selecting Winning Photographs for Publication." In *Proceedings of the 13th Practical Conference on Communication.* Knoxville, TN: East Tennessee Chapter, Society for Technical Communication, 1989, pp. 1-9.

169 Krebs, M. J., J. D. Wolf, and J. H. Sandvig. *Color Display Design Guide* (ONR-CR213-136-2F). Minneapolis: Honeywell Systems and Research Center, 1978.

170 Kruk, R. S. and P. Muter. "Reading Continuous Text on Television Screens." *Human Factors*, 26 (3), 1984, pp. 339-345.

171 Krull, Robert. "Communicative Functions of Icons as Computer Commands." In *Proceedings of the IEEE Professional Communication Society*. New York: Institute for Electrical and Electronics Engineers, 1985, pp. 207-210.

172 Krull, Robert. "If Icon, Why Can't You?" In *Effective Documentation: What We Have Learned from Usability Research*. Cambridge, MA: MIT Press, 1988, pp. 255-273.

173 Krull, Robert. "Task-Oriented Communication: Providing Information about Physical Performance." In *Proceedings of the 38th Technical Writers' Institute*. Troy, NY: Rensselaer Polytechnic Institute, 1990, pp. 55-69.

174 Lalomia, Mary J. and Alan J. Happ. "The Effective Use of Color for Text on the IBM 5153 Color Display." In *Proceedings of the Human Factors Society*. Santa Monica, CA: Human Factors Society, 1987, pp. 1091-1095.

175 Land, Edwin H. "Experiments in Color Vision." In *Perception: Mechanisms and Models*. San Francisco: W. H. Freeman and Company, 1972, pp. 286-298.

176 Landau, Terry. *About Faces: The Evolution of the Human Face*. New York: Anchor Books, 1989.

177 Laner, Frances J. "Readability Techniques for Authors and Editors." In *Directions in Technical Writing*. Farmingdale, NY: Baywood Publishing, 1978, pp. 117-129.

178 Larkin, J. H. and H. A. Simon. "Why a Diagram is (Sometimes) Worth Ten Thousand Words." *Cognitive Science*, 11, 1987, pp. 65-99.

179 Lazzari, Margaret R. and Clayton Lee. *Art and Design Fundamentals: A Text for Cultural Production*. New York: Van Nostrand Reinhold, 1990.

180 Lefferts, Robert. *How to Prepare Charts and Graphs for Effective Reports*. New York: Barns & Noble, 1982.

181 Levy, W. Howard and Richard Lentz. "Effects of Text Illustrations: A Review of Research." *Educational Communication and Technology Journal*, 30, 1982, pp. 195-232.

182 Lew, A. "In the Emulation of Flowcharts by Decision Tables." *Communications of the ACM*, 25 (12), 1982, pp. 895-905.

183 Little, Raymond and Michael Smith. "Improving FOMM Troubleshooting." *Technical Communication*, 30 (1), 1983, pp. 20-23.

184 Littman, D. and T. Moran. "Automating Connectivity." *MacWorld*, January 1990, p. 135.

185 Lockard, William Kirby. *Drawings as a Means to Architecture*. New York: Van Nostrand Reinhold, 1971.

186 Los Angeles Times News Service. "Nearly 1 Billion Adults are Illiterate." *Los Angeles Times*, 7 December 1989, Section F, p. 1.

187 Luria, S. M. and David F. Neri. "The Effects of Set Size on Color Matching Using CRT Displays." In *Proceedings of the Human Factors Society*. Santa Monica, CA: Human Factors Society, 1986, pp. 49-61.

188 Luther, Arch C. "You Are There ... And in Control." *IEEE Spectrum*. September 1988, pp. 45-50.

189 Macaulay, David. *The Way Things Work*. Boston: Houghton Mifflin, 1988.

190 Macindoe, C. Scott. "An Assessment of Functionally Oriented Maintenance Manuals (FOMMS)." *Technical Communication*, 32 (3), 1985, pp. 7-11.

191 Mailey, Thomas F. "The Psychology of Visual Perception: Is Cueing Important in Concept Formation?" In *Proceedings of the 26th International Technical Communication Conference*. Arlington, VA: Society for Technical Communication, 1979, pp. V 62-64.

192 Mann, Gerald A. "How to Present Tabular Information Badly." In *Proceedings of 31st International Technical Communication Conference*. Arlington, VA: Society for Technical Communication, 1984, pp. WE 48-51.

193 Marcel, T. and P. Barnard. "Paragraphs of Pictographs: The Use of Nonverbal Instructions for Equipment." In *Processing of Visible Language*. New York: Plenum, 1979, pp. 510-523.

194 Marcus, Aaron. "Sign Language: Graphic Designers Try to Break the Language Barrier with Icons." *Unix World—International Supplement*, May 1991, pp. 63-67.

195 Martin, James. *Design of Man-Computer Dialogues*. Englewood Cliffs: Prentice Hall, 1973.

196 Martin, James and Carma McClure. *Diagramming Techniques for Analysts and Programmers*. Englewood Cliffs, NJ: Prentice Hall, 1984.

197 Martin, Marilyn. "Visual Development of Documents." In *Proceedings of the 35th International Technical Communication Conference*. Arlington, VA: Society for Technical Communication, 1988, pp. VC 48-50.

198 Martin, Marilyn. "The Visual Hierarchy of Documents." In *Proceedings of the 36th International Technical Communication Conference*. Arlington, VA: Society for Technical Communication, 1989, pp. VC 32-34.

199   Mascelli, Joseph V. *The Five C's of Cinematography.* Hollywood: Cine/Grafic Publications, 1965.

200   Mattingly, William A. and Marilyn Whitesell. "Comprehending Complex Patterns of Information Using Visual Techniques." In *Proceedings of the 32nd International Technical Communication Conference.* Arlington, VA: Society for Technical Communication, 1985, pp. VC 34-37.

201   Mays, Lonne Lee. "How to Write a Technician's Level New Look Maintenance Manual." In *Proceedings of the 29th International Technical Communication Conference.* Arlington, VA: Society for Technical Communication, 1982, pp. W 78-81.

202   Mazzatenta, Louis. "Getting the Picture at *National Geographic.*" *Technical Communication,* 24 (2), 1977, pp. 9-10.

203   McGee, Brad. *Documenting Software.* Cincinnati, OH: Writer's Digest Books, 1984.

204   McKee, John B. "Computer User Manuals in Print: Do They Have a Future?" In *Proceedings of SIGDOC'85.* New York: Association for Computing Machinery, 1985, pp. 11-16.

205   McKellar, P. "The Investigation of Mental Images." In *Penguin Science Survey.* London: Penguin, 1965, pp. 199-217.

206   McKim, Robert H. *Thinking Visually: A Strategy Manual for Problem Solving.* Belmont, CA: Lifetime Learning Publications, 1980.

207   McLuhan, Marshall. *Understanding Media: The Extensions of Man.* New York: McGraw-Hill, 1964.

208   Merrill, Paul F. "Structured Outline Representations for Procedures or Algorithms." In *The Technology of Text: Principles for Structuring, Designing, and Displaying Text.* Englewood, NJ: Educational Technology Publications, 1982, pp. 233-251.

209   Meyer, Benjamin. "The ABCs of New-look Publications." *Technical Communication,* 33 (1), 1986, pp. 16-20.

210   Miller, George A. "Information and Memory." In *Perception, Mechanisms and Models.* San Francisco: W. H. Freeman and Company, 1972, pp. 17-21.

211   Miller, Ralph and Edward Read. "Developing Illustrations for Technical Manuals from a Writer's Viewpoint." *Technical Communication,* 26 (2), 1979, pp. 4-9.

212   Miller, Wendy. "The Technical Writer's Role in On-Line Documentation." In *Proceedings of 33rd International Technical Communication Conference.* Arlington, VA: Society for Technical Communication, 1986, pp. 61-64.

213   Modley, Rudolf. *Handbook of Pictorial Symbols.* New York: Dover, 1976.

214   Moret, B. "Decision Trees and Diagrams." *Computing Surveys,* 14 (4), 1982, pp. 593-623.

215   Morris, Desmond. *Manwatching: A Field Guide to Human Behavior.* New York: Harry N. Abrams, 1977.

216   Morrison, Claire and William Jimmerson. "Business Presentations for the 1990s." *Video Manager,* 4, 1989, p. 18.

217   Muir, John. *How to Keep Your Volkswagen Alive: A Manual of Step by Step Procedures for the Compleat Idiot.* Santa Fe, NM: John Muir, 1990.

218   Murch, Gerald. "Color Displays and Color Science." In *Color and the Computer.* Boston: Academic Press, 1987, pp. 1-25.

219   Muse, Ken. *The Secrets of Professional Cartooning.* Englewood Cliffs, NJ: Prentice Hall, 1981.

220   Nakanishi, Akira. *Writing Systems of the World: Alphabets, Syllabaries, Pictograms.* Rutland, VT: Charles E. Tuttle Company, 1980.

221   Nassi, I. and Ben Shneiderman. "Flowchart Techniques for Structured Programming." *ACM SIGPLAN Notices,* 8 (8), 1973, pp. 12-26.

222   Neisser, Ulric. "The Processes of Vision." In *Perception: Mechanisms and Models.* San Francisco: W. H. Freeman and Company, 1972, pp. 252-259.

223   Nelms, Henning. *Thinking with a Pencil.* Berkeley, CA: Ten Speed Press, 1981.

224   Neurath, Marie. "Isotype: Education Through the Eye." In *Symbol Sourcebook: An Authoritative Guide to International Graphic Symbols.* New York: Van Nostrand Reinhold, 1984, pp. 24-25.

225   Neurath, Marie and Robert S. Cohen, eds. *Otto Neurath: Empiricism and Sociology.* Boston: D. Reidel Publishing, 1973.

226   Nickerson, R. S. "Short-Term Retention of Visually Presented Stimuli: Some Evidence of Visual Encoding." *Acta Psychologica,* 40 (2), 1976, pp. 153-162.

227   Noake, Roger. *Animation Techniques.* Seacaucus, NJ: Chartwell, 1988.

228   Noton, David and Lawrence Stark. "Eye Movements and Visual Perception." In *Image, Object, and Illusion.* San Francisco: W. H. Freeman and Company, 1974, pp. 113-122.

229   O'Neill, J. O. "Prodigal Genius: The Life of Nikola Tesla." In *Experience in Visual Thinking.* Monterey, CA: Brooks/Cole, 1972, p. 8.

230   Ogilvy, David. *Ogilvy on Advertising.* New York: Vintage Books, 1985.

231   Olsen, Gary R. "Eideteker: The Professional Communicator in the New Visual Culture." *IEEE*

Transactions on Professional Communication, 34 (1), 1991, pp. 13-19.

232 Oren, Tim. "The Architecture of Static Hypertexts." In *Hypertext'87 Papers*. Chapel Hill, NC: University of North Carolina, 1987, pp. 291-306.

233 Osborne, D. J. *Computers at Work: A Behavioral Approach*. New York: John Wiley & Sons, 1985.

234 Ota, Yukio. "LoCos." *Graphic Design*, June 1971, pp. 90-101.

235 Paivio, Allan. *Imagery and Verbal Processes*. New York: Holt, Rinehart, and Winston, 1971.

236 Paivio, Allan. "Mental Imagery in Associative Learning and Memory." *Psychological Review*, 76, 1969, pp. 241-263.

237 Pegg, Barry M. "Diesel Print and Turbo Visuals or Text as Image, Image as Text." In *Proceedings of the 33rd International Technical Communication Conference*. Arlington, VA: Society for Technical Communication, 1986, pp. VC 38-40.

238 Pegg, Barry M. "Technical Writing Means the Visual Display of Organization." In *Proceedings of the 32nd International Technical Communication Conference*. Arlington, VA: Society for Technical Communication, 1985, pp. VC 38-40.

239 Pegg, Barry M. "Visual Organization of Text— Breaking the String." In *Proceedings of the 30th International Technical Communication Conference*. Arlington, VA: Society for Technical Communication, 1983, pp. G&P 43-44.

240 Perkins, D. N. "Pictures and the Real Thing." In *Processing of Visual Language*. New York: Plenum, 1980, pp. 259-278.

241 Peterson, W. Wesley. "Icons Set Computer Science Back 4,000 Years." *IEEE Computer*, 21 (12), 1988, p. 75.

242 Piaget, J. and B Inhelder. *Mental Imagery and the Child*. New York: Holt, Rinehart, and Winston, 1971.

243 Pinelli, Thomas E., Virginia M. Cordle, Myron Glassman, et al. "Report Format Preferences of Technical Managers and Nonmanagers." *Technical Communication*, 31 (2), 1984, pp. 4-8.

244 Pinelli, Thomas E., Virginia M. Cordle, and Robert McCullough. "A Survey of Typography, Graphic Design, and Physical Media in Technical Reports." *Technical Communication*, 33 (2), 1986, pp. 75-80.

245 Plotnik, Arthur. *The Elements of Editing: A Modern Guide for Editors and Journalists*. New York: MacMillan, 1982.

246 Plunka, Gene A. "The Editor's Nightmare: Formatting Lists Within the Text." *Technical Communication*, 35 (1), 1988, pp. 37-44.

247 Polya, G. *How to Solve It: A New Aspect of Mathematical Method*. Princeton, NJ: Princeton University Press, 1988.

248 Pomerantz, J. R. and S. D. Schwaitzberg. "Grouping by Proximity: Selective Attention Measures." *Perception and Psychophysics*, 18, 1975, pp. 355-361.

249 Potosnak, Kathleen. "Do Icons Make User Interfaces Easier to Use?" *IEEE Software*, May 1988, pp. 97-99.

250 Price, Jonathan. "Creating a Style for Online Help." In *Text, ConText, and HyperText: Writing with and for the Computer*. Cambridge, MA: The MIT Press, 1988, pp. 330–341.

251 Quiepo, Larry. "User Expectations of Online Information." *IEEE Transactions on Professional Communication*, PC-29 (4), 1986, pp. 11-15.

252 Radl, R. W. "Experimental Investigations for Optimal Presentation-Mode and Colours of Symbols on the CRT-Screen." In *Ergonomic Aspects of Visual Display Terminals*. London: Taylor & Francis, 1980, pp. 137-142.

253 Rakyta, Charlene A. "The Technical Manual— Charting a Course for the User." In *Proceedings of the 29th International Technical Communication Conference*. Arlington, VA: Society for Technical Communication, 1982, pp. W 91-94.

254 Ramsey, Richard David. "Audience Reactions to Two Visual Formats." In *Proceedings of the 30th International Technical Communication Conference*. Arlington, VA: Society for Technical Communication, 1983, pp. G&P 39-42.

255 Raven, Mary Elizabeth. "A Survey of Diagrams in CAD Documentation." *IEEE Transactions on Professional Communication*, 32 (3), 1989, pp. 200-204.

256 Redish, Janice C. "Integrating Art and Text." In *Proceedings of the 34th International Technical Communication Conference*. Arlington, VA: Society for Technical Communication, 1987, pp. VC 4-7.

257 Reid, S. "Toward a Grammar of the Image." *Psychological Bulletin*, 81, 1974, pp. 319-333.

258 Reising, John M. and Anthony J. Aretz. "Color Computer Graphics in Military Cockpits." In *Color and the Computer*. Boston: Academic Press, 1987, pp. 151-169.

259 Robertson, Bruce. *How to Draw Charts and Diagrams*. Cincinnati, OH: North Light Books, 1988.

260 Rock, Irvin. "The Perception of Disoriented Figures." In *Image, Object, and Illusion*. San Francisco: W. H. Freeman and Company, 1974, pp. 71-78.

261 Rock, Irvin and Charles Harris. "Vision and Touch." In *Perception, Mechanisms and Models*. San Francisco: W. H. Freeman and Company, 1972, pp. 269-277.

262   Rockmann, John. *Lessons that Work*. New York: Dell Publishing, 1962.

263   Rogers, Yvonne. "Evaluating the Meaningfulness of Icon Sets to Represent Command Operations." In *People and Computers: Designing for Usability*. Cambridge, England: Cambridge University Press, 1986, pp. 586-603.

264   Rohr, G. "Understanding Visual Symbols." In *Proceedings of IEEE Computer Workshop on Visual Languages*. New York: Institute for Electrical and Electronics Engineers, 1984, pp. 184-191.

265   Rosenstiel, Thomas B. "Newspaper Rivals Taking Ad Revenues." *Los Angeles Times*, 27 April 1989, Part IV, pp. 1, 5.

266   Rubens, Philip. "Creating Useable Information Displays to Support Tasks." In *Proceedings of the 38th Technical Writers' Institute*. Troy, NY: Rensselaer Polytechnic Institute, 1990, pp. 43-53.

267   Rubens, Philip. "Online Information, Hypermedia, and the Idea of Literacy." In *Hypertext, Hypermedia, and the Social Construction of Information*. Cambridge, MA: MIT Press, 1989, pp. 3-21.

268   Rubens, Philip. "A Reader's View of Text and Graphics." *Journal of Technical Writing and Communication*, 16, 1986, pp. 73-86.

269   Rubenstein, Richard. *Digital Typography: An Introduction to Type and Composition for Computer System Design*. Reading, MA: Addison-Wesley, 1988.

270   Rude, Carolyn D. "Format and Typography in Complex Instructions." In *Proceedings of the 32nd International Technical Communication Conference*. Arlington, VA: Society for Technical Communication, 1985, pp. RET 36-38.

271   Russell, Peter. *The Brain Book*. New York: E. P. Dutton, 1979.

272   Sadowski, Mary A. "Elements of Composition." *Technical Communication*, 34 (1), 1987, pp. 29-30.

273   Salomon, G. *Interaction of Media, Cognition, and Learning*. San Francisco: Jossey Bass, 1979.

274   Salomon, Gitta. "New Uses for Color." In *The Art of Human-Computer Interface Design*. Reading, MA: Addison-Wesley, 1990, pp. 269-278.

275   Schmandt, Christopher. "Color Text Display in Video Media." In *Color and the Computer*. Boston: Academic Press, 1987, pp. 255-266.

276   Schmid, Calvin F. and Stanton E. Schmid. *Handbook of Graphic Presentation*. New York: John Wiley & Sons, 1979.

277   Search, Patricia. "Structural Design: Movement in Art." In *Proceedings of the 37th International Technical Communication Conference*. Arlington, VA: Society for Technical Communication, 1990, pp. VC 18-20.

278   Semple, Marlene C. "The Electronic Blue Pencil: Editing Online Information." In *Proceedings of 34th International Technical Communication Conference*. Arlington, VA: Society for Technical Communication, 1987, pp. ATA 140-142.

279   Sewell, E. H. and R. I. Moore. "Cartoon Embellishments in Informative Presentations." *Educational Communication and Technology Journal*, 28, 1980, pp. 39-46.

280   Shapiro, Linda and Steve Rubin. "The Audiovisual Capabilities of Computers." *Technical Communication*, 35 (1), 1988, pp. 16-22.

281   Shelton, S. M. "The Eyes Have It." *Technical Communication*, 38 (2), 1991, pp. 168-177.

282   Shneiderman, Ben. "Control Flow and Data Structure Documentation: Two Experiments." *Communications of the ACM*, 25 (1), 1982, pp. 55-63.

283   Shneiderman, Ben. *Designing the User Interface: Strategies for Effective Human Computer Interaction*. Reading, MA: Addison-Wesley, 1987.

284   Shneiderman, Ben, R. Mayer, D. McKay, et al. "Experimental Investigations of the Utility of Detailed Flowcharts in Programming." *Communications of the ACM*, 20, 1977, pp. 373-381.

285   Shorper, Steven. "Pump and Circumstance." *Social Studies of Science*, 14, 1984, pp. 492-493.

286   Shurtleff, D. A. "How to Make Displays Legible." *Contemporary Psychology*, 27 (1), 1982, p. 46.

287   Silverstein, Ann Parker. "Working with Images: Applying Writing Principles to Photography." In *Proceedings of the 29th International Technical Communication Conference*. Arlington, VA: Society for Technical Communication, 1982, pp. G 53-56.

288   Silverstein, Louis D. "Human Factors for Color Display Systems: Concepts, Methods, and Research." In *Color and the Computer*. Boston: Academic Press, 1987, pp. 27-61.

289   Simon, H. A. *The Sciences of the Artificial*. Cambridge, MA: MIT Press, 1981.

290   Smith, Sandra B. "Space, Time, and Color." In *Proceedings of the 36th International Technical Communication Conference*. Arlington, VA: Society for Technical Communication, 1989, pp. VC 12-15.

291   Smith, Wanda. "Ergonomic Vision." In *Color and the Computer*. Boston: Academic Press, 1987, pp. 101-113.

292   Snyder, H. L. and G. B. Taylor. "The Sensitivity of Response Measures of Alphanumeric Legibility to Variations in Dot Matrix Display Parameters." *Human Factors*, 21, 1979, pp. 457-471.

293   Soderston, Candace. "An Evaluative and Prescriptive Look at Graphics Research." In

Proceedings of the 30th International Technical Communication Conference. Arlington, VA: Society for Technical Communication, 1983, pp. RET 87-90.

294 Solomon, Charles. "The Comic Book Grows Up." *Los Angeles Times,* 16 April 1989, Calendar Section, pp. 6-7.

295 Spielman, Howard A. "Color and Business Graphics." In *Color and the Computer.* Boston: Academic Press, 1987, pp. 267-284.

296 Standing, Lionel. "Learning 10,000 Pictures." *Quarterly Journal of Experimental Psychology,* 25 (2), 1973, pp. 207-222.

297 Steichen, Edward. *A Life in Photography.* New York: Bonanza Books, 1985.

298 Steinbeck, John. *The Log from the Sea of Cortez.* New York: Penguin Books, 1976.

299 Stermer, Dugald. "A Desert Island Question Concerning Type." *Communication Arts,* September/October 1983, pp. 84-85.

300 Stern, Kenneth R. "An Evaluation of Written, Graphics, and Voice Messages in Proceduralized Instructions." In *Proceedings of the Human Factors Society.* Santa Monica, CA: Human Factors Society, 1984, pp. 314-318.

301 Stockton, James, ed. *Designer's Guide to Color.* San Francisco: Chronicle, 1984.

302 Strawhorn, J. M., E. C. Fake, and B. D. Huybrects. *Improving the Dissemination of Scientific and Technical Information: A Practitioner's Guide.* Rockville, MD: Capitol Systems Group, 1978.

303 Sullivan, Patricia. "Teaching Writers to Create Visual Texts." In *Proceedings of the 35th International Technical Communication Conference.* Arlington, VA: Society for Technical Communication, 1988, pp. RET 127-129.

304 Sussman, David. "Composing Photographs for Technical Journals." *IEEE Transactions on Professional Communication,* PC-28 (1), 1985, pp. 3-12.

305 Taylor, Joann M. and Gerald M. Murch. "The Effective Use of Color in Computer Graphics Applications." 1986, pp. 515-521.

306 Tedford, W. H., S. L. Berquist, and W. E. Flynn. "The Size-Color Illusion." *Journal of General Psychology,* 97 (1), 1977, pp. 145-149.

307 Theodos, Roger D. "White Space: Planning for the Affective Response." In *Proceedings of the 36th International Technical Communication Conference.* Arlington, VA: Society for Technical Communication, 1989, pp. VC 28-31.

308 Thomas, Frank and Ollie Johnson. *Disney Animation: Illusion of Life.* New York: Abbeville Press, 1981.

309 Thorell, Lisa G. and Wanda J. Smith. *Using Computer Color Effectively: An Illustrated Reference.* Englewood Cliffs, NJ: Prentice Hall, 1990.

310 Tinker, Miles A. *Bases for Effective Reading.* Minneapolis: University of Minnesota Press, 1965.

311 Tinker, Miles A. *Legibility of Print.* Ames, IA: Iowa State Univeristy Press, 1963.

312 Trimble, John. "Cartoons Can Add Punch to Your Technical Manual." *Technical Communication,* 23 (1), 1976, pp. 10-11.

313 Trollip, S. and G. Sales. "Readability of Computer-Generated Fill-Justified Text." *Human Factors,* 28, 1986, pp. 159-164.

314 Tufte, Edward R. *Envisioning Information.* Cheshire, CT: Graphics Press, 1990.

315 Tufte, Edward R. *The Visual Display of Quantitative Information.* Cheshire, CT: Graphics Press, 1983.

316 Tullis, Thomas. "An Evaluation of Alphanumeric, Graphic, and Color Information Displays." *Human Factors,* 23, 1981, pp. 541-50.

317 Twyman, M. "Using Pictorial Language: A Discussion of the Dimensions of the Problem." In *Designing Usable Texts.* New York: Academic Press, 1985, pp. 123-149.

318 Van Dam, Andries. "Hypertext'87 Keynote Address." *Communications of the ACM,* 31 (7), 1988, pp. 887-895.

319 Van Nes, F. "Space, Color, and Typography on Visual Display Terminals." *Behaviour and Information Technology,* 5 (2), 1986, pp. 99-118.

320 Vaughn, Frank. "Color WYSIWYG Comes of Age." *Byte,* December 1990, pp. 275-279.

321 Vogt, Herbert E. "Graphic Ways to Eliminate Problems Associated with Translating Technical Documentation." In *Proceedings of the 33rd International Technical Communication Conference.* Arlington, VA: Society for Technical Communication, 1986, pp. 330-333.

322 Vogt, Herbert E. "Wordless Instructions—Say It with Pictures." In *Proceedings of the 31st International Technical Communication Conference.* Arlington, VA: Society for Technical Communication, 1984, pp. VC 23-26.

323 Waite, Robert. "Making Information Easy to Use: A Summary of Research." In *Proceedings of the 29th International Technical Communication Conference.* Arlington, VA: Society for Technical Communication, 1982, pp. E 120-123.

324 Wald, George. "Eye and Camera." In *Perception: Mechanisms and Models.* San Francisco: W. H. Freeman and Company, 1972, pp. 94-103.

325   Walker, R. E., R. C. Nocolay, and C. R. Stearns. "Comparative Accuracy of Recognizing American and International Road Signs." *Journal of Applied Psychology*, 49, 1965, pp. 322-325.

326   Wallach, Hans. "The Perception of Neutral Colors." In *Image, Object, and Illusion*. San Francisco: W. H. Freeman and Company, 1974, pp. 28-35.

327   Waller, Robert. "Text as Diagram: Using Typography to Improve Access and Understanding." In *The Technology of Text: Principles for Structuring, Designing, and Displaying Text*. Englewood, NJ: Educational Technology Publications, 1982, pp. 137-166.

328   Watson, J. D. *The Double Helix*. New York: Atheneum, 1968.

329   Weadon, Mark P. "Visualization in the Technical Writing Classroom." In *Proceedings of the 35th International Technical Communication Conference*. Arlington, VA: Society for Technical Communication, 1988, pp. RET 124-126.

330   Weiss, Edmond H. *How to Write a Usable User Manual*. Philadelphia: ISI Press, 1985.

331   Welford, A. T. "Theory and Application in Visual Displays." In *Information Design: The Design and Evaluation of Signs and Printed Material*. New York: John Wiley & Sons, 1984, pp. 3-18.

332   Wheildon, Colin. *Communicating or Just Making Pretty Shapes: A Study of the Validity—or Otherwise—of Some Elements of Typographic Deisgn*. North Sydney, Australia: Newspaper Advertising Bureau of Australia, 1986.

333   White, Jan V. *Color for the Electronic Age*. New York: Watson–Guptill, 1990.

334   White, Jan V. *Editing by Design: Word-and-Picture Communication for Editors and Designers*. New York: R. R. Bowker, 1974.

335   White, Jan V. *Graphic Design for the Electronic Age*. New York: Watson-Guptill, 1988.

336   Whitney, Margaret A. "Toward a Cognitive Theory of Visual Processing." In *Proceedings of the 35th International Technical Communication Conference*. Arlington, VA: Society for Technical Communication, 1988, pp. VC 15-18.

337   Williges, Beverly H. and Robert C. Williges. "Dialogue Design Considerations for Interactive Computer Systems." In *Human Factors Review*. Santa Monica, CA: The Human Factors Society, 1984, pp. 167-208.

338   Wingfield, A. "Effects of Frequency on Identification and Naming of Objects." *American Journal of Psychology*, 81, 1968, pp. 226-234.

339   Winn, William. "Encoding and Retrieval of Information in Maps and Diagrams." *IEEE Transactions on Professional Communication*, 33 (3), 1990, pp. 103-107.

340   Winn, William. "The Role of Graphics in Training Documents: Toward and Explanatory Theory of How They Communicate." *IEEE Transactions on Professional Communication*, 32 (4), 1989, pp. 300-309.

341   Winn, William and William Holiday. "Design Principles for Diagrams and Charts." In *The Technology of Text: Principles for Structuring, Designing, and Displaying Text*. Englewood, NJ: Educational Technology Publications, 1982, pp. 277-299.

342   Winsberg, Freya Y. "Online Documentation: Tutorials That Are Easy to Take." In *Proceedings of 34th International Technical Communication Conference*. Arlington, VA: Society for Technical Communication, 1987, pp. ATA 101-104.

343   Wong, Wucius. *Principles of Color Design*. New York: Van Nostrand Reinhold, 1987.

344   Wood, William T. and Susan K. Wood. "Icons in Everyday Life." In *Social, Ergonomic and Stress Aspects of Work with Computers*. Amsterdam: Elsevier, 1987, pp. 156-184.

345   Wright, Patricia. "Behavioral Research and the Technical Communicator." *Technical Communication*, 24 (2), 1978, pp. 6-12.

346   Wright, Patricia. "A User-Oriented Approach to the Design of Tables and Flowcharts." In *The Technology of Text: Principles for Structuring, Designing, and Displaying Text*. Englewood, NJ: Educational Technology Publications, 1982, pp. 317-341.

347   Wright, P. and A. Lickorish. "Proof-reading Texts on Screen and Paper." *Behaviour and Information Technology*, 2 (3), 1983, pp. 227-235.

348   Yuen, Elsie C. "Loose Ends of the Scientific Paper—Figure and Caption Titles." In *Proceedings of the 27th International Technical Communication Conference*. Arlington, VA: Society for Technical Communication, 1980, pp. W 159-162.

349   Zimmerman, Margot L. and Gordon W. Perkin. "Instructing Through Pictures: Print Materials for People Who Do Not Read." *Information Design Journal*, 3, 1982, pp. 119-134.

350   Zimmerman, Muriel. "Reducing by Design: A Checklist for Editors." In *Proceedings of the 30th International Technical Communication Conference*. Arlington, VA: Society for Technical Communication, 1983, pp. W&E 18-20.

INDEX

Symbols

 Activities

Defined, vii

Occurrences, 5, 7, 9, 10, 16, 17, 19, 48, 85, 108, 235, 238, 239

 Color

Defined, vii

Occurrences, 105, 176, 212

 International audiences

Defined, vii

Occurrences, 4, 67, 81, 92, 109, 125, 166, 242

 Online display

Defined, vii

Occurrences, 81, 83, 105, 246, 267, 272, 273

 Readings

Defined, vii

Occurrences, 2, 14, 42, 61, 66, 92, 100, 155, 175, 189, 220, 223, 228

 Tips

Defined, vii

Occurrences, 14, 18, 28, 60, 64, 66, 67, 69, 70, 74, 76, 84, 85, 100, 109, 121, 153, 190, 195, 196, 236, 239, 243, 249, 266, 269, 272

Numbers

30-3-30 rule of time to read graphic, 80

7±2, magic number for size of human short-term memory, 87

A

Aberration, chromatic, 228

Abbreviations, avoid in multilingual documents, 209

Abstract ideas, showing, 38, 88, 166

Abstracting in process of scanning a page, 266

Accuracy

    Self-correcting graphics, 10

    Of observation, 17

    Setting objectives for, 64

Achromatic colors, 220

Action-response table, 120

Active blank space, 273

Activities to motivate detailed study, 197

Adams, Ansel, photographer, 100

Additive desaturation, color illusion, 227

Advantages

    Of color in graphics, 223-225, 237

    Of graphics, 2-10

    Of words and graphics together, 172, 247

    Of visual thinking, 16

Aggregation to simplify graphics, 44

Alexander Christopher, creator of Pattern Language, 28

Alternatives, showing, 25, 123-131, 137, 140, 143-144, 153

American cultural expectations for graphics, 213

Analogy in designing graphics, 43, 161, 169

Angle. *See also* Orientation

    Of view in pictures, 95

    Representing quantity, 54

Animals, as visual symbols, 166

Animation, in computer displays, 189-192

Annotations

    Avoiding deception, 78

    Labeling objects in graphics, 251-257

Symbolic meaning of, 213, 241

Z

Zavalani, Tom, creator of visual language, 28
Zooming in and out, 79, 182, 183, 188, 190